CREATING HEAVEN ON EARTH

CREATING HEAVEN ON EARTH

The Psychology of Experiencing Immortality in Everyday Life

Paul Marcus

KARNAC

First published in 2015 by
Karnac Books Ltd
118 Finchley Road
London NW3 5HT

British Library Cataloguing in Publication Data

A C.I.P. for this book is available from the British Library

ISBN-13: 978-1-78220-178-6

Typeset by V Publishing Solutions Pvt Ltd., Chennai, India

Printed in Great Britain

www.karnacbooks.com

For Raphael and Gabriela
"May the Lord cause His Presence to shine upon you."

"One has to pay dearly for immortality; one has to die several times while one is still alive."

—Friedrich Nietzsche

CONTENTS

Contents

CHAPTER ONE

Introduction
The quest for earthly immortality

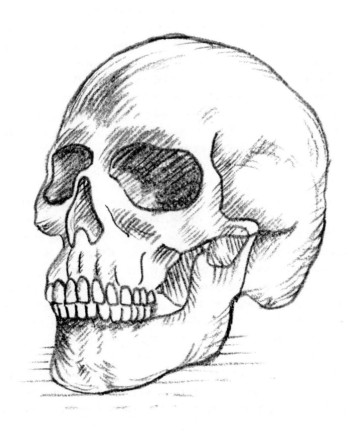

Creating Heaven on Earth

"The best argument I know for an immortal life is the existence of a man who deserves one."

—*William James* (Esar, 1995, p. 413)

Known for his unrestrained optimism, Ralph Waldo Emerson said that if he were banished to hell, he would "make a heaven there" (Nichols, 2006, p. 29). Indeed, we all know people, enviably so, who, despite the sham, drudgery, and broken dreams of everyday life manage to find and create situations that are a fertile psychological breeding ground for joyful self-assertion and personal transcendence. It is these transformational and deeply satisfying moments that reflect what psychoanalyst Margaret Mahler described as a typical experience for the well-looked-after toddler, that "love affair with the world" (Mahler, Pine, & Bergman, 1985, p. 74) that constitutes what I metaphorically refer to as making a choice of "heaven" on earth. Robert Jay Lifton has described this process as striving for "symbolic immortality", an "experiential transcendence", that intense feeling when "time and death disappear". Such experiences of being enamoured with existence centrally involve "losing oneself" and can occur in a number of enthralling contexts: in religious and secular forms of mysticism, and "in song, dance, battle, sexual love, childbirth, athletic effort, mechanical flight, or in contemplating works of artistic or intellectual creation" (Lifton, 1976, pp. 33–34).

My claim in this book is that the capacity to find and create frequent moments of joyful self-assertion and personal transcendence in part constitutes what Aristotle, in his *Nicomachean Ethics*, called *eudaimonia*—"human flourishing and well-being" (Cooper, 2006, p. 86), also called the art of living the "good life". By "good life" I mean, following Freud, a life of deep and wide love, creative and productive work, that is guided by reason and ethics and is aesthetically pleasing (that is, attentive and appreciative of sensuous experiences). While the notions of enjoying the small things in life, sparks of divinity (to continue with my heaven on earth metaphor), and "taking time to smell the roses" are part of conventional wisdom about how to live well, in this book I want to go beyond simply stating these significant truisms. Most important, I want to describe the nuts and bolts of how the average person can actually find and create a heaven on earth, those manifold moments that evoke a sense "of exhilaration or acute sensory activity" (Bennett, 2001, p. 5), of being pleased and grateful to be alive, what William James aptly called "enchantment" (Sexton, 2013, p. 10).[1] The art of living the "good life" ultimately involves fashioning the *petite bonne heures*, the small pleasures one finds and creates into a larger narrative of self-identity, giving one the profound and powerful sense that life is meaningful, satisfying, and justifiable. This self-fashioning process requires a fine-tuned capacity for "noticing"—the ability to become aware of something or somebody and register the fact in the mind. This capacity of awareness, or "mindfulness" as the Buddhists have famously called it, means noticing "the idiosyncrasies" and "the specialness, of the 'this-ness' of the moment" (Miller, 2010, p. 190). There is an inner calm and serenity, a therapeutic ripple effect, associated with such experiential "attunement, engagement and endorsement" (O'Brien, 2010a, p. 201), the micro-perceptual skilfulness that constitutes embracing life without reserve. O'Brien, drawing from Daniel Haybron's *The Pursuit of Unhappiness: The Elusive Psychology of Well-Being*, describes the many aspects of this sharpened sense-perception and the "happiness" that it evokes, within the context of common gardening:

> There is first attunement. This is manifest in feelings of tranquility or inner surety ... As one leans against one's shed after a heavy bout of digging one feels "psychically ... at home in one's life"—one's day-to-day

3

anxieties have floated away. Such attunement leads to engagement. One steps inside the shed and becomes engaged in activity—potting on, cleaning one's tools, organizing one's seed trays. One can become lost in such activity, unaware of the passage of time, and even of oneself ... Before one knows it the sun is setting and one must pack away one's tools. Lethargy or listlessness have melted away in activity ... Engagement then leads to endorsement, and here pleasurable feelings are important. One becomes conscious of one's activity, and perhaps of the productivity on one's plot or the beauty of one's blooms. (ibid., pp. 200–201)

The overall impact of such moments of enchantment is an enhanced mood, a sense "of fullness, plentitude, or liveliness ... of having had one's nerves or circulation or concentration power tuned up or recharged" (Bennett, 2001, p. 5). Put more colloquially, such moments feel like "a shot in the arm", similar to that delight that calls to mind childhood play (ibid.). Indeed, in a world that often feels overwhelmingly brutal and dehumanising, a literal "death world"—just glance at the morning newspaper headlines—and where most of us feel unable and/or unwilling to engage in sustained political action to bring about humane global changes, we can at least resist these dark forces, or what Freud called Thanatos (the death instinct), by engaging in ethically animated, life-affirming, everyday activities that make our world a little bit better. As Jean-Paul Sartre noted, "Everything has been figured out, except how to live" (Parker & Austin, 2011, pp. 2–3).

Rather than focus on familiar peak experiences, those usual suspects that overwhelm the senses with rapture, like making sexual love, gazing at a beautiful sunset, or childbirth, I have chosen to explore the phenomenology of five of the more ordinary, subtle experiences of life that many people take for granted, though they can be said to reflect the "hiddenness of the divine" (Buber, 1999b, p. 44). They include gardening, going to a baseball game, having a cup of coffee with a friend, listening to music, and telling or listening to a story. These common experiences are usually felt to be less immediately euphoric than peak experiences in that they often require more internal "work"—like exacting preparation and examination, critical self-reflection, and accurate empathy—these qualities of mind and heart being some of the conditions for the possibility of the upsurge of transcendent joy. In each one of these illustrative chapters I provide a "thick description" of what it is like to engage in these activities skilfully, with the fullness of one's being, and always with an eye to fostering a sense of transformative, joyful self-assertion and personal transcendence. Moreover, as with any thick description, I have tried to not only delineate the literal behaviour that constitutes the activity in question, but also its broader psychological and social context, such that someone who has never engaged in, for example, seeding a garden, sitting in the "centerfield bleachers" (central stands) at a baseball game, or listening to "The Boss" (the nickname for Bruce Springsteen) or the "blues", would understand and appreciate their complexities and evocative sway.

Thus, the capacity to engage ordinary experience along these lines is no easy matter, for it requires considerable effort, know how, and the fashioning of a rich internal world that, paradoxically, is other-directed, other-regarding, and other-serving rather than strictly "for oneself". Such ethical deepening, characterised by kindness and generosity, is the lynchpin, or at least an important prerequisite, for the self-mastery, self-discipline, and self-propulsion that is the royal road to finding and creating that earthly sense of paradise and immortality. As Heinrich Heine said, "The grandeur of the universe is commensurate with the soul that surveys it" (Marcus, 2010, p. 175).

Defining psychoanalysis

In the remainder of this introductory chapter, I want to briefly contextualise the gist of my focus and methodology by providing a few comments on what I mean by psychoanalysis and artful self-fashioning.

I conceive of psychoanalysis as a form of life, a resource for individuals who can appropriate the life- and identity-defining narrative of psychoanalysis when they seek to understand, endure, and conquer the problems that beset the human condition: despair, loss, tragedy, anxiety, and conflict. In effect, they try to synthesise, come to grips with the emotionally painful experiences of life through a psychoanalytic outlook. In other words, psychoanalysis can be viewed as what Michel Foucault called a "technology of the self": "an exercise of the self, by which one attempts to develop and transform oneself, and to attain a certain mode of being" (1989, p. 433). As philosopher Pierre Hadot notes about ancient Greek philosophy in another context, psychoanalysis can be understood as a "spiritual exercise" (1997, p. 83), a tool for living life skilfully and wisely. The aim of a spiritual exercise is to foster a deep modification of an individual's way of "seeing and being" (ibid., p. 103), a decisive change in how he lives his practical, everyday life. The main objective of a spiritual exercise is "a total transformation of one's vision, life-style, and behavior" in the service of increased personal freedom and peace (ibid., p. 14). According to this view, as philosopher Emmanuel Levinas described "Jewish humanism", psychoanalysis is "a difficult wisdom concerned with truths that correlate to virtues"—in other words, it is a powerful tool for the art of living a good life (Levinas, 1989, p. 275) as one construes and fashions it.

Most important for my study, it is such a psychoanalytic outlook and sensibility that both expresses and potentiates being radically emotionally and intellectually open, to being ready, receptive, responsive, and responsible to what a person encounters. Like cultivating a garden, if approached skilfully, empathically, and compassionately, the world "is a willing, receptive partner" (Roach, 2013, p. 50); it finds and creates the openness to new experiences in us. Philosopher Gabriel Marcel called such a mode of comportment a "spiritual attitude": a way of being in the world that is passionately devoted to intellectual and moral virtues, to Beauty, Truth, Goodness and Justice, while at the same time being aware of the often conflicted, ambiguous, and ambivalent nature of such a way of being (Marcus, 2013b, p. 4). Moreover, such a spiritual attitude is characterised by humility and gratitude in the face of the mystery of being, to those enigmatic moments of what believers call "grace", of "pure disclosure", and of "sudden epiphany" (O'Donohue, 2004, p. 12). In religious language, a language that I am to some extent aligned with, this is the experience of God's sublime, spontaneous, and, perhaps most important, unmerited love. For the secular reader who might find this "God talk" ill-conceived and ill-fated, we can say that such a spiritual attitude involves being responsible and receptive, creative and imaginative, and most important, responsible, as one engages the subtle weave of the luminous and numinous presences in the world (Marcus, 2013b, p. 69). As New York University President John Sexton shows in his lovely co-authored book, *Baseball as a Road to God: Seeing Beyond the Game*, the gist of this spiritual attitude, of fashioning a deeper and more meaningful life, involves a form of religious perception, of noticing and thoroughly appreciating those ineffable, mystical, and "sacred" moments that occur around us, like in our secular national pastime.

This book, then, is an attempt to help the reader learn how to become more attuned to, and grateful for, the plenitude of possibilities (Buber, 1999d, p. 24) for joyful self-assertion and personal transcendence—if only he throws open his mind, heart, and spirit—to fully engage what is quite literally right in front of him.

Note

1. Enchantment, said Jane Bennett, "is a feeling of being connected in an affirmative way to existence; it is to be under the momentary impression that the natural and cultural worlds *offer gifts* and, in so doing, remind us that it is good to be alive" (2001, p. 157; italics in original).

CHAPTER TWO

"Take time to smell the roses"
The delights of gardening

Creating Heaven on Earth

> "No occupation is so delightful to me as the culture of the
> earth, and no culture comparable to that of the garden."
>
> —*Thomas Jefferson* (Betts, 1999, p. 461)[1]

Elton John may well be a lone voice when he said in an interview, "I can't bear gardening, but I love gardens" (see "Inside 'Gnomeo and Juliet'"). Researchers have estimated that in a typical weekend, about 78% of American households are involved in some form of gardening activity (Francis & Hester, 1990, p. 8). What motivates so many people to want to painstakingly work an unassuming plot of ground where herbs, fruits, flowers, or vegetables are cultivated?[2] Or to make the point a trifle more graphic, gardening as a practical action "can hardly be done without getting hands dirty and getting earth under fingernails and blisters on palms" (ibid., p. 6). Indeed, as we shall see, there is a complex set of interrelated, interdependent, and interacting motivations and practices that allow gardeners, and, in a different way, garden spectators, to experience the life-affirming, nurturing, and enchanting forces of nature that are responsibly animated by human inventiveness and shaped by human intervention. As English garden writer and designer Penelope Hobhouse noted, gardening, conceived as "the result of a collaboration between art and nature", is essentially about "editing nature, not dictating to it … painting a picture to create" beautiful, harmonious, and delightful "visions of nature" (2008).[3] Moreover, gardening is a human endeavour that involves many important psychological, sociological, and philosophical questions that have bearing on practical wisdom and human flourishing (O'Brien, 2010b, p. 1), the "good life", as I have called it. For example, gardens help individuals distinguish themselves from others by working on and intervening in that which they control and over which they have a direct positive influence—"We must cultivate our garden" is the famous last line of Voltaire's *Candide*.

10

The act of cultivating a garden is thus a form of self-cultivation or self-fashioning. The incomparable English garden designer, Gertrude Jekyll, my intellectual touchstone and "master" garden-maker that I will refer to often,[4] noted nearly a hundred years ago, "I think there are few things so interesting as to see in what way a person, whose perceptions you think fine and worthy of study, will give them expression in a garden" (Lawrence, 1964, p. 6).[5] Like a painting that reveals the inner workings of its painter, a garden is a living Rorschach;[6] it also is a way to improve one's biography.

Gardens also help differentiate in-group and out-group in terms of literal and symbolic territory. One only has to consider the garden from the point of view of social status, as a way to affirm social, economic, and intellectual power (Miller, 1993, p. 54). For example, in 1661, Louis XIV commissioned André Le Nôtre with the design and implementation of the gardens of Versailles, gardens that to the king were equally as significant as the already existing château. The gardens took forty years to build and became Europe's archetypal royal residence, the primary dwelling of French kings and the epitome of royal power and authority. Persian kings valued garden making and horticultural activities as much as military pursuits, and viewed them as vital to the prospering state (Ray, 2010, p. 30). In ancient Greece and Rome, where plants were valuable booty, gardens were venues to display military competence and success, spaces to plant spoils of war (Day, 2010, p. 76).

Perhaps most important for our discussion, as Jekyll noted, the garden is "a never ending parable of Life and Death and Immortality" (Massingham, 1973, p. 180). Gardens negotiate many of the existential polarities and tensions that shape human experience in a wide range of contexts: "Man and Nature, the natural and the artificial, indoor and outdoor, private and social, duty and pleasure, action and contemplation" (Miller, 1993, pp. 56–57); and perhaps most obviously, change versus permanence. Moreover, as I shall discuss, there are numerous other seemingly irreconcilable human oppositions, if not paradoxes, that are endemic to Western society, which gardens attempt to mediate: "male versus female, good versus evil, reaction versus revolution, self versus community, consumerism versus self-reliance, connectedness versus anomie, integration versus segregation, rich versus poor, real versus surreal, bigness versus smallness, sacred versus profane, science versus intuition, higher versus folk art" (Francis & Hester, 1990, p. 4). As landscape architects and designers Francis and Hester further noted, gardens are ways of resolving these dialectical tensions, or at least learning to live more comfortably with them. Gardens are very "powerful settings for human life, transcending time, place, and culture". They "are mirrors of ourselves, reflections of sensual and personal experience". Moreover, it is through gardens, "both using or admiring them, and dreaming them", that "we create our own idealized order of nature and culture" (ibid., p. 2).[7] As novelist/ journalist Mary Cantwell noted, "Gardeners, I think, dream bigger dreams than emperors" (Robbins, 1998, p. 49).

In this chapter I will be mainly focusing on two questions: (1) What makes gardening and garden appreciation compelling to so many people from all walks of life, even having a therapeutic effect,[8] and how does it create the psychological conditions of possibility for the average person to experience a glimpse of immortality? As Jekyll noted, the gratification of original garden composition is "the nearest thing we can know to the mighty forces of creation" (Jekyll, 1983, p. 6). (2) How does gardening and garden appreciation help make people better human beings? That is, how does it contribute to ethical deepening, to increased kindness and generosity, to enhancing one's capacity to be more "for the other" rather than "for oneself"? As ethical philosopher Emmanuel Levinas has claimed, such an other-directed, other-regarding, other-serving way of being can be the "staging" ground, "the phenomenological circumstances" when "God 'comes to mind'", when one senses

12

the divine (Marcus, 2008, pp. 204, 207). To quote Jekyll again, "The garden is a grand teacher"—like a good parental caregiver, "it teaches patience and careful watchfulness; it teaches industry and thrift; above all it teaches entire trust" (Lawrence, 1964, p. 25).[9] For Jekyll, trust meant both the gardener's confidence in, and reliance on, the good qualities of "Mother Nature" and the gardener's responsibility to take good care of her herbs, fruits, flowers, or vegetables. Jekyll, who viewed "Mother Nature" as a manifestation of God's beneficence—she even quotes 1 Corinthians 3:6, "Paul planteth and Appolos watereth, but God giveth the increase"—further clarifies:

> The good gardener knows with absolute certainty that if he does his part, if he gives the labour, the love, and every aid that his knowledge of his craft, experience of the conditions of his place, and exercise of his personal wit can work together to suggest, that so surely as he does this diligently and faithfully, so surely will God give the increase [i.e., God is the ultimate minister of growth and flourishment]. Then with the honestly-earned success comes the consciousness of encouragement to renewed effort, and, as it were, an echo of the gracious words, "Well done, good and faithful servant." (Lawrence, 1964, p. 25)[10]

As Freud and his followers have shown, trust begins with one's relationship to one's mother (or main parental caregiver), the psychological parent that most symbolises nurturance and stability, from which our moral strivings ultimately begin, including devotion to a beneficent God. Thus, the gardener's relationship to his garden simultaneously expresses, affirms, and reinforces trust in "Mother Nature" as a nurturing and stable (though always changing) other, but only if one is responsive and responsible to her everyday needs and growth potential. As the psychologically astute Jekyll further opined,

13

"The size of the garden has very little to do with its merit. It is the size of the owner's heart and brain and goodwill that will make his garden either delightful or dull" (Bisgrove, 1992, p. 19).[11]

I. What makes a gardener tick?

In order to get the gist of how and why gardening can be therapeutic, if not provide a glimpse of immortality, it is important to understand how a master gardener typically thinks, acts, and feels. I say glimpse of immortality because, as Freud suggested, we are threshold beings of deep-seated ambivalence and troubling ambiguity, and when the beautiful garden picture touches our innermost sense of selfhood, it can only do that before we emotionally close down (O'Donohue, 2004, p. 21). As Jekyll noted, "For the very essence of good gardening is the taking of thought and trouble" (Lawrence, 1964, p. 203). Gardeners, like analysands, have a special way of seeing the world, one that has "layers of complexity and nuances" (Will, 1990, p. 3). In other words, gardeners, like analysands, embody a way of being, a way of doing life, and while every gardener is a unique person that comes to his garden by way of a highly idiosyncratic trajectory, some common characteristics of the typical gardener can be cautiously delineated. While a book can be written on this interesting and important subject (Kaplan & Kaplan, 1989), I will only discuss four characteristics that may be said to constitute the typical gardener, mainly to further contextualise my primary focus on how gardening can be both therapeutic and hint at immortality.

First, a gardener can be described as the ultimate Freudian devotee, that is, he is allied (almost always unknowingly) with the best of the Freudian outlook on the human condition— man as pleasure-seeking in an erotically tinged universe. For Freud, who viewed living as a "harsh" undertaking, one of the goals of psychoanalysis was to live according to the pleasure principle, that is, to maximise sexual and aggressive gratification (the id), though in accordance with the reality principle, that is, in ways that are realistic and socially acceptable (the ego), all in the service of obtaining a modicum of happiness. Sublimation is Freud's technical term for the way a relatively healthy individual resolves intrapsychic conflict between the id, ego, and superego (roughly, the conscience), this being the basis for experiencing the modicum of happiness that the pessimistic Freud famously thought was possible. The purpose of psychoanalysis, Freud said, was to "transform neurotic misery into common unhappiness". Sublimation involves "changing the sexual or aggressive aim of an urge and finding a substitute gratification", one "that implies a constructive or socially admirable outcome that is satisfying and flexible" (Person, Cooper, & Gabbard, 2005, p. 560). All sublimation relies on symbolisation, and gardening requires just such instinctual redirection and refashioning, that is, engaging in adaptive desexualised and "deaggressified" psychic processes. For example, voyeuristic wishes are satisfied by becoming a psychoanalyst; or, the wish to hurt or kill is satisfied by becoming a surgeon. In other words, gardening represents one very good venue for the individual to negotiate the conflicting demands between desire, that is, instinctual gratification, and culture, the requirements of normative social reality.

While Jekyll was writing from an entirely different intellectual perspective and context, her understanding of what motivates a gardener nevertheless strongly resonates with Freud's hedonistic/sublimatory outlook: "The main purpose of a garden is to give its owner the best and highest kind of earthly pleasure." Moreover, Jekyll said, "I hold that the best purpose of a garden is to give delight and to give refreshment of mind, to soothe, to refine ('through the representation of the best kind of pictorial beauty of flower and foliage') that can be combined and invented, and to lift up the heart in a spirit of praise and thankfulness." Finally, Jekyll wrote:

> When I see this [a novice gardener who thinks that more plants in a garden means more pleasure], I try to put myself into the same mental attitude, and so far succeed, in that I perceive that it represents one of the earliest stages in the love of a garden, and that one must not quarrel with it, because a garden is for its owner's pleasure, and whatever the degree or form of that pleasure, if only it be sincere, it is right and reasonable, and adds to human happiness in one of the purest and best ways. (Lawrence, 1964, pp. 6, 24, 29, 89)

Thus, the first characteristic of the typical gardener is that he has a vigorous hedonic aptitude, though he also graciously honours the reality principle, as he has the "patience of a saint", being willing and able to delay gratification for months, even years, in his quest to create a beautiful, harmonious, and delightful garden. "All good gardening is the reward of well-directed and strongly sustained effort," said Jekyll (ibid., p. 182). About hardy flower gardening she said, "It is not easy at all. It has taken me half a lifetime merely to find out what is worth doing, and a good slice out of another half to puzzle out the ways of doing it" (ibid., pp. 171–172). In other words, no gardener gardens only for today (Miller, 1993, p. 56); he is always leaning into the future. As gardening involves a lot of uncertainty and trial and error, it is a continuous "testing of what will hold with what" within a hugely complex, interactive environment of plants, trees, rocks, water, and the like (Macdonald, 2010, p. 133).[12] As Jekyll observed, gardening, especially for the beginner, is characterised by a feeling of "perplexity and helplessness" (Lawrence, 1964, pp. 44, 72), and thus it requires not only a robust capacity for self-control and consequential thinking, but a powerful sense of self-efficacy, that all-important belief that one can positively influence one's thoughts and behaviour in the service of achieving one's goal. In the case of gardening it is to create an "optical gastronomy," that is, "brilliantly-beautiful pictures … of the most refined and poetical quality" (ibid., pp. 56, 211).

A second quality of mind and heart of a typical gardener is that he has the imaginative capacity to view plants as what botanist Matthew Hall evocatively calls "ensouled life" (2009, p. 22). That is, in the mainly unconscious mind of a garden-maker, plants are roughly equivalent to "other-than-human persons" (ibid., p. 13). To some degree, garden-makers are similar in sensibility to indigenous peoples in Australia, North America, and Aotearoa (New Zealand) who view plants as living beings that have "awareness, intelligence, volition, and communication" (ibid., p. 10). Indeed, recent scientific evidence has shown that plants are in fact "communicative, relational beings—beings that influence and are influenced by their environment", and as Hall noted, that they have numerous "capacities of sentience and mentality" (ibid., p. 158). In short, for the garden-maker, plants are to be respected in their "absolute otherness", and depending on how they are treated they can either be harmed or flourish (ibid., p. 5).[13] As Johann Wolfgang von Goethe noted, "A plant is like a self-willed man, out of whom we can obtain all which we desire, if we will only treat him his own way" (Robbins, 1998, p. 8).

Jekyll, for example, has described her relationship to plants in a manner that affirms Hall's notion of plant personhood, of relating to plants as "other-than-human persons". When she was eighty-eight she wrote in a letter to a friend that it was very difficult for her not to be able to physically do "all the little things about the garden that want doing directly you notice them", and to have to be pushed in a wheelchair rather than having "leisurely solitary prowls of *close intimacy with growing things*" (Lawrence, 1964, p. 19; italics added). In another passage she criticised a certain type of rock garden with "… little square or round enclosures of stones placed on end, with the plant inside conspicuously labeled. It always makes me think of cattle-pens in a market, and the surrounding stones are placed prison-wise, *less for the plant's comfort* than for its forcible detention" (ibid., p. 226; italics added). Elsewhere Jekyll described "the Dahlia's first duty in life is to flaunt and to swagger and to carry gorgeous blooms well above its leaves, and on no account to hang its head" (she also speaks of the "dignity" of the lily (ibid., pp. 144, 147)). In another passage, she wrote, "Nothing is more deplorable than to see a neglected, overgrown plant at the last moment, when already half blown down, tied up in a tight bunch to one stake" (ibid., pp. 148–149). Jekyll referred to giving away a few plants, "[T]hough beautiful and desirable, they were *unhappy and home-sick* in my dry soil, and it was quite evident that they were no plants for me" (ibid., p. 26; italics added). And one of my favourite quotations:

> But it is a curious thing that many people, even among those who profess to know something about gardening, when I show them something fairly successful—the crowning reward of much care and labour—refuse to believe that any pains have been taken about it. They will ascribe it to chance, to goodness of my soil, and even more commonly to some supposed occult influence of my own—to anything rather than to the plain fact that *I love it well enough to give it plenty of care and labour*. (ibid., p. 33; italics added)

As these quoted passages indicate, especially the italicised phrases, for Jekyll and, I believe, for the typical garden-maker, plants are a "significant other" to be loved and nurtured, though not simply as an "other-than-human person", but most often they are cherished as if they were one's real or imagined "children". Jekyll spoke as kind-heartedly of a misshapen pear as one might of some crippled child: "One is so sorry for a poor fruit" (Massingham, 1973, p. 157). Cooper, for example, has noted that there is a plausible analogy between raising children and tending to one's plants in a garden.[14] The joy that parents feel is their "essential participation in the development of their children, creatures who are, moreover, never going to be 'finished products'". Cooper further noted, like with raising children, gardening is not viewed as a task, for it is the act of caring for the garden that is an important reason for having the garden in the first place. In many ways, perhaps with some qualifications, this is how a gardener views his plants in his garden (2006, pp. 71–72); the plants are beloved children in whose welfare he is highly ego-invested throughout his gardening life. This analogy is not as far-fetched as it may sound. The Achuar peoples of Amazonia regard their garden plants "as their children, and nurture them with the same responsibilities that childrearing entails". Not only are the plants experienced as "animated and dynamic", thus fostering identification with them as personified living beings, they are also regarded as deserving "of moral consideration through the recognition and responsibility of direct kinship" (Hall, 2010, p. 42).

Third, the typical gardener not only has a pronounced capacity to love and nurture his garden plants as if they were his beloved children, but like a good mother or parental caregiver, this centrally includes being able to engage with his children in creative, fantasy play. While most adults, at least in Western culture, are too bound, tied, and gagged by societal and personal restrictions, if not neuroses, the gardener is able to live playfully in his everyday life amid his garden. Frances Hodgson Burnett's 1911 childhood novel, *The Secret Garden*, superbly depicts the magical healing power of a living garden. Such activities are pleasurable sublimations of childhood play and have important cultural functions. What gardening does for the adult is something rooted in re-finding the aliveness and joy associated with play activities engaged

19

in for their own sake, for the pleasure they give, most often without any serious aim or end and without much conscious anxiety, inhibition, and/or guilt. Jekyll, for instance, wrote in *Children and Gardens*, that "Nothing is so delightful as any sort of playing with water," and she described paddling in a shallow river amid the wild flowers where the sticky mud was "like thick chocolate." Indeed, Jekyll's entire book, and much of her other writings, are characterised by typical childhood sentiments, of "magic, adventure and laughter" (Massingham, 1973, pp. 110–111). Perhaps it is for this reason that psychoanalyst Donald Winnicott famously argued that, in part, the goal of psychoanalysis at its best is to transform "the patient from a state of not being able to play into a state of being able to play ... It is in playing and only in playing that the individual child or adult is able to be creative and to use the whole personality, and it is only in being creative that the individual discovers the self" (1971, p. 10). To be able to play is thus a sign of "mental health", an expression of autonomy and integration. It is also self-healing and therapeutic, and yet sadly, for most people in our society, it is regarded more as a luxury than a necessity. Finally, through play one can learn a lot about people if one knows what to look for. Sounding more like a psychoanalyst than the wise philosopher he was, Plato noted, "You can discover more about a person in an hour of play than in a year of conversation" (Brooke, 2006, p. 56).

For the gardener, the garden is his "playground of the mind"; it is the place where he can engage in a highly personalised mode of creative expression that depicts the world as he imaginatively apprehends it, or more accurately, as he would like it to be. For example, "Plants were ... Jekyll's paint, the earth her canvas and nature was her inspiration" as she experimented and adapted in her garden playground (Wood, 2006, p. 8). Thus, gardening embraces the heartfelt value that most adults need to be reminded of, namely, deepening and expanding the capacity to play or have fun. The notion of fun is rarely taken seriously in scholarly discourse, including in psychological discourse, though it is mentioned in passing in the literature on play. Fun, as I am using the notion, is more than simply having a feeling of enjoyment or amusement. In addition, as in gardening at its best, it refers to a way of being in the world in which one uses one's ingenuity and inventiveness in the service of life-affirmation. That is, the whole person is awakened and attentive to the problem of living—mind, body, intelligence and creativity, spontaneity and intuition are all utterly responsive to the moment, and I think, to the other, as in plant personhood, a reflection of the otherness of life.

In a similar manner, the typical gardener, mainly unconsciously, also tends to view his garden as a comforting "home world", a place where he can feel like a child at play with his best childhood chums, his "plant friends", one might say. Jekyll, for example, noted in *Children and Gardens,*

> Now if you will take any flower you please and look it carefully all over and turn it about, and smell it and feel it and try and find out all its little secrets; not of flower only but of leaf, bud, and stem as well, you will discover many wonderful things. This is how to make friends with plants, and very good friends you will find them to the end of your lives. (1908a, p. 80)[15]

While the garden/home connection is one that I will later discuss in greater detail, it is worth mentioning that garden-makers frequently speak about how they are attempting to recreate in their adult gardens the gardens they fondly recall from their childhood (Miller, 1993, p. 172). As the prominent Victorian art critic John Ruskin noted, "No man ever painted [including the garden-artist], or ever will paint, well, anything but what he has early and long seen, early and long felt, and early and long loved" (Festing, 1992, p. 31). In many instances, plants and flowers are associated with particular people and have nostalgic meaning. These gardens often were places where, as children, they happily played alone and with their friends, sometimes in view and earshot of their kitchen where their mother or parental caregiver was cooking, or near other emotionally important parts of their home. As one gardener noted, "If the hearth is the heart of the household, the kitchen garden is its spirit" (Francis & Hester, 1990, p. 144). Jekyll noted that when she was about sixty-five she would still, when no one was noticing, climb over a five-barred gate or jump a ditch. "I think it is because I have been more or less a gardener all my life ... that I still feel like a child in many ways, although from the number of years I have lived I ought to know that I am quite an old woman" (Lawrence, 1964, p. 18).[16] Another interesting observation that is in sync with the above formulation that in the unconscious mind of the gardener plants are equated with childhood playmates, is that researchers have found that urban gardeners almost always desire songbirds in their gardens, not only because nature is highly valued in the concrete jungle, but, I believe, because it gives the gardener a lovely sense that she is joyfully playing with her childhood friends (Dawson, 1990, p. 138). Jekyll made a similar point when she wrote in *Children and Gardens*, "My garden would not be half the pleasure it is to me without the pussies [cats]. I hope you love them as much as I do. They are perfect garden companions" (1908a, p. 164) whom she also called "playmates" (p. 175). Birds and cats and other animals are primal companions; they have a fluency of presence that is graceful and beautiful (O'Donohue, 2004, pp. 118–119, 245). Presence can be thought of as "the 'soul texture' of the person", and, more generally, the way a person's or thing's individuality or otherness engages or strikes you (O'Donohue, 1997, p. 135). One only has to think of venerated Saint Francis of Assisi, the saint of animals and the environment. Legend has it that one morning, as he was journeying with some friends, they came upon a location in the road where chirping birds packed the trees on both sides. Francis said to his friends to "wait for me while I go to preach to my sisters the birds" (Jewett, 2005, p. 45). The birds encircled him, fascinated by the power of his gentle, lilting voice, and not one of the mesmerised birds flew away. There is probably at least a little bit of Francis in every garden artist, as his love of animals and the environment and his belief that nature is the signature of God are sentiments that resonate with many gardeners.

The fourth general quality of the typical gardener is his uncanny ability to create new realities, to actualise what is unthinkable and unimaginable, what is "not yet". Jekyll, for example, designed many of her 400 gardens without ever visiting the site of the garden; rather she worked from site plans, photographs, and samples of soil. In a certain sense, all of us produce and co-produce new realities as we go through our everyday lives, for most of what we say and do with others is not rehearsed, but is a function of responding in the moment to what is happening. And yet, when we see great gardens we feel there is something rather extraordinary going on, as if what is a normative aspect of physical reality, of the environment, has morphed into something appealingly different, something new, if not magical. Great gardening is fundamentally great storytelling, or rather, in a word, "storymaking" (Wiener, 1994, p. 89) through the use of plants, flowers, trees, and water to paint glorious, living pictures that evoke a sense of paradise re-found.

II. The garden as paradise

The word paradise comes from the Persian root meaning "wall enclosing a garden or orchard". In the Hebrew Bible, paradise is famously depicted as a fruit garden. The Garden of Eden is a place of ideal beauty and loveliness, where the just and righteous souls reside—in a word, heaven. In Christianity, Eden is an intermediate resting place for righteous souls awaiting the Resurrection. Other religious traditions also equate paradise with a heavenly garden. Thus, from earliest times, gardens strove to recreate, to psychologically re-find paradise, developing "ever more elaborate versions of the rational mind's vision of heaven" (Francis & Hester, 1990, p. 25).[17] What is it about a garden that transports a person into another dimension of the spirit, infused with feelings associated with the experience of what believers call divine presence?

What the garden and gardening most likely represent in the mainly unconscious mind of the garden-maker is the return to his beloved mother after being separated from, if not abandoned by, her. Freud, in his *Introductory Lectures on Psycho-Analysis* (1916–1917) drew on Otto Rank's theory of "birth trauma", the notion that the anxiety experienced at birth is the template for all anxiety later in life, to emphasise that early separation from the mother is a traumatic experience.[18] On some level all adults feel estranged from their symbolic mother, that primordial sense of existential grounding that helps us defend against our ontological fear of annihilation, or death anxiety, and against our aggressive wishes associated with this real or imagined maternal separation/abandonment, which provides us with the thoroughly unrealistic, though necessary fantasised sense that all is well and will continue to be well. As Victor Hugo wrote in *Les Misérables*, "A garden to walk in and immensity to dream in—what more could he ask? A few flowers at his feet and above him the stars."

In a letter from the Nobel Prize-winning French dramatist Roman Rolland to Freud, Rolland used the term "oceanic feeling" to describe this mystical, cosmic sentiment which Rolland believed was the ultimate basis for religious feelings, and as the many religiously inspired Jekyll quotations have suggested, for the transcendent aspects of garden making. In *Civilization and Its Discontents* Freud conceptualised the oceanic feeling in terms of marked ego regression in which the adult re-experiences the contented pleasure associated with breastfeeding prior to his awareness that he and his mother are separate beings or, for that matter, that he and the external world are different (Rycroft, 1995, p. 118). By unconsciously equating the garden with the breast, the garden-maker is able to feel that thoroughly pleasurable sense of merging and timelessness that has been described as "narcissistic bliss". Gardening is unconsciously equated with the "fantasy of psychic oneness with the mother" (Moore & Fine, 1990, p. 133). As Pulitzer Prize-winning author Alice Walker noted, "In search of my mother's garden, I found my own."

Hobhouse noted that at Munstead Wood where Jekyll lived, she "planned her garden planting to melt into the surrounding woodland". There were no sudden "transitions", instead "a gradual drift from colourful planting to more muted shades beyond" (1993, p. 17). As Jekyll wrote, "At the beginning of all these paths I took some pains to make the garden melt imperceptibly into the wood ..." (Massingham, 1973, p. 64). This "melting into" design quite likely unconsciously evoked the sense of merging and narcissistic bliss mentioned above. Hobhouse quoted a colleague of Jekyll who aptly describes the latter's garden. Listen with the "third ear" for the unconscious resonances, especially in the last two sentences, that point to the "psychic oneness with the mother" theme I describe:

> Every glade and clearing has become a lovely picture, a gratifying surprise. Here a narrow mown way winds between aboriginal fern and grass and colonized shrub and plant; there rhododendron and azalea, with just such shade and shelter as they desire, cover their wide stretching boughs with bloom. And everywhere there is composition. The wood approaches the border area or billows on to the lawn without intrusions or abruptness. All is suave and engaging, all is friendly and beautiful. It is a home of undisputed peace. (1993, p. 17)

A second quote from Jekyll, the artist garden writer at her most eloquent, further suggests this desired experience of merging with the loved and soothing maternal presence as one of the likely unconscious factors that animated the creation of her beautiful living pictures. In *Color in the Flower Garden*, Jekyll delineated gardening that can be called a "fine art" from "commonplace gardening":

> Given the same space of ground and the same material, they may either be fashioned into a dream of beauty, a place of perfect rest and refreshment of mind and body—a series of soul-satisfying pictures—a treasure of well-set jewels; or they may be so misused that everything is jarring and displeasing. (1908b, p. vii)

Thus, for the garden-maker the garden is paradise re-found, in part because it provides a compelling real-life context for the calling to mind of the merging experience with the idealised, all-good mother, the archetypal source and symbol of magical-like nurturance, stability, and existential grounding ("re-rooting" one might say), and that longed for sense of having no beginning and no end, of timelessness. Rather ironically, Jekyll, who late in her life was somewhat reclusive, a "spinster" who "never had any love life" or children (Festing, 1992, pp. 58, 77),[19] seemed to inspire the fantasy of the "big breasted" mother who made plants grow and flourish. Sir Edwin Lutyens, perhaps the greatest British architect of his time, who collaborated with Jekyll in her landscape compositions, playfully nicknamed Jekyll "Aunt Bumps, Mother of All Bulbs" ("In Bloom Again", n.d.).[20] Sometimes this nickname was shortened to "Mab" (Festing, 1992, p. 133). "Mab" was the queen of fairies in English and Irish folklore (referred to in *Romeo and Juliet*); rather interestingly, she was said to create and control men's dreams.

III. Timelessness in the garden

"What then is time?" St. Augustine famously asked in his *Confessions*. "If no one asks me, I know: if I wish to explain it to one that asketh, I know not" (Schaff, 2004, Part 1, n.p.). What Augustine was saying was that experientially he knows what time is, but it is so infused with paradox that he cannot rigorously define it except, perhaps, by saying what it is not. The only thing we actually know, said Augustine, is that time is experienced as residing in us, and is construed and measured in the mind (Marcus, 2003, pp. 139–158). Indeed, the subject of time is a tremendously complex one with a long and contradictory philosophical history. However, we can learn something interesting about how people creatively use time, even play with it, and in other ways reckon with it in everyday life when we consider the garden-maker cultivating his garden. For wisely and skilfully engaging the many forms of everyday time is to also engage the changeability of the emotional life (Kunitz, with Lentine, 2005, p. 75), an important part of the art of living the "good life". As Mara Miller noted, gardens "exploit time in various ways, purposely directing our attention, incorporating the rhythms and tempi of natural phenomena or deliberately discarding them" (1993, p. 128). Moreover, in part by shaping how we psychologically experience time, gardens create the "illusion of timelessness, the illusion of paradise" (Miller, 2010, p. 178).[21]

Miller noted that artistically animated gardens involve at least six types of time, each having their unique structural properties, dynamics, and practical implications, and evoking a slightly different emotional sense in the garden-maker and spectator.

Scientific time is objective, quantifiable time used by scientists; it is directional, interchangeable, uniform, and predictable. It flows from present to the future and its course commences in the past. For the garden-maker this notion of time is extremely important, though of little aesthetic value. However, without his taking into exacting consideration scientific time, plants are unlikely to survive, let alone flourish, and the garden-maker would be frustrated beyond what is psychologically tolerable. For example, the amount of days until germination, the number of hours of sunlight needed for a plant to fruit, and other seasonal changes related to sprouting and flowering are crucial considerations. As Miller further noted, "there is for gardeners a vibrant interplay between scientific time and subjective time. The desire for plants to bloom or ripen may make us experience time slowing down (subjective time), but that is in sharp contrast with the plants' scientifically predictable time" (ibid., p. 180). Put differently—and this is one of the important psychological "take home" points about scientific time in the gardening context—scientific time teaches the utmost respect for the reality principle, the adaptive ego exerting control over behaviour to satisfy the circumstances imposed by external reality, and thus acts as a modulating influence on the pleasure principle. In other words, as Freud noted, living according to the reality principle involves transforming "free energy" into "bound energy", phantasised wish-fulfilment—the beautiful garden I imaginatively long for—into realistic appreciation of the "facts" of the external world—the garden that is doable according to the setting-specific spatio-temporal parameters.

The second form of time, said Miller, is subjective time, "time as it *feels* to us", a highly individualised experience. "The fifteen minutes [measured time] of a physicist and the last fifteen minutes of a [n impatient] student's school day are very different quantities indeed." These temporal experiences are felt quite differently both qualitatively and quantitatively, and in some sense subjective time is also objective time in that it is a predictable shared experience. In this chapter's context, gardens have the capacity to evoke varying experiences of subjective time. For example, a well-positioned bench to be used to observe a sunrise or sunset tends to suggest a particular kind of temporal experience compared to an intricately designed fountain that is meant to evoke appreciation of its technical perfection. Moreover, the way gardens manifest and exploit time depends on the cultural context: a "dry garden", such as a Japanese rock garden or a zen garden, is a space decorated with sand, rocks, and other natural materials in lines or patterns to create a meditative environment; it is meant for slow and mindful walking, to enter a different dimension of the spirit, one that is impervious to clinging desire, intentionality, and concept (O'Donohue, 2004, p. 226), and hints at eternity. As Jekyll noted, being "observant ... is one of the ways of being happy" (1908a, p. 95). The fifteenth-century Italian Renaissance garden also had a contemplative function; however, given that it was primarily designed with ancient Greek and Roman principles of order and beauty, its main function was to give aesthetic pleasure associated with gazing at the garden and the outlying landscape, allowing spectators to take pleasure in the various things they saw, heard, and smelled. Visitors thus tended to walk this garden faster than in a zen garden, going from one pleasurable sensation to the next.

Shared time, the third form of time, is the experience of time common within society. Since it is experienced or felt, it may be described as subjective, yet it is also objective in that it is taken for granted and shared. For example, as Miller further noted, to legitimate his time in power during a period when challenges to monarchy were being experienced through-out Western Europe, Louis XIV's garden-makers at Versailles "reconciled familiar daily and annual changes within nature's cycles with the seemingly eternal constraints of the celestial realm by juxtaposing themes from the four seasons and the course of the sun through the sky with Apollo and other fig-ures and themes from classical mythology". These felt reso-nances between nature and monarchy, and among Apollonian sun and God and king, were not solely for his and his courtiers' pleasure. In addition, said Miller, Versailles was a centralised designed public garden that expressed a shared sense of time as "eternal and historic and recurring" as well as concurrently "divine and mundane" (Miller, 2010, p. 184). Thus, the garden-maker's design both expresses the values of a society—in the case of Versailles, monarchical power—but perhaps even more important it is meant to have a relational impact that shapes the visitor's internal reality. Garden-making in this context is "a way of delimiting, inscribing, marking, and coding a territory", and by doing so, it advocates specific normalising "forms of movement appropriate for the bodies which move within or through it". As a result of this "diagram of the picturesque" (Shapiro, 2010, pp. 152, 154), a kind of road map, the spectator has the inner experience that correlates with the heartfelt value that the garden-maker's living assemblage personifies and wants reinforced as the spectator moves through the garden.

"Timing is all," Hamlet famously mused. *Kairos*, the fourth form of time, is a notion of time rooted in Greek thought. It refers to situational awareness, intuitively reading the apt time to act to achieve one's goal. For gardeners, this sense of timeliness is a question of knowing "what to plant and when" (Ray, 2010, p. 35). Jekyll's famous rule was "always choosing the plant for the place and the conditions" (Way, 2012, p. 28)[22] and this sense of "rightness" and "sympathy with the place" (Festing, 1992, pp. 142, 162) was, to a large extent, based on having a capacity for detailed observation and critical judgment: "Throughout my life I have found one of the things most worth doing was to cultivate the habit of close observation" (Lawrence, 1964, pp. 30, 66). It is extremely important, for it can mean the difference between a plant living or dying. For example, most seeds should be planted after the last frost, but the daunting challenge of knowing when that will be is a matter of fine-tuned intuition. In Taoist thought, such intuition is usually discussed in terms of "wu-wei", or non-action. While wu-wei has many subtle meanings, it includes patiently waiting for the spontaneous transformation of things, and then acting in a manner that is in sync with, and supports, this natural development. For the garden-maker wu-wei means accepting that "things happen in their own time" (Brook, 2010, p. 20). For example, one must accept impotence in directly determining a successful outcome, like a plant's trajectory to fruit, not with anxiety or sadness, but with equanimity, because this is the way "Mother Nature" has prescribed the parameters of the plant/human encounter. Therefore, as Alan Watts said, wu-wei is better translated as "don't force it". Wu-wei does not mean complete passivity, whether inside or outside the garden, but rather it is the development of a suitable sensibility for every situation. Like a master gardener does, the idea is to intuitively feel the action that is required in a particular context. This is done intuitively because we are not capable of discovering the best response to a situation strictly analytically, conceptually, and consciously. Responding (not reacting) spontaneously to all things as they come, flowing with the natural currents of the world and with the Tao, is the goal. Most important, again both inside and outside the garden, is that this does not mean the suppression of feelings, but rather the integrated use of one's emotions and increased sensitivity to general context, specific setting, and timeliness.

Cyclical time, the fifth form of time, refers to "the time of the seasons, the life cycles of animals (including human beings), of agriculture" (Miller, 2010, pp. 185–186). In general, cyclical time, especially when compared with linear time associated with science, often evokes the serene feeling of "having time". Consequently, this diminution or loss of time consciousness creates a stronger relationship to space, to the feeling of enmeshment with the environment, such as the relationship of "Native Americans [with] sacred mountains and lakes" (ibid.). This feeling of enmeshed relatedness is often experienced as a kind of spiritually elevating mode of connection, for it points to the infinite flow of things with which one is merged ("Cyclical Time"). Garden-makers, said Miller, "integrate the cyclical time of their plants' internal calendar and the seasons with scientific time" (2010, pp. 185–186). For example, the garden-maker's knowledge of the cyclical nature of particular plants powerfully impacts how the garden will develop and how, and to what extent, the spectator favourably experiences the garden picture. As Barwell and Powell have pointed out, the time the cycles take in a garden "is the same as the time experiencing them would take, if we were to watch them continuously". Moreover,

> This is a way in which changes in gardens are like [musical] performances. However, we do not usually sit and watch the grass grow or oak trees mature. This is because we would feel that the experience was taking even longer than the time it does take. We would experience it as intolerably long because it would be very tedious. This is an example of the difference between experiential [subjective] and chronological [scientific] time. (2010, p. 141)[23]

Finally, according to Miller, there is historical time, that is, the way "society's and our own personal histories" are structured and expressed. Historical time "is superimposed upon our awareness of the cycle of the seasons, the cycle of day and night, and the history of the developments of the plants in their own cycle"; this is human history. For example, gardens choreograph our experience of time through their configuring of spaces for strolling, resting, picnicking, and musical and theatrical performances. Moreover, said Miller, these experiences of strolling or resting in the garden tend to be similar to those of other spectators, regardless of the year or age in which the spectator moves, thus we get a sense of the predecessor's experience of "internal time" (2010, pp. 178, 190). This is another example of identification with the garden-maker's heartfelt value that he wants us to appropriate. More generally, there is a communal intimacy between the garden visitor with the real and imagined, and the people who created and/or worked the garden (Cooper, 2006, p. 81).

Thus, the artist-gardener works with different forms of time to emotionally affect the experience of his beautiful living paintings enjoyed by the spectator. Most important, since gardens are not still phenomena—they are always in process, always changing—they are intimately connected to the experience of the movement of time. As Barwell and Powell further noted, when we engage a garden not only pictorially, but also "presenting the passing of time" with its inevitable changes, we immensely enlarge our enjoyment and appreciation of the garden. For example, gardens are "designed real-time worlds" that allow the skilled spectator to "see birth, senescence, and death; we see slow and fast cyclical changes, and we see 'offspring' and 'parents'". In this way gardens promote musings on some of the perennial existential polarities and tensions that constitute everyday human experience, like "permanence or transience, stability or instability, mortality or regeneration, growth or decay, health and sickness" (Barwell & Powell, 2010, p. 146). Similar to how the gardener who confronts the vagaries of the natural world must "learn to play the hand he's been dealt" (Cooper, 2006, p. 107), the garden visitor is encouraged to learn to realistically accommodate the existential polarities and tensions that characterise the human condition.

Perhaps most profoundly, what the living garden-picture suggests to the visitor is that he can actually go beyond the mere realistic, creative, and inspired accommodation of these polarities and tensions. He can glimpse something more, something beyond the immanence of the garden-picture. In addition, the wise and skilful garden visitor can imaginatively use these accommodated-to polarities and tensions as a fertile breeding ground, as an enlivening psychological context, for being transported to a different "depth dimension" of the spirit that points to the transcendent. Such an internal space opens one up to a non-objectifiable, transcendent moment, to the sense of receiving a gift of astonishing beauty, a gift of "absolute presence", as Gabriel Marcel called it (Marcus, 2013b, p. 74). Such "creative receptivity", said Marcel, points to "an other order of being", an existential modality that usually operates below the level of everyday awareness and problem-solving, technique-oriented living. Rather, such a "depth dimension", as it has been called, "is experienced as a release from ourselves by giving us access to the hidden mystery that surrounds the everyday and that corresponds to our hidden depths" ("open ourselves to those infiltrations of the invisible ... the radiance of that eternal Light", Marcel (2005, p. 31) beautifully put it). Cooper noted that while "the garden exemplifies a co-dependence between human endeavor and the natural world", this mutual depend-ence is best conceived of as between human existence and the unfathomable, primordial "'deep ground' of the world and ourselves". (Cezanne called this "the very roots of being, the intangible source of sensation".) Thus, concluded Cooper, "[T]he garden ... is an epiphany [and embodiment] of man's relationship to mystery," and it is precisely this relationship to this source of absolute presence and being that points to its transcendent meaning (2006, p. 145). As George Bernard Shaw no doubt said tongue in cheek, though there is at least a grain of psychological truth to his words, "The best place to see God is in a garden. You can dig for him there" (Pratt, 2013, p. 11). What, in part, makes this garden-emanating sense of transcendence so compelling is that it is experienced as a "living vibration", a "deep pulsing" of the universe (Kunitz, with Lentine, 2005, p. 100). In other words, the garden is an erotically tinged longing for belonging in the eternal presence of Eros. It is to this subject that I now briefly turn.

IV. Garden erotica

My wife, a child psychoanalyst trained by Anna Freud, told me about a patient of hers, a sassy urban teenage girl, who dyed her pubic hair green and had tattooed above it, "Keep off the grass"! Indeed, what this anecdote insinuates is that the garden, both as actuality and metaphor, can be viewed as an erotic activity that is "saturated with impulse" (ibid., p. 103). Importantly, it is a way to transform impulse, that is, nature, especially its wildness and fluency of presence (O'Donohue, 2004, pp. 229, 240) that strongly resonates with the uncharted regions of our turbulent psyches, into a thing of controlled spontaneity, as exemplified in the artistic beauty of Jekyll's garden-pictures. Her garden-pictures maintain "the fluency of continual change" while holding their form (O'Donohue, 1998, p. 174).

As I have stated, most elementally, the garden is often unconsciously equated in the adult mind with the real or imagined, loved and loving childhood mother (or one's other parental caregiver), as in "Mother Earth" or "Mother Nature". Thus the garden is a way of emotionally connecting, if not communing, to the "Earth Mother", the mythological goddess symbolising fertility and the source of life. In this formulation the garden is the psychical umbilical cord to the archetypically sensual and maternal woman, to her utterly enlivening and nurturing spirit (Thayer, 1990, p. 197). The garden as a manifestation of "Mother Nature" is not simply immanent matter, though the garden earth, like all earth, has "a stable presence and thereness" (O'Donohue, 1998, p. 101). In addition, it is a manifestation of Eros, a "luminous and numinous presence that ha[s] depth, possibility and beauty". The garden, in other words, caresses human presence and thus evokes a soulful "erotic charge" that calls to mind a mystical, divine, or eternal presence (O'Donohue, 1997, pp. 76, 100–101, 131).

Eros, as I am using the term, is not merely lustful desire, but it is a divine or eternal force that animates the earth, including the garden. While Freud viewed Eros as the primordial life force and sexual instinct, its meaning can be plausibly enlarged and deepened to include a "sacred force": Eros "is the light of wisdom that awakens and guides the sensuous … the energy that illuminates the earth". Without it the earth, even the garden-picture, would feel like a bare, cold, inhospitable place, without soul (O'Donohue, 2004, p. 152). O'Donohue further noted,

> In the embrace of Eros, the earth becomes a *terra illuminata*. Amidst the vast expanse of field and seas, the providence of Eros awakens and sustains the longing of the earth. This is the nerve source of all attraction, creativity and procreation. Eros is the mother of life, the force that has brought us here. It constantly kindles in us the calm of beauty and the desire for the Beautiful as a path towards growth and transformation. (ibid., pp. 152–153)

Thus, the garden reminds us that "we belong to the earth", whether we are a garden-maker or a visitor to the garden; its strong psychological pull is not simply to its brilliant colours[24] or forms and textures. It stimulates a powerful urge to return to the "intimate unity of belonging", said O'Donohue, the sense of self-belonging that was first experienced in relation to our own bodies. Freud called this feature of the ego the "body ego". It emanates "from the self's self-perceptions", in contrast to externally perceived objects. Said Freud: "The ego is ultimately derived from bodily sensations, chiefly from those springing from the surface of the body" (Rycroft, 1995, p. 15). This is the "deeper rhythm" and serenity that we unconsciously long for and in which we would like to eternally dwell. This short-lived return to a secure and protective presence, to one's sheltering inner centre of gravity, is experienced as a kind of joyful homecoming (O'Donohue, 1998, pp. 19, 102, 104, 122). As the well-known saying goes, "We come from the earth, we return to the earth, and in between we garden."

If the garden/"Earth Mother"/Eros linkage is psychologically plausible, then gardening can be viewed as a viable way of reworking one's erotically tinged relationship to one's childhood mother and/or other main parental caregiver, via the symbolic means of creating the perfect garden for which one longs. Gardens are often the place where authors like D. H. Lawrence and Virginia Woolf situated a specific scene to evoke the character's "memories, nostalgia, and regrets".

As Cooper further noted, "The garden is peculiarly receptive to the exercise of reverie, memory, and imagination" (2006, p. 122). For the gardener, these often melancholy psychological moments have a duality of structure: on one hand they express the gardener's wish to be, or at least to be like, the fertile, life-giving "Earth Mother", nurturing and loving his "plant children", and on the other, they allow the gardener to feel like the adored "plant child" that is loved and nurtured by a bountiful and beautiful "Mother Earth". Taken together, these moments point to the Eros that permeates the world, a "call to life and creation that quickens the soul and captures the heart" (O'Donohue, 2004, p. 69).

As the psychoanalyst Bruno Bettelheim brilliantly showed in his *Uses of Enchantment*, fairy tales that take place in a forest or jungle, especially a dark one, often evoke in children fantasies of uncontrolled primordial sexuality that is both thrilling and terrifying. Indeed, as Riley further noted, there has been an evolution "from forest, to forest glade, to meadow, to garden, to lawn as a metaphor of increasing control over, or sublimation of, the raw sexual content of nature". In this evolution, the garden can be said to exist in the "middle ground, where sexuality is controlled but still potent and available" (Riley, 1990, p. 67). As Jekyll and others have claimed, the garden is a venue where the wildness of nature can be controlled and artistically edited for pleasurable purposes. Riley elaborated thus:

> If the jungle is a symbol of sex beyond human control and
> the lawn a symbol of sex corseted and over-controlled,
> then the garden is a place where sex is available for
> human delight in a controlled context. (ibid.)

While the garden as a metaphor for sexuality has a long history in literature and painting, a subject beyond the scope of this chapter, the literal, mainly unconscious use of the garden by the garden-maker as an expression of sexuality is both direct and indirect. As English writer and author H. E. Bates blatantly noted in his celebrated novel, *A Love of Flowers*, "Gardens ... should be like lovely, well-shaped girls: all curves, secret corners, unexpected deviations, seductive surprises and then still more curves" (Slung, 2005, p. 11). The French novelist Colette noted, "How can one help shivering with delight when one's hot fingers close around the stem of a live flower, cool from the shade and stiff with newborn vigor" (Robbins, 1998, p. 110). The New York Botanical Garden head horticulturist, Francisca P. Coelho, noted about the noble chrysanthemum, "It is wild when you think about it. These plants love to be tortured. The more you manipulate them, the more they give" (Grimes, 2013, p. C21). More subtly, Jekyll's "drifts", what has been described by Riley as a "sensual drift" (Robbins, 1998, p. 110), suggests a more refined sexuality. Jekyll explained the origin of her term:

> Many years ago I came to the conclusion that in all flower borders it is better to plant in long rather than block-shaped patches. It not only has a more pictorial effect, but a thin long planting does not leave an unsightly empty space when the flowers are done and the leaves have perhaps died down. The word "drift" conveniently describes the shape I have in mind and I commonly use it in speaking of these long-shaped plantings. (Lawrence, 1964, p. 64)

What made Jekyll's "drifts", these "long, thin, flowering groups" of plant associations sensual is that they gave the visitor the feeling of his senses being highly aroused and gratified. It was, for instance, the complex, though lyrical, interplay of presence and absence, the repeating upsurge and downturn of colour which, said Jekyll, gives "a fresh spring of vitality in the life of the garden" (1983, p. 272). This garden vitality correlates with the individual's internal longing for a sense of aliveness, his wish to make contact with the "the primal presence" of his own vitality. It is that part of himself that makes him feel most alive (O'Donohue, 1998, p. 130). As Bisgrove explains,

> Jekyll's drifts are very apparent in her flower borders, but they can also be seen in the interweaving groups of holly, oak thorn and other natives in her woodland plantings, and in the interplay of plant groups and open space in her wild gardens. In her borders, the drifts have a practical purpose in that while a considerable quantity of each plant is revealed when in flower, its thin trail disappears as it ceases to flower and other plants come into prominence. (Bisgrove, 1992, pp. 44–45)

Through the use of these "sensual drifts", continued Bisgrove, the visitor has the experience of a unified garden with a "repetitive flow". As Jekyll noted, "The whole border becomes a picture instead of a scattered collection of unrelated colourings" (Wood, 2006, p. 28). The drift allows the plants that are blossoming at any one particular time to evolve into beautifully colourful compositions, while earlier and later blossoming plants recede into the background, creating a strong sense of primal rhythm and harmony. It is precisely Jekyll's exquisite "balance of discipline and generosity, harmony and contrast" that characterises her drifts and keeps our "desire alive in its freshness, passion and creativity" (Bisgrove, 1992, pp. 44–45). Like in sexuality on the rigorously sexual level, the beautiful garden-picture "is not a deadener but a quickener" (O'Donohue, 2004, p. 4).

V. Gardening as ethically deepening

"We have descended into the garden and caught three hundred slugs," wrote Christian mystic Evelyn Underhill. "How I love the mixture of the beautiful and the squalid in gardening, it makes it so lifelike" (Robbins, 1998, p. 197). Indeed, while we have focused on the garden as a nurturing, sensuous, maternal presence, a living, pulsating manifestation of Eros, the gardener also apprehends that what makes garden-making so therapeutic and ethically deepening is that it also requires a confrontation of the dark side of Mother Nature, a manifestation of destructive Thanatos. For it is mainly through reckoning with the squalid in life, with the struggle, if not downright suffering that it entails, that we are most likely to grow, develop, and flourish. In short, suffering is the mother of all wisdom. In the garden this struggle with Thanatos is evoked when one faces the "dwindling, drooping, falling and decaying" (Barwell & Powell, 2010, p. 145), the precursors to death and dying with which the garden-maker must continually contend. "Winterkill", for example, is a plant's death as a result of exposure to winter conditions. Nature has an unkind, if not cruel side, hence there is often pathos to a garden, a poignancy that can stir compassion in the spectator. In fact, one might say that the garden-maker is attempting to transform the pathos and poignancy of the garden into something beautiful. As Jekyll noted, "For a love of flowers, of any kind, however shallow, is a sentiment that makes for human sympathy and kindness, and is in itself uplifting, as everything must be that is a source of reverence and admiration" (Lawrence, 1964, p. 235).

Likewise, the garden-maker engages in acts of considerable crude but controlled violence for the sake of his beloved plantings—the weed killing and insect poisoning, the cutting and chopping that constitute so much of his art of cultivating and tending to a garden. As Stanley Kunitz noted, "When the time comes for cutting, gathering, moving, removing" in the garden, "one has to be pretty ruthless" (Kunitz, with Lentine, 2005, p. 5). Thus, it is not simply coincidental that gardening is often conceptualised in military metaphors. As the journalist and gardener James Shirley Hibberd noted, "Gardening is always more or less a warfare against nature. It is true we go over to the 'other side' for a few hints, but we might as well abandon our spades and pitchforks as pretend that nature is everything and art nothing" (1871, p. 223). A trifle less fatalistic, May Sarton, an American novelist and poet, wrote, "A garden is always a series of losses set against a few triumphs, like life itself" (Henneberg, 2010, p. 137). Thus, gardening both demands and teaches incredible patience, determination, Stoic-like fortitude, and humility. After all, how else can one cope with being routed by a dumb little cabbage fly or slug (O'Brien, 2010b, p. 3)? Such praiseworthy qualities of character, especially the narcissistic downsizing that patience, determination, fortitude, and humility imply, are necessary to be a successful garden-maker and have their obvious application in other domains associated with the art of living the "good life". The English author, poet, and gardener, Vita Sackville-West, caught the gist of the gardener's outlook in saying, "The most noteworthy thing about gardeners is that they are always optimistic, always enterprising, and never satisfied. They always look forward to do something better than they have ever done before" (Rushing, 1997, p. 181).

Gardening also profoundly teaches the garden-maker something about the process of separation/individuation and identity development; in short, of becoming a person. It puts into sharp focus how one engages the "otherness", the differences of plants and humans, and deferentially, if not reverentially, uses this knowledge as a basis for personal growth and development. There are at least two ways of engaging the otherness of the world as it relates to developing and elaborating a wholesome, life-affirming sense of self throughout life. In Western thought, "difference", especially between people, is conceptualised "as radical and is the basis of a drive toward separation and exclusion", such as in the development of one's unique ego, identity, and cognitive abilities. However, in animist societies, for example, "[T]he response to difference occurs within a relational framework and so is one engagement and inclusion" (ibid., p. 111). In this view, gardening can be conceived as an activity in which one recognises both similarity and difference between humans and plants, but in a context of greater appreciation for the otherness of the plant world as part of a larger web of significant relations, that if approached respectfully and with curiosity, we can learn from. By choosing to responsibly nurture the beloved plant in all of its otherness we affirm and strengthen our personal agency and autonomy. Responsibility for the other, said Levinas—and I believe this can be extended to plants—does not limit freedom; on the contrary, it sets a person free. "True belonging", the kind of belonging the garden-maker feels in his beloved garden, is welcoming "to difference for it knows that genuine identity", what can be called authentic selfhood, "can only emerge from the real conversation between self and otherness. There can be no true self without the embrace of the other" (O'Donohue, 1998, p. 59), and in the garden context, this involves one's "Earth Mother", and plant "children" and "friends", as described earlier.[25]

Perhaps most important, gardening cultivates a care ethic, one that puts the "other-than-human persons", that is, plants, before oneself, especially in the early and middle phases of the human-to-plant relationship. Such an orientation to the plant, conceived as a beloved other, is an instructive counterpoint to the more typical human-to-human form of intimate social interaction, one that is mainly based on the norm of reciprocity, a "tit for tat", returning-benefits-for-benefits way of relating (e.g., "I scratch your back, you scratch mine"). While the garden-maker looks forward to the possibility of his plantings becoming the living medium for his beautiful pictures, so therefore they are giving him something back for loving them, for taking good horticultural care of them, he nevertheless loves them from their seed existence without getting anything obviously in return from them, and with no guarantee that they will become the fruiting, flowering, blooming basis for his beautiful pictures. In a sense then, as Levinas has suggested, the decision to care for a garden implies an asymmetrical human/plant relationship characterised by an ethic of "responsibility for the other" that is more commanding than "being for oneself". One of the reasons the garden-maker can voluntarily gravitate towards this kind of selflessness, or at least proto-selflessness, is likely because, as with raising children, the joy the parent gets is through the quality of the children's presence in and of itself and mainly on its own terms. "We love the things we love for what they are," said Robert Frost (ibid., p. 56). That is, the ultimate purpose of children and plants is "to live and blossom for themselves" (Hall, 2009, p. 22). The act of nurturing the child or seedling is experienced by the garden-maker as a form of what has aptly been described as a sacred stewardship of a divine or divine-like potentiality, one that can hopefully be beautifully actualised through one's love. The gardener experiences his plantings as a gift from Mother Nature and/or from God, which demands a "gracious receptivity" (O'Donohue, 1998, p. 3). This provides motivation enough for the gardener, like a parent, to keep giving until it hurts. And hurt it does, as Charles Dudley Warner, an American essayist and novelist, wryly noted, "What a man needs in gardening is a cast-iron back, with a hinge in it" (www.quotegarden.com/gardens.html).

VI. Conclusion: the art of glimpsing immortality in the garden

From a psychoanalytic point of view, gardening, especially when viewed as a form of landscape painting as Jekyll and others have described it, offers great satisfaction, and is in some ways therapeutic, because it (1) satisfies instinctual needs and the wishes stirred up by them: this gardening is mainly about the vicissitudes of sex and aggression and its sublimations; (2) reinforces various defensive needs: this is the garden that defends against sexual and aggressive/sadistic drives and other negative emotions associated with death, like death anxiety; (3) satisfies the need for mastering external and internal stimuli: this is the garden that fosters a sense of self-efficacy and control amid a feeling of weakness and vulnerability as one effectively intervenes, taking care of one's plantings in the real and symbolic landscape. In the context of these three functions, gardening can be said to be an attempt to "restore and recreate inner images and objects" that have been either destroyed or tainted by unconscious aggressive and/or sexual wishes and fantasies. Hence, landscape gardening is concerned with "order, harmony and beauty", with making outer order out of inner chaos, and turning ugliness/the sense of inner badness into beauty/the sense of inner goodness. In short, the garden-maker is wholly capable of transfiguring primary process into secondary process and back again, ad infinitum, as the garden is a living, ever-changing artistic medium of sublime integrated gratification, all in the service of guaranteeing the triumph of Eros over Thanatos (Noy, 2013, pp. 562, 574, 578). Jekyll, for example, noted "… the enduring happiness that the love of a garden gives. For the love of gardening is a seed that once sown never dies" (Wood, 2006, p. 8). Moreover, not even the sense that death was around the corner muted her life-affirming experience of the garden as Eros. "And as the quick years pass and the body grows old around the still young heart, and the day of death grows ever nearer; with each new springtide the sweet flowers come forth and bloom afresh …" (Way, 2012, p. 47). There is much food for thought in these psychoanalytic formulations meant to account for what is so satisfying about creating garden-paintings and visiting a garden. However, there is something more to gardening than mere instinctual gratification and/or defence, and this gets to the ineffable, immortal spirit of what makes gardening so compelling to the garden artist and visitor.

Jekyll once suggested one of her core convictions about life was "that things worth doing are worth doing well" (Bisgrove, 1995, p. 147).[26] Indeed, to reach her remarkable level of garden-making, perhaps above all else, one had to have a trained eye, especially to see colour, but also other physical details of the landscape. Even more important, the garden-maker has to grasp the totality of the landscape's spatio-temporal circumstances as a basis for imagining the beautiful garden-pictures that will be creatively drawn. For Jekyll this principle of integration and unity involved "knitting house, garden and landscape as a background to man's body and soul" (Festing, 1992, p. 159).

What Jekyll was able to do was to use her trained eye in a manner that accessed the variety of depth presences of the landscape, presences that call to mind the eternal, or what I have called glimpsing immortality—those uplifting inklings of universal spirit that can fleetingly be apprehended both inside and outside us if we are graciously receptive of them. As Jekyll noted, the training of the eye to see colour "enable[s] one to see pictures for oneself … and the pictures so seized by the eye and brain are the best pictures of all for they are those of the great Artist, revealed by Him direct to the seeing eye and receiving heart" (Bisgrove, 1995, p. 147). In another passage, Jekyll wrote, "The Grey garden is seen at its best by reaching it through the orange borders … making the eye eagerly desirous for the complementary colour, so that … suddenly turning to look into the Grey garden—the effect is surprisingly—quite astonishingly—luminous and refreshing" (ibid., p. 148). Sometimes Jekyll's love of the physicality of the garden had a mystical[27] aspect to it: "When in our hills a moss-grown thorn or juniper dies of old age the woodbine will give it a glorious burial covering the hoary branches with a freshness of young life and a generous and gladly-given wreath of sweetest bloom" (ibid., p. 150). Jekyll also spoke of the "infinite beauty of colour of the air", "the clouds (eternal mine of divinest colour)", and the "infinitely varied hues" of living plants (Wood, 2006, p. 67). And finally, she reflected that the "sense of beauty is the gift of God, for which those who have received it in good measure can never be thankful enough" (Bisgrove, 1988, p. 11). Taking these quotations as a whole, it is clear that gardening for Jekyll, especially the art of skilful combination of plants, was the closest she could get to the spirit of divine "creation" (1983, p. 6).

Notwithstanding the religious language that Jekyll used to describe her experience of gardening, in particular as an emotionally open and skilfully observant visitor quietly dwelling in the garden, I believe that Jekyll is suggesting the contours of what potentially makes gardening and the garden a living medium for glimpsing immortality.

"Peace! Peace! To be rocked by the Infinite," wrote poet Stanley Kunitz in his poetic memoir on his experience of gardening. The garden as a manifestation of "Mother Nature" beckons us to return to our primal "rhythms of perception and attunement to the world"; and by doing so, we re-find our inner centre of gravity and relinquished peace of mind. Especially when we feel under siege, or simply down and out, the garden evokes, and invokes, what has been described as a "quiet eternity" that "restores your lost tranquillity". It does so in part by renewing one's sense of existential grounding, being rooted, or re-rooted in something that transcends one's clamouring personal ego and often petty, everyday concerns. The garden as landscape, especially a self-edited one, with its "silence, solitude and stillness" (O'Donohue, 1998, pp. 22, 60), and most of all, its beauty, transports us to another dimension of being, one that deeply satisfies our longing to belong in a web of lovely presences and nurturing relations. After all, as I have suggested, in the unconscious mind of the gardener, his garden is pleasantly inhabited with his favourite "other-than-human" persons, and most of all, he has his comforting and compelling memories of being sheltered by an infinitely loving maternal presence.

Thus, it is not surprising that when a gardener lost his beloved wife he filled his whole vegetable garden with flowers (Francis, 1990, p. 208). The garden is a kind of sacred space that "transfigures some of the forsakenness" of one's life and of the world, and there are few moments when one feels the absence of companionship, protection, and support more than after the death of a loved one. The garden, as a manifestation of "Mother Nature", does not despair the permanent separation that death brings, for she is ever renewing herself in her own seasonal presences, an ode to resurrection. In the mind of the bereaved gardener or visitor—and we are all in a state of bereavement in one form or another—of sorrow, affliction, deprivation, or stress—the garden is a place of an other-than-ordinary sense of time, a "deeper, eternal order" (O'Donohue, 1998, pp. 266, 287) that is tremendously comforting. As O'Donohue poetically puts the point,

> The deepest longing of the mind is for real presence. Real presence is the ideal of truth, love and communication. Real presence is the ideal of prayer here and beatific vision in the hereafter. Somewhere deep in the soul, our longing knows that we break through to the eternal when we are gathered in the shelter of presence. These are the moments of deepest belonging.

In short, it is in the garden that such a profoundly nurturing moment occurs, one that is a deeply gratifying, revitalising experience, for it "nourishes us to the roots" (ibid., p. 322) of our innermost being. It is in these precious moments that we create beauty out of our suffering and are blessed with a glimpse of immortality, for we are communing with the eternal presences that we have forgotten we have always been part of (Kunitz, with Lentine, 2005, p. 137). This moment has been described by former Auschwitz inmate, Viktor Frankl, who tells the story of a young woman who knew that she would die in a few days. Despite her grim situation, when Frankl spoke to the woman she appeared to be cheerful. "I am grateful that fate has hit me so hard," she said to Frankl. "In my former life I was spoiled and did not take spiritual accomplishments seriously." The woman then pointed through the window of her hut and said, "This tree here is the only friend I have in my loneliness." "Through that window," said Frankl, "she could see just one branch of a chestnut tree, and on the branch were two blossoms." "I often talk to this tree," the woman said, an utterance that startled Frankl, who did not know how to interpret her troubling words. At first Frankl thought she was delirious, or that maybe she was hallucinating. "Anxiously I asked her if the tree replied. 'Yes.' What did it say to her? She answered, 'It said to me, 'I am here—I am here—I am life, eternal life'" (1963, pp. 109–110).

Notes

1. Jefferson, an astonishingly refined man who designed his own house in Monticello and some of the buildings of the University of Virginia, was a serious garden devotee, both in terms of "a practical horticultural as well as an aesthetic point of view". He kept an extensive garden notebook from the age of twenty-five until two years before he died (Taylor, 2006, p. 254).

2. A working definition of a garden is, "Any purposeful arrangement of natural objects (such as sand, water, plants, rocks, etc.) with exposure to the sky or open air, in which the form is not fully accounted for by purely practical considerations such as convenience" (Miller, 1993, p. 15).

3. Hobhouse has been strongly influenced by English garden legend Gertrude Jekyll's ideas about gardening, especially the notion of the gardener as a "garden-artist" who creates "garden-pictures" (Lawrence, 1964, pp. 29, 49). Jekyll and Hobhouse follow Kant, the "father of modern aesthetics", who maintained that landscape gardening is a sub-species of painting, one of the visual arts (Barwell & Powell, 2010, p. 135).

4. Gertrude Jekyll (1843–1932) was a horticulturist, garden designer, artist, and writer. She is "recognized as the most significant influence in the design of today's gardens"

(Bisgrove, 1992, p. 6). As Tankard notes, "Her theories of planting in naturalistic drifts, using harmonious colors and contrasting textures of foliage, were revolutionary in her day and still resonate among garden designers today" (Shoemaker, 2001, p. 664). Christopher Hussy, an expert on British domestic architecture, characterised Jekyll as "the greatest artist in horticulture and garden-planting that England has produced", while the English humorist and essayist, E. V. Lucas, wrote that Jekyll "changed the face of England more than any, save the Creator himself, and perhaps, Capability Brown" (Taylor, 2006, p. 254).

5. Jekyll is quoting from a friend's letter.

6. One is reminded of Erma Bombeck's humorous quip, "Never go to a doctor whose office plants have died."

7. Jekyll also wrote about the garden as fantasy-wish: a "cherished garden picture, the consummation of some long-hoped-for wish, the crowning joy of years of labour" (Jekyll, 1983, p. 278).

8. Horticultural therapy is a sub-discipline that deals with the application of gardening to clinical populations. I will not be considering this literature in any detail. For more details, see Simson and Straus, 1998. It is worth noting that from its onset the famed psychoanalytically oriented Menninger Clinic used horticultural therapy as part of its hospital treatment (ibid., pp. 161–162).

9. Jekyll also noted that, "No artificial planting can ever equal that of nature but one may learn from it the great lesson of moderation and reserve, of simplicity of intention, and directness of purpose, and the inestimable value of the quality called 'breadth' in painting" (Festing, 1992, p. 105). In her discussion of working with climbing plants, Jekyll noted, "The lesson is generally one that teaches greater simplicity—the doing of one thing at a time; the avoidance of overmuch detail" (Lawrence, 1964, p. 154). Jekyll further elaborated in *Wall and Water Gardens* that, "In garden arrangements, as in all other kinds of decorative work, one has not only to acquire a knowledge of what to do, but also to gain some wisdom in perceiving what it is well

to let alone." It is this acute sensitivity to knowing where to stop that was her "touchstone" (Massingham, 1973, p. 108).

10. Elsewhere Jekyll noted, "The whole garden is singing this hymn of praise and thankfulness" (1901, p. 67).

11. Bertold Brecht also noted, "A clever gardener can do much with a small patch of ground" (Miller, 1993, p. 21).

12. Enchantment is a notion that Jekyll refers to in her book, *Children and Gardens,* and alludes to throughout her writings (1908a, p. 13).

13. In Jekyll's discussion of "staking" (supporting the plant), she noted, "They must be so arranged that they give the needful support, while allowing the plant its natural freedom," this being an example of Jekyll as an advocate for respecting the plant's otherness (Lawrence, 1964, p. 70).

14. Garden-makers may also relate to their gardens as if they were companion animals or pets.

15. Sally Festing, Jekyll's biographer, noted that Jekyll spent hours in her first big garden, "befriending trees, shrubs and flowers" (1992, p. 15). Jekyll was "thoroughly trained to the smell of flowers"; for example, she could determine the different flowers in a garden without ever seeing them (1982, pp. 75, 77). Her hearing was also finely honed. At an early age she could correctly identify a tree simply from the sound of the wind in its foliage (Festing, 1992, p. 287). Jekyll would have agreed with her brother's friend, the author Robert Louis Stevenson, who wrote, "It is a golden maxim to cultivate the garden for the nose, and the eyes will take care of themselves." Incidentally, Stevenson used the name Jekyll in his famous book, *Dr. Jekyll and Mr. Hyde.*

16. Jekyll has been described by one garden historian as someone who had a "love of innocent and childish pleasures" (Way, 2012, p. 51).

17. The editors are quoting from Jeff Cox.

18. Rank's "birth trauma" theory is mainly of historical relevance in contemporary psychoanalytic thought.

19. Interestingly, as her book on *Children and Gardens* suggests, Jekyll had a good grasp of the psychology of children; said

Festing, "Children were always deeply in awe of her" (1992, p. 70). A previous biographer noted that Jekyll had a "profound understanding of children" and she "loved" them (Massingham, 1973, p. 31).

20. Actually, it was Edwin Lutyens's wife, Emily, who pronounced that Bumps was an apt nickname, for Jekyll was "very fat and stumpy, dresse[d] like a man, little tiny eyes, very nearly blind, and big spectacles". The Lutyens's children called Jekyll "Aunt Bumps" (Way, 2012, p. 21). Their collaboration has been described as a brilliant "combination of architectural form with impressionist painting". Jekyll hugely admired the Impressionists (Massingham, 1973, p. 162). Lutyens designed Jekyll's house in Munstead Wood.

21. I have drawn generously from Miller's excellent essay.

22. This notion has been expanded by horticulturist Melinda Myers (2013): "the right plant, the right purpose, the right place, the right look".

23. As Festing noted, Jekyll's concern with harmony in her plantings suggests a musical analogy to gardening. Her own garden, "Gertrude's inner sanctuary", was like a "self-contained melody or perhaps an interlude" (1992, p. 184).

24. I will not be dealing with the subject of the psychology of colour, including the symbolic meanings of various colours in the garden. I will also not discuss the possible symbolic meanings of particular flowers and plants, like the red rose or the carnivorous Venus flytrap, both of which are a psychoanalyst's field day.

25. While I have not discussed in any detail the role of gardens and gardening in fostering a sense of community and other feelings of "we-ness", there is a large literature on the "garden as cultural expression", notably that "The garden is a record of the uniqueness of a culture in time and space" (Francis & Hester, 1990, p. 14).

26. Jekyll's philosophy of life has been summarised by Massingham: "The regard for nature, the reverence for detail, the appreciation of the veining in a small leaf just as much as for a fine lily, the persistence and respect for work,

the faith and trust in the ordering of life" (1973, p. 179). This being said, with a degree of ironic distance, Jekyll, the driven perfectionist, wrote in her book, *Home and Garden*, "Are the people happier who are content to drift comfortably down the stream of life, to take things easily, not to *want* to take pains or give themselves trouble about what is not exactly necessary? I know not which, as worldly wisdom, is the wiser" (ibid., p. 55).

27. In her biography of Jekyll, Festing described Jekyll's "mystical experience" when, as a young girl, she saw a primrose copse: "Looking at the yellow flowers with their green spread of leaves, it seemed suddenly as if they were part of the earth, as if we too are part of a hidden pattern, and both are parts of a work of art" created by God. As Festing further noted, "There was genuine humbleness in Gertrude's deference to her Maker. In later life, an Italian picture of two praying nuns hung in her sitting room" (1992, pp. 13–14).

CHAPTER THREE

"Magical myths"
The passion for sport

"In our sundown perambulations of late through the outer parts of Brooklyn, we have observed several parties of youngsters playing 'base,' a certain game of ball ... The game of ball is glorious ... I see great things in baseball. It is our game, the American game."

—*Walt Whitman* (Sexton, with Oliphant & Schwartz, 2013, p. 215)

"But those of us who were lucky enough to see [Pelé] play received alms of extraordinary beauty: moments so worthy of immortality that they make us believe immortality exists."

—*Eduardo Galeano*, 2009, p. 152[1]

Baseball", wrote syndicated columnist and baseball rhapsodist George F. Will, "is heaven's gift to struggling mortals" (Will, 1998, p. 64). Indeed, baseball, to some extent like other sports, is "a way of looking at life", one that teaches a subtle form of exquisite pleasure (Giamatti, 1998a, p. 82). Exactly what constitutes baseball's pleasure-giving qualities to its players and spectators, qualities that point to the possibility of glimpsing immortality, is what this chapter is mainly about.[2] Baseball, similarly to religion, has a "systematic coherence, spiritual luminosity, and transcendent character" (ibid., p. 43), which has a strong interpretive grip on millions of people, not only in the United States, but also in many other parts of the world. One Gallup poll from 2006 indicated that nearly half of Americans are baseball fans (Jones, n.d.), while it is one of the most popular sports in Japan and parts of Central and South America.[3]

In addition to baseball appealing to the "common man" (and woman), its diehard fans include some notable intellectuals like the late president of Yale University and baseball commissioner, A. Bartlett Giamatti, the late Harvard palaeontologist and historian of science, Stephen Jay Gould, and most recently, the president of New York University, John Sexton, who teaches a popular course on baseball as a spiritual journey. The seriousness of many intellectuals' baseball devotion is in sync with the well-known observation that baseball is the "thinking person's sport", it is "graceful, subtle, elegant, inexhaustibly interesting and fun" (Will, 1998, p. 50).[4] While some may find baseball to be boring compared to football and basketball, the American broadcaster Red Barber quipped, "Baseball is dull only to dull minds."[5] To the aficionado, however, it is the "green fields of the mind". The great English novelist and essayist, John Fowles, explained, "Though I like the various forms of football in the world, I don't think they begin to compare with these two great Anglo-Saxon ball games for sophisticated elegance and symbolism. Baseball and cricket are beautiful and highly stylised medieval war substitutes, chess made flesh, a mixture of proud chivalry and base—in both senses—greed. With football we are back to the monotonous clashing armor of the brontosaurus" (izquotes. com/quote/291919).[6] In other words, baseball is mainly about "nuances and anticipations", while football is about "vectors and forces" (Will, 1990, p. 250).[7] Psychoanalytically speaking, we can say that baseball is about the psychological struggle between sons and fathers, while football is about sibling rivalry, brothers whacking each other in the back garden or play area. Most important for this chapter, as the wonderful baseball films like *Field of Dreams* (my favourite), *The Natural*, *Bull Durham*, and *It Happens Every Spring* suggest, baseball is "one of the best settings for metaphorical tales of the human spirit and character" (Sexton, 2013, p. 160). It can aptly be conceived as a "parable of life", as a "moral fable" (Robson, 1998, pp. 3, 14), one that has much to teach us about how to live the "good life".[8] Most important, this requires developing a greater baseball literacy and attunement to the way the craft is performed at its highest level of excellence, for this is the most fertile point of entry for embracing baseball's magic, its beautiful immortality.[9]

I. Home plate: the internal place where you must reckon with yourself

Baseball has a powerful emotional bond and tie to home plate, both literally and symbolically, as it is the centre of the baseball universe. It is perhaps for this reason that it is not simply called "fourth base". Home plate is the place where the batter begins his existential odyssey, that is, his high octane, "man-to-man" battle against the pitcher and secondarily, the fielders, and hopefully hits the rocketing ball and scores a run, signified when he victoriously crosses home plate. In baseball, the only safe passage around the four bases is the "home run", otherwise the challenge of safely and victoriously returning to home plate requires nearly superhuman powers. As Ted Williams, the left fielder of the Boston Red Sox (nicknamed "the greatest hitter who ever lived"), famously said, hitting a baseball is the most difficult task in any sport, it "is the only field of endeavor where a man can succeed three times out of ten and be considered a good performer" (Palmer, Gillette, & Shea, 2006, p. 7). The best hitters manage to score a bit more than 100 runs a season in roughly 650 times at bat (Kraus, 2004, p. 10).[10] Home plate is often a place of shattered dreams of greatness, if not immortality. To quote Ted Williams again, "All I want out of life is that when I walk down the street folks will say, 'There goes the greatest hitter who ever lived'" (Will, 1990, p. 329). Interestingly, Williams psyched himself up before batting by saying to himself, "My name is Ted fucking Williams and I'm the greatest hitter in baseball" (Dickson, 2008, p. 599). Baseball, like all sports, involves the wish for immortality in its players, and in a different way, in its fans (Giamatti, 1998b, p. 15).[11]

What is baseball's obsession with home plate all about, and what does it suggest about the art of living the "good life", including pointing to something deeper and more profound, that can plausibly be the staging ground to sensing the ineffable or transcendent? (Sexton, 2013, pp. 3, 21).

It was A. Bartlett Giamatti, a Renaissance scholar and the "metaphysician of American sport" (Will, 1990, p. 100), who has perhaps best captured the allegorical meaning of home plate in baseball. As a narrative, baseball is "an epic of exile and return, a vast, communal poem about separation, loss, and the hope for reunion". That is, said Giamatti, baseball is a "... story of going home after having left home, the story of how difficult it is to find the origins one so deeply needs to find. It is the literary mode called Romance" (1998b, pp. 90, 95). Giamatti beautifully explained,

> Baseball is about homecoming. It is a journey by theft and strength, guile and speed, out around first to the fair island of second, where foes lurk in the reefs and green sea suddenly grows deeper, then to turn sharply, skimming the shallows, making for a shore that will show a friendly face, a color, a familiar language and, at third, to proceed, no longer by paths indirect but straight, to home.
>
> Baseball is about going home, and how hard to get there and how driven is our need. It tells us how good home is. Its wisdom says you can go home again but that you cannot stay. The journey must always start once more, the bat an oar over the shoulder, until there is an end to all journeying. (1998a, pp. 30–31)

Citing Homer's *Odyssey*, and the many literary romances that have grown from it, Giamatti made the thoughtful observation that while the goal of Odysseus, and the batter, is to return home and put things right, it "is rarely glimpsed, almost never attained". One of the main reasons for this is that once one leaves home, one is "thrown" into inhospitable real life, that is, one has to negotiate the many challenges and hardships, the pain and sorrow, emanating from what often feels like an uncooperative, hostile world (Giamatti, 1998b, pp. 92–93). While a residue of this "hunger for home" (Giamatti, 1998a, p. 42) may survive the ordeal of separating and venturing into the world, the home whence one began is mainly an imagining that rarely corresponds with the reality of returning home, especially when one remains home over time. Indeed, Thomas Wolfe was onto something psychologically important when he wrote his famous novel, *You Can't Go Home Again*. In baseball, however, you can literally go home again, which is part of baseball's promise of redemption. Everyone longs "to arrive at the same place, which is where they start", home plate. While home is a literal possibility in baseball, ironically, just about everything has psychologically changed for the batter and spectator during and after this journey "of leaving and seeking home" (ibid., pp. 94, 103). It is this point that is often underappreciated by Giamatti and others who embrace baseball as an Odysseus-like, spiritual journey.

In real life, home, the place one lives permanently, is usually experienced as a refuge from the harshness of the outside world, as a place of security and happiness, of comfort and relaxation, and competence and familiarity—in short, it is unconsciously equated with a real or imagined warmth, protectiveness, and love of one's mother.[12] For most people, this is only one side of being at home, especially in terms of an adult remembrance of one's childhood home. Home is also a place of familial discord, conflict, rivalry, and frustrated desires. If, as I do, you believe Freud was right, for the boy growing up in a traditional family (of baseball fanatics), home is a place of subtle, and sometimes not so subtle, fears, especially of the imposing, "larger than life" father. Freud conceptualised this problematic aspect of the father/son relationship with one's real or imagined, powerful and "castrating" oedipal father, as a struggle against helplessness.

Home thus can be conceived as having a duality of structure; it can be the basis of experiencing one's childhood home, to use an apt religious expression, as a "blessing"—the comforting fantasised maternal presence alluded to above—or a "curse"—the threatening side of the paternal presence. Most often, however, one's home world is regarded as situated in the "grey zone", full of emotional half-tints, that is, mixed and conflicted feelings often associated with both parents. For instance, interest in baseball is often a point of memorable father/son bonding. As Sexton noted, "Just as I had once forged a powerful bond with my father through a ball club, so too, I decided, must my son be given the opportunity to experience such wonders with me" (2013, p. 48). I have had many patients who have reported that their fondest memories of their father was playing a simple game of baseball "catch" with each other.[13]

In baseball, this duality of structure to the felt experience of home is dramatically depicted: home plate is where one can hit a home run and feel like a conquering hero,[14] yet it is also a place where one can strike out and feel publicly humiliated and furious. Home, especially one's childhood home, is thus an ambiguous and ambivalent place of personal identity, of growth and development and the opposite. This duality of structure, in particular the two emotion clusters most associated with home plate and batting, maternally tinged security versus paternally tinged insecurity, a nest of self-belonging versus a crucible of fear, calls to mind Freud's notion of the uncanny, which he defined as "that class of the frightening which leads back to what is known of old and long familiar". Moreover, he said, "[A]n uncanny experience occurs either when infantile complexes [e.g., castration and womb fantasies] which have been repressed are once more revived by some impression, or when primitive beliefs which have been surmounted seem once more to be confirmed" (1919h, pp. 220, 249).[15] Freud mentioned the eerie and unsettling examples of *déjà vu*, perceiving one's double, and feeling that someone who has died has come back to life.

As already insinuated, in the context of baseball, the experience of the uncanny is in sharp focus during the batter's duel with the pitcher at home plate. Similar to much of ordinary life which feels like a battle, "[B]aseball life is an endless series of skirmishes about who will control the periphery of the plate, batters or pitchers" (Will, 1990, p. 95). The great Yankees slugger, Mickey Mantle, once told shortstop Tony Kubek that at least once a year, and maybe more often, "I wake up screaming in the middle of the night, sweating a cold sweat, with the ball coming right at my head" (ibid., p. 176). As is well known, though often underplayed and/or denied, downright fear of the pitcher is an intrinsic aspect of batting. In fact, in Little League, children just starting to learn the game often have incredible anxiety about being hit by the ball, especially in the head. One six-year-old I treated would obsessively touch his penis before he had to bat. His visceral response to fear is no surprise, as a pitcher throws a hard ball at about 90 mph (60 mph in Little League), and yet all the batter has to defend himself with, as it were, is a thin wooden or aluminum bat and some plastic equipment. If the ball hits him it usually hurts terribly. Moreover, the speeding ball can do serious bodily harm, and it can, in a worst case scenario, actually be lethal. Not only this, the pitcher is well aware that he is at a huge advantage in terms of the power dynamics over the batter: he is on the "mound", the small hill on which the pitcher stands, thus appearing bigger and more formidable than he actually is; he is collaborating with the catcher (and other fielders) to outsmart the batter, and the catcher is nerve-rackingly squatting directly behind the batter who is "boxed in", having to stay inside the "batter's box" while batting. To make matters even more threatening, behind the catcher is the law, the umpire, who is an imposing figure of absolute judgment. As Will evocatively puts it, "Umpires are carved from granite and stuffed with microchips. They are supposed to be dispassionate dispensers of Pure Justice, icy islands of emotionless calculation" (ibid., p. 58). "Call 'em fast and walk away tough," home plate umpire Richie Garcia famously said (ibid., p. 64).[16] Most important, the pitcher is willing and able to use fear to intimidate the batter into submission, that is, to get him out of his routine, so self-doubting, that a conceptual disarray is induced. As the great pitcher Don Drysdale noted, "The pitcher has to find out if the hitter is timid, and if he is timid, he has to remind the hitter he's timid" (Dickson, 2008, p. 150). Will further noted,

> Even the most gentlemanly pitchers can be provoked to use fear. Kubek says that Sandy Koufax "who could throw a baseball maybe better than anybody in history," once threatened Lou Brock [left fielder, St. Louis Cardinals] just because Brock stole a base in a crucial situation. As Brock was dusting himself off at second, Koufax turned to him and, according to Kubek, said, "Next time you do that I'm going to hit you right in the head." Brock stole another base against Koufax. He then became the only man Koufax ever hit in the head. Brock stole no more bases off Koufax (ibid., p. 177). [In fact, Koufax said, "Pitching is the art of instilling fear" (Price, 2006, p. 128).]

"If you've got them by the balls, their hearts and minds will follow," said President Theodore Roosevelt. Indeed, intimidation is an all-important constituent of being a great pitcher, and both the pitcher and batter viscerally know this (Dickson, 2008, p. 608).[17] Said one of the most daunting fastball pitchers, Early Wynn: "A pitcher will never be a big winner until he hates hitters … [he] has to look at the hitter as his mortal enemy" (ibid., p. 606). Alternately, Ted Williams said, "There's only one way to become a hitter. Go up to the plate and get mad. Get mad at yourself and mad at the pitcher" (Seidel, 1991, p. xix). Like David facing Goliath, the batter hopes that his trusty slingshot/bat will protect and prevail. What makes the duel between the batter and pitcher so thrilling, if not nerve-racking to both the batter and the spectator, is that it re-enacts the oedipally tinged struggle between the more powerful and "castrating" father and the weaker and near helpless son, who is fighting for his freedom to be his own person and for his self-respect, if not for his life, symbolised by returning safely and victoriously home to the "mother of all bases", home plate. Indeed, the symbols of this struggle saturate the erotically tinged psychological context of the batter facing—"man to man"[18]—the pitcher, all within a decidedly masculine "gang up": the catcher is behind the batter calling to mind a sense of vulnerability to the powerful phallic father, while the ultimate symbol of paternal judgment and punishment is evoked in the stern rulings of the heartless umpire. From the onset of the duel, the pitcher has the clear advantage of power; in the batter's unconscious mind he appears bigger, stronger, and faster than the batter. He throws a "hard ball", an unconscious sex organ equivalent, at the batter who holds a small, thin bat, another unconscious reference to the phallus, and who most of the time will strike out, that is, be "struck down" by the pitcher's precise ferocity. Remember, as a Yale professor of physics noted, a pitcher's fastball is thrown with an initial velocity of 97 mph and it crosses home plate in 0.4 seconds. Batters therefore have 0.17 seconds to make the decision to swing. To make matters even more daunting, if they swing 0.0005 seconds early, they forego the maximum bat velocity. Incredible skill and timing is required of the batter like in no other sport (Will, 1998, pp. 58, 243–244). It is for this reason that the spectator has a degree of identification with the batter's underdog status, if not his helplessness, and this is why when he gets a hit, a way of "hitting back" at the oedipal father, there is a sense of relief, if not overwhelming joy. Perhaps this moment has been best captured in the famous "called shot" of the incomparable Yankees slugger, Babe Ruth.

Ruth's "called shot" was the home run he hit in the fifth inning of the third game of the 1932 World Series played at Chicago's Wrigley Field. While at-bat against pitcher Charlie Root, the Chicago Cubs' "bench jockeys" and fans were mercilessly heckling Ruth, including fans who were yelling insults and throwing lemons. Allegedly, someone even spat on Ruth's wife, Claire. Rather than paying no attention to the taunting and trash talk, the angry Ruth was ridiculing the dugout and fans through his words and gestures. With two strikes against him in a tied game, he then made a pointing gesture at either the centerfield bleachers, at the Cubs' dug-out, or at Charlie Root (this is hotly disputed),[19] seemingly proclaiming that he would hit a home run to that part of Wrigley Field. On the following pitch, Ruth hit a home run to "center field". The 50,000 fans watching the game went wild.[20] Thus, in this intensely anti-Yankees, anti-Ruth context, Ruth asserted his will to power, reclaiming his and his wife's dignity, just as his mythological status, his immortality, was guaranteed in the annals of baseball history. Indeed, what is uncanny about this is that when "the Babe" completed his victory run and crossed home plate, it was unconsciously understood by fans that that the Yankees "son" had slain the Cubs' "father", thus calling to mind the oedipal struggle. The roaring spectators, even the diehard Cubs fans and dugout were cheering, thoroughly identified with the Babe's guilt-free self-affirmation of his wish to defeat the fearful, dominating, hate-filled father/pitcher and return home as conquering hero to the loved and loving "mother", symbolically named home plate. Such inspired self-affirmation is radically transforming to both the batter and spectator. It has a transcendent spiritual intensity that makes you feel completed and perfected and want to rejoice. As the Yale professor of history and classics and baseball lover, Donald Kagan, put it, "A dramatically heroic and potentially tragic confrontation stands at the heart of this most poetic game" (ibid., p. 148). The exalted melancholy of the batter's fate is that the exhilaration associated with this so-called "oedipal victory" lasts only briefly, reminding us of the truth that nothing remains the same. More important, the batter and spectator are reminded that forever possessing the mother is not the way things are supposed to be. At best, we are permitted to "re-find" our mother symbolically, whether it is in the real-life choice of a partner who unconsciously calls to mind the best of one's real or fantasised mother, or hitting a home run. Indeed, the whole oedipal drama repeats itself when the batter returns to home plate for his next at-bat.[21] Baseball loves these beautiful repetitive rhythms and patterns, especially those that signify "something more", something beyond and greater than oneself, that hints at a transcendent realm of values, meanings, and feelings. It is to this subject that I now turn.

II. The aesthetics of baseball

"Baseball, of course, is beautiful," wrote philosopher Eric Bronson. That is, on the elemental level it has a lilting aesthetic appeal: "The stadium and uniforms are visual treats, the sounds of the ball hitting the bat or popping into the catcher's mitt takes us back to a more innocent time, as does the smell of peanuts on a hot summer day" (Bronson, 2004, p. 319).[22] The American broadcaster Red Smith made a similar point when he famously quipped, "Ninety feet between home plate and first base may be the closest man has ever come to perfection" (Dickson, 2008, p. 504). Cohen has further elaborated what constitutes the beauty of baseball:

> The structure of baseball is its art. It's a structure that admits of infinitely complicated possibilities and combinations, within the rigid framework of rules in common, of distances to fences, of worked-out angles, of human proportions. Man is the measure of all things. The Major

League ballplayer is the measure of the distances on his
field of trade. Given these, he must do or die, win or lose.
It's the majesty that dignity imparts. (1974, p. 3)

What these baseball pundits are implicitly saying is that to
appreciate the beauty of baseball you need to learn the art of
disciplined observation lodged in a repository of accumu-
lated knowledge. The spacing of the players, the pace of the
game, the fact that there are flashes of discrete action rather
than being a game of flowing action like basketball (Will, 1998,
pp. 241, 311) makes baseball a sport that is most conducive
and best appreciated via disciplined observation. It requires
"thoughtfulness", that is, "attention to detail" (ibid., p. 147).
"Baseball people", said poetry professor Giamatti, "have the
keenest eyes for details I have ever known" (ibid., p. 211).
Often this learning process takes place amid the father/son
bonding relationship when they go to watch a game. In W. P.
Kinsella's *The Iowa Baseball Confederacy*, a father urges his son,
Gideon, to carefully observe the exacting choreography of a
play:

> Gideon, there's a lot more to watching a baseball game
> than keeping your eye on the ball ... [t]he real movement
> doesn't start until the ball is in play. *After* the ball is hit,
> *after* it has cleared the infield, especially if it is going for
> extra bases, you've got to train yourself to look back at the
> infield. While the outfield is running down the ball, watch
> who is covering which base, watch to see who is back-
> ing up third and home. You'll be amazed at the amount
> of movements. Ah, Gideon, when everyone is in motion
> it's like watching those delicate, long-legged insects skim
> over the calm water ...

The father further presses his son to see the more subtle details
of the play, the "purposeful watching" that allows one to see

the "game within the game" (Will, 1990, pp. 49, 288), as it has been called:

> You've got to watch the pitcher, Gideon … and you'll appreciate why baseball is a combination of chess and ballet. Watch him back up the bases, watch him get across to first on a grounder to the right side, see how the first baseman leads him, tossing to an empty sack, trusting him to be there … . It takes a lot of years watching baseball to learn *not* to follow the ball every second. The true beauty of the game is the ebb and flow of the fielders, the kaleidoscopic arrangements and rearrangements of the players in response to a foul ball, an extra-base hit, or an attempted stolen base. (Sexton, 2013, pp. 19–20)[23]

What is it about playing or watching a baseball game that feels like one is doing or watching great art, like going to a great theatre performance, and having the uplifting experience of participating in the "immortal force" of beauty, as Plato described it (Bronson, 2004, p. 319)?[24] To give a plausible answer to this important question, I need to say something about the psychological experience of beauty in terms of the analogy between doing and/or watching a great baseball player and actor performing his craft at the highest level of excellence. As Willie Mays noted, "Baseball players are no different from other performers. We're all actors, when you come right down to it, so I always thought I had to put a little acting into the game—you know, make it more interesting to the fans" (Dickson, 2008, p. 356).[25] Giamatti pointed out, "Athletes and actors … share much." Through years of perfecting their craft they achieve "complete intensity and complete relaxation—complete coherence or integrity between what the performer wants to do and what the performer has to do". The performer has achieved a kind of absolute freedom that operates automatically and naturally (Giamatti, 1998b, p. 40).[26]

The call of beauty

Beauty, most simply defined, is the combination of qualities that make something pleasing and impressive to listen to or touch, or especially to look at. While this definition is a serviceable one, it does not connote what the engagement with beauty, and its internalisation in terms of one's feeling, thinking, and acting, actually means for one's general comportment, one's way of being in terms of living the "good life". As the incomparable actor, theatre director, and developer of method acting, Constantin Stanislavski, advised to singers who were training as actors, "Learn to see, hear, love life—carry this over into art, use it to fill out the image you create for yourself of a character you are to play" (1958, p. 31). This recommendation also applies to the baseball player.

According to Catholic philosopher and poet John O'Donohue, beauty is a kind of "invisible [and] eternal embrace", a tender but pressing call to awaken to the world of the spirit, that vital force that characterises a living being as he embraces life without reserve (2004, p. 13). As Stanislavski said, "Our ideal should always be to strive for what is *eternal* in art, that which will never die, which will always remain young and close to human hearts" (1936, p. 192). For O'Donohue, like Stanislavski, beauty is not so much a thing "out there" that we experience through our senses, though it is that too, rather, like any mystery, it tends to erode the sense of a distinction between "what is in me and what is before me" (Treanor, n.d.). However, more important, as the actress and teacher Stella Adler described acting, the capacity to perceive, feel, and create beauty is a different, more refined way of imaginatively "seeing and describing" the world and one's experience of it (Marcus & Marcus, 2011, p. 44). As O'Donohue noted, "Beauty inhabits the cutting edge of creativity—mediating between the known and unknown, light and darkness, masculine and feminine, visible and invisible, chaos and meaning, sound and silence, self and others" (2004, p. 40). In this context, beauty can be adequately defined for the actor and baseball player as "human subjectivity expressed in ideal form"; in other words, "It is an aspect of experience of idealization in which an object(s), sound(s), or concept(s) is (or are) believed to possess qualities of formal perfection" (Hagman, 2005, p. 87). In most instances, the experience of beauty is enjoyable and can evoke a gamut of emotional states, "from a gentle sense of disinterested pleasure to awe and excited fascination" (e.g., like watching a tidal wave on television). Moreover, while the observer usually believes that the beautiful object or baseball game is inherently beautiful, it is the appropriate and skilful subjective involvement in the object of beauty that is crucial to experience its beauty (ibid.).

The capacity to experience and, most important, create beauty is thus a huge subjective accomplishment that implies a high-level mode of psychological functioning. Indeed, psychoanalysis and other psychological perspectives have elaborated in thousands of books and professional articles the psychology of creativity. For our purposes, I want to simply suggest some of the internal conditions of possibility for a person to experience and create the beautiful, whether in the performing arts, in baseball, or in the art of living the "good life".

George Hagman, a psychoanalyst, has aptly summarised much of the psychoanalytic literature on the sense of beauty. He notes that the main contribution of psychoanalysis has been carefully explicating "the nature, sources, and functions of the subjective experience of beauty" (ibid., p. 94). His integrated findings are worth thinking about as they relate to acting, baseball, and living the "good life", though not surprisingly, as with Stanislavski, much of what has been written by psychoanalysts on creativity has to do with unconscious processes. Stanislavski asked, "How can we come closer to this nature of creation? This has been the principal concern of my whole life" (1949, p. 287). His answer: "Through the conscious to the unconscious, that is the motto of our art and technique" (1961, p. 9). Mainly drawing from Hagman, this brief review of some of the most interesting psychoanalytic formulations about the sense of beauty are provided to give the reader a feel for the internal accomplishments that experiencing and creating beauty seem to entail. Whether actor, baseball player, or ordinary person, Hagman's insights provide much food for thought in terms of understanding why baseball excellence feels so utterly beautiful to both the player and spectator.

Sublimation

For Freud, beauty was understood as a sublimation of sexual and aggressive wishes. Sublimation can be simply defined as a "developmental process by which instinctual energies [i.e., sex and aggression] are discharged in non-instinctual forms of behavior" (Rycroft, 1995, p. 176). Put differently, for any creative, artistic person, whether a baseball player or actor, sublimation is "a resolution of intrapsychic conflict [conflict between two parts of the psyche] by changing the sexual and aggressive aim of an urge and finding a substitute gratification" (Person, Cooper, & Gabbard, 2005, p. 560). Sublimation by definition involves a socially approved result that is gratifying, supple, and judged to be personally and socially beneficial. For example, an actor may have had a childhood in which he was rarely genuinely listened to, appreciated, or otherwise validated by his parents; his need to be heard and admired gets sublimated in his choice of an acting career, of playing to an adoring audience. In the context of baseball, the player's and spectator's involvement in the game is often enmeshed in his childhood experiences, and not only in terms of the father/son bonding and the oedipal drama I have earlier described. Baseball is often a child's first introduction to the adult world, and its heroes are great men whose remarkable accomplishments can be grasped and internalised (Robson, 1998, p. x).

Such identification with a hero evokes in the child, and for that matter in the adult fan, the fantasy that they too can have their transcendent moment of astonishing achievement (Gould, 2003, p. 101). In authentic sublimation, the original strong desire always comes through in the substitute activity. Meryl Streep and Marlon Brando have superbly described sublimation, the former with a pinch of humour, the latter acerbically: "Let's face it, we were all once three year olds who stood in the middle of the living room and everybody thought we were so adorable. Only some of us grow up and get paid for it"; "Acting is the expression of a neurotic impulse. It is a bum's life. The principal benefit acting has afforded me is the money to pay for my psychoanalysis." Paul Newman and Al Pacino, respectively, have also regarded their acting careers as a kind of sublimation: "To be an actor you have to be a child"; "My first language was shy. It's only by having been thrust into the limelight that I have learned to cope." And finally, Stanislavski perceptively noted in his autobiography, "Actors often use the stage to receive what they cannot get in real life" (Marcus & Marcus, 2011, p. 239).

In baseball we also hear sentiments that call to mind child-hood longings and urges. One of the greatest catchers of all time, Roy Campanella, made this exact point: "There has to be a lot of little boy in a man who plays baseball" (Will, 1990, p. 5). Former first baseman Wes Parker captured the child-hood wish to be big and powerful in a larger than life way: "Players believe the mystique about big league baseball prob-ably more than kids or fans do. It's those two words that are not applied to any other sport—big league" (Dickson, 2008, p. 150). With amusing, ironic distance, third baseman Graig Nettles expresses exhibitionistic wishes that are common in childhood: "When I was a little boy, I wanted to be a baseball player and join a circus. With the Yankees I've accomplished both" (ibid., p. 379). Pitcher John "Blue Moon" Odom voiced the wish to remain embedded in the ambivalent comfort and protection of a nuclear family: "We liked the idea that we were a family. We could fight each other in the clubhouse and fight together outside the clubhouse. That's what made us good. You went to the ballpark never knowing what was going to happen" (ibid., p. 403). Joe DiMaggio captured the pure magic of childhood play in saying, "You always get a special kick on opening day, no matter how many you go through. You look forward to it like a birthday party when you're a kid. You think something wonderful is going to happen" (ibid., p. 144). And finally, Willie Mays and Ty Cobb spoke of baseball as a venue for childhood-originating, sublimated aggression,[27] such as sibling rivalry and/or father/son competition: "Baseball is a game, yes. It is also a business. But what it most truly is, is disguised combat. For all its gentility, its almost leisurely pace, baseball is violence under wraps" (Dickson, 2008, p. 356); "Baseball is a red-blooded sport for red-blooded men. It's no pink tea, and mollycoddles had better stay out. It's a struggle for supremacy, a survival of the fittest" (ibid., p. 111). Thus, baseball players, like actors and others, come to their career choice by way of a highly idiosyncratic trajectory that has its psychological roots in childhood wishes, conflicts, and deficits.[28]

Idealisation

The experience and creation of beauty always involves the capacity to idealise. Idealisation, a lifelong process, especially observed when one is in love, is an unrealistic overstatement of a person's qualities. It involves the capacity for illusion; the other person or activity, like acting on a stage, is regarded as living perfection and magnificence. It goes without saying that children and adults idealise their baseball heroes. Stephen Jay Gould wrote that a foul ball that Joe DiMaggio hit and autographed "remains my proudest possession to this day" (2003, p. 133). Idealisation can be a defence against

71

ambivalence ("I love and hate my wife", "I love and hate the profession of acting [or, baseball]"); it is a way of warding off disenchantment, sadness, guilt, and other negative emotions. However, idealisation in the context of beauty can represent a healthy need to be connected to someone or something that is experienced as perfect or ideal. As Babe Ruth said, "Baseball was, is and always will be to me the best game in the world" (Dickson, 2008, p. 473). Pete Rose quipped, "I'd walk through hell in a gasoline suit to play baseball" (ibid., p. 463). And Mickey Mantle said, "Well, baseball was my whole life. Nothing's ever been as fun as baseball" (Andrews, 2012, p. 43).[29] This being said, idealisation of the other, whether a beautiful person, thing, or activity, like baseball, is a delicate and fleeting enterprise. Hagman states,

> The yearning that we experience before beauty is for an experience that is ultimately unattainable, which is already lost, perhaps forever. This is what makes beauty at times unbearable: the simultaneous sense of the ideal as both recovered and lost. (2005, pp. 95–96)

Thus, the experience and creation of beauty is at times a painful and subjectively wounding process, something of which Stanislavski was acutely aware:

> Life [and the creative process] is an unremitting *struggle*, one overcomes or one is defeated. Likewise on the stage, side-by-side, with the through action there will be a series of *counter-through actions* on the part of other characters, other circumstances. The collision and conflict of these two opposing through actions constitute the dramatic situation.[30] (1961, p. 80; emphasis in original)

To be a great baseball player is also an "unremitting struggle" in that it fundamentally is a game of "failure"—just think of the odds of getting a hit. Moreover, there is a pronounced struggle between one team's desire to create opportunities to score, which often comes literally down to inches—"Baseball is a game of normal proportions and abnormally small margins" (Will, 1990, pp. 1, 34)—and the other team's utter commitment to stop them dead in their tracks.

Active engagement

To experience and create beauty is not a passive undertaking; it requires marked involvement, energy, and action. In acting and baseball, achieving excellence requires a total commitment of mind, body, and soul. Only in this way, when the doer merges with the beautiful animate or inanimate other, is he liberated from his limited, subdued, or truncated sense of himself. The experience of beauty and its creation involves an intellectual, emotional, and spiritual engagement, an "interactive and inter-subjective" process (Hagman, 2005, p. 96), one that tends to foster a sense of self-transcendence. In baseball, where fortune can change in a flash, especially disastrously, where memories of such disastrous moments are easily recollected by players and fans, victory is that much sweeter, for "Hope builds slowly to success in a way that makes success more beautiful" (Sexton, 2013, p. 14). Perfect self and perfect world, creator and observer, loss/disappointment and abundance/satisfaction constitute, in part, the psychological landscape of the sense of beauty. In a way, as D. W. Winnicott pointed out, the experience of beauty, and for that matter all forms of art, takes place between the above-mentioned dualities and polarities, in the overlapping "halfway" space between subjective and objective, the psychic and the external worlds. Residing in this "between-ness" psychic space results in a wide range of emotions, such as "awe, joy, excitement, optimism and contentment" as well as "anger, sexual excitement and fear", as this range of emotions is embedded within the "formal structure" of the experience of beauty (Hagman, 2005, p. 97). Indeed, as insinuated earlier, baseball is chock-full of dualities and polarities and emotional swings and roundabouts, and this is why when we observe a great player integrating these ambiguous if not conflicting forces, we are in awe. Giamatti noted, for example, that the great pitcher Tom Seaver "pitched as much with his head as with his legs and right arm, a remarkably compact, *concentrated* pitcher, brilliantly blending control and speed, those twin capacities for restraint and release that are the indispensable possession of the great artist" (1998a, p. 17). Seaver claimed that at the height of his pitching control, "[H]e could pitch within a quarter of an inch of a spot nine times out of ten" (Will, 1990, p. 149).[31] To observe such professional craftsmanship, such excellence, is akin to experiencing a kind of "spiritual epiphany" (Sexton, 2013, p. 94), a sudden manifestation of the essence or meaning of athletic perfection.

Giving way to the healing and self-enhancing experience of beauty

In order to yield to the self-transcendent, transformative experience of beauty and its creation, one must be able to "let go", to hurl oneself into the invisible embrace. This "letting go" can be done in many different ways and intensities depending on the context, from passionately surrendering to the allure of a beautiful person or to the felt presence of God through prayer, to quietly admiring a lovely sunset or the elegance of a mathematical equation. This letting go is what separates the baseball fan from the observer who finds the game dull or boring. As Hagman noted, following Emmanuel Ghent, it is "through this experience of surrender that we break out of the confines of our false selves and allow ourselves to be known, found, penetrated, and recognized—it is a vital, natural force toward psychological and spiritual growth" (2005, p. 98). This capacity to be open and responsive sounds easier than it actually is. As the great Roman lyric poet Horace wrote, "If you would

have me weep, you must first of all feel grief yourself" (www.
eng.aphorism.ru/author/horace/).[32] There are many people
who are twisted up like pretzels, so inhibited, defended, and
in other ways internally restricted that they cannot appreciate
beauty or creatively imagine and produce something beautiful.
For them, life lacks the "presence and possibility" of a "real"
encounter with the mysteriously beautiful, which is also always
a striking self-encounter. O'Donohue said, "Yet ultimately
beauty is a profound illumination of presence, a stirring of the
invisible in visible form and in order to receive this, we need to
cultivate a new style of approaching the world" (2004, p. 23).
Thus, when beauty and its creation touches the "matrix of
human selfhood" (ibid., p. 21), whether gently or disruptively,
it always enlarges, expands, and enriches consciousness—it is
"an encounter of depth and spirit" (ibid., p. 23).

The encounter with the beautiful, whether as an observer
or a creator, thus has a healing aspect to it. It is capable of
facilitating a feeling of "harmony, balance, and wholeness"
(Hagman, 2005, p. 99), better ways of experiencing and engaging the self and the world. Moreover, it can "repair the feared
fragmentation or damage done to internal objects by aggressive wishes". (An internal object is "that towards which action
or desire is directed; that which the subject requires in order
to achieve [sexual or aggressive] satisfaction; that to which
the subject relates himself" (Rycroft, 1995, p. 113).) Put more
simply, beauty helps the person subdue, transform, or undo
the aggressive fantasies that we all consciously or unconsciously periodically have towards others (think of the anger
the pitcher and batter feel towards each other; each sees the
other as the "enemy"). It can also reduce the anxiety associated
with death by putting the person "in touch" with a transcendent belief, value, and self-experience that is regarded as definitively, overwhelmingly, and eternally truthful and good.[33] As
Hagman noted, "Beauty is not illusory, nor does it stand in or
cover up something else" (though it can). Rather, beauty may

express "man's search for perfection, transcendence and hope ..." It is "one of the most exquisite forms of human meaning that exists" (2005, p. 101).[34] In the context of baseball playing and/or spectatorship, Hagman has it exactly right. Giamatti's title to his scholarly baseball book, *Take Time for Paradise* and John Sexton's title to his, *Baseball as a Road to God*,[35] superbly capture Hagman's important observation about the nature of beauty. First-baseman and manager Buck O'Neil made the same point, though using rather earthier language: "Baseball is better than sex. It is better than music, although I do believe jazz comes in a close second. It does fill you up" (1996, p. 63).

III. Baseball as moral instruction

"Baseball", said former catcher and announcer Joe Garagiola, "gives you every chance to be great. Then it puts every pressure on you to prove you haven't got what it takes" (Dickson, 2008, p. 192). The all-time greatest no-hitter pitcher who regularly threw pitches at 100 mph, Nolan Ryan, said something very similar, "One of the beautiful things about baseball is that every once in a while you come into a situation where you want to, and where you have to, reach down and prove something" (Stewart, 2012, p. 39). Proving something, especially to oneself, perhaps even more than to real and imagined others, is mainly a question of character, that is, moral and ethical excellence. As sports columnist Thomas Boswell wrote, "We are drawn to baseball because, while it may not always teach character, it usually reveals it" (Will, 1998, p. 48). Indeed, baseball is a game that brings out the best, and sometimes the worst, in its players, managers, and spectators. For example, think of the tragic grandeur of Lou Gehrig's "farewell speech" at Yankee Stadium after he was diagnosed with the fatal disease named after him—"Yet today I consider myself the luckiest man on the face of the earth," versus the nastiness, if not sadism, of Ty Cobb, whom baseball scholar Stephen Jay Gould calls both the "finest player in the history of baseball" and "the meanest star in the history of American sport" (Gould, 2003, pp. 328–329).[36] As pitcher great Jim Bouton wrote in *Ball Four Plus Ball Five*, "There's pettiness in baseball, and meanness and stupidity beyond belief, and everything bad that you'll find outside of baseball" (1984, p. xix).[37] Most important for this chapter, baseball is a venue of moral insight, for it articulates and instantiates life-affirming values and commitments that point to what really matters in life; that is, to the importance of embracing transcendent values that can enhance one's autonomy, integration, and humanity. Such attachments often reflect rather finely nuanced moral reasoning: As one batter who was brushed back by a pitcher's fastball quipped, "They shouldn't throw at me. I'm the father of five or six kids!" (Will, 1998, p. 68).

What existential philosopher Albert Camus (who played goalie for the University of Algiers) said about sports readily applies to baseball: From "sports … I learned all I know about ethics" (1960, p. 242).[38] What Camus was getting at is that from the moral perspective, baseball, like all sports that are played honourably, should have the same objective as great art. "The aim of art, the aim of a life can only be to increase the sum of freedom and responsibility to be found in every man and in the world" (ibid., p. 240).[39]

Like with Adam and Eve before their fall, unrestricted, unrestrained freedom is as close to "paradise" as one can get. Baseball, according to Giamatti, speaks to American moral identity like no other sport, for it "best mirrors the condition of freedom", that amalgamation of intense energy and complex order, "that Americans ever guard and aspire to" (Sexton, 2013, p. 83). Similar to all sports, baseball assumes equality for the reason of creating inequality, a level playing field on which the best will assert their superiority (Will, 1998, p. 220). It teaches us how to win based on excellence.[40] However, as in everyday life, there can be a rough justice in baseball. Sometimes "good guys" come in last, reminding us that life often feels grossly unjust.[41] Baseball also teaches us how to lose graciously. Moreover, Giamatti claimed, "Our national plot is to be free enough to consent to an order that will enhance and compound—as it constrains—our freedom. That is our grounding, our national story, the tale America tells the world" and itself (1998b). Commenting on Giamatti's important point, Will noted that baseball perfectly duplicates the challenge of freedom that Americans so cherish, especially through those who impartially protect the rule of law and dispense justice—the quintessential constrainers of baseball freedom, the umpires (Will, 1998, p. 220). As an angry Babe Ruth told hard-nosed umpire Babe Pinelli who called him out on strikes, "There's 40,000 people here who know that last one was a ball, tomato head." Pinelli famously replied, "Maybe so, but mine is the only opinion that counts" (Will, 1990, p. 64). The point is that truth may be inflexible and inviolable, but ironically, it is also context-dependent and setting-specific, that is, "Truth is a circumstance, not a spot" (Gould, 2003, pp. 48–49).

As in real life, in baseball, freedom is knotted to responsibility, for it is not only a matter of individual self-affirmation and personal accountability, but it centrally includes actions that strengthen and deepen moral community.[42] Baseball values individual achievement but never at the expense of the common good and the team's overarching goal of a fair win. That is, baseball values actions that are, to paraphrase ethical philosopher Emmanuel Levinas, firstly "for the other" rather than "for oneself". These are the instances where one's crude narcissism, the egotistical search for individual immortality, must give way to the more commanding needs of the team.[43] In baseball, this being for the other before oneself is manifested in many ways, but most obviously it is personified in the notion of "sacrifice", especially the "sacrifice bunt" or "sacrifice hit". A sacrifice bunt is when a batter purposely bunts the ball (that is, the batter loosely holds the bat in front of home plate and intentionally lightly taps the ball into play) before there are two men out to permit a runner on base to proceed to another base. The batter is usually sacrificed, which is the purpose of the bunt, though occasionally he gets to first base because of a fielder's error or strategic decision. Young further elaborates other instances of baseball sacrifice:

> ... a sacrifice fly, advancing to draw a throw so a runner may score, or pitching deep into a ball game to let the bullpen rest. A batter may let himself be hit by a pitch, to give his team a base runner; or, if an opposing team pitches the batter's inside, a pitcher may throw at the opposing team, risking ejection or retaliation to protect the other players. (2004, p. 61)[44]

Indeed, baseball's notion of sacrifice is so compelling that it has become a metaphorical way of affirming the personal meaning of this moral virtue in other critical contexts. As the admiral said to Lt. Brickley in John Ford's 1945 film classic, *They Were Expendable*, "Listen, son, you and I are professionals. If the manager says, 'Sacrifice,' we lay down a bunt and let somebody else hit the home runs ... Our job is to lay down that sacrifice. That's what we were trained for, and that's what we will do" (TCM, n.d.).

While the notion of "sacrifice" is a hugely complex and multifaceted philosophical and psychological notion, I want to briefly focus on the most obvious, though often underappreciated, aspect of sacrifice in baseball, namely, that the game has evolved so that the very notion of "sacrifice" is central to its play. As the saying goes, baseball is "almost the only place in life where a sacrifice is really appreciated".

What a "sacrifice bunt" in baseball puts into sharp focus is the importance of committing yourself to something beyond yourself, beyond what psychoanalyst Karen Horney called the narcissistically driven individual "search for glory". Whether for player, manager, or fan, baseball at its best should be about fashioning a close tie with others who share similar transcendent-pointing values (Senor, 2004, p. 55), like the importance of teamwork. As Yogi Berra allegedly said, "When you sacrifice, you stand beside your teammates, by putting them in front of yourself" (Young, 2004, p. 57). Cal Ripkin noted, "I was raised to play for the team, not for yourself" (Will, 1990, p. 233). It is precisely this being for the other, or "being-for-us", that is foundational to the important narrative role that baseball has in American life, and to all others who love the game, including because of "the moral community it inspires" (Morgan, 2004, p. 167). The power of baseball is that it draws "people together for something more than merely baseball" (Sexton, 2013, p. 192), something beyond one's self-serving, selfish needs.[45] Morgan further elaborated this point just right: "The goods [that is, the moral standards and sensibility] of baseball are very much like those of friendship, in which an important part of what is valued is the very fact that they are shared." In a similar manner, Morgan said, "Becoming a member of the baseball fraternity also requires us to transform our own desires for the sake of the common good of the game" (2004, pp. 163–164). It is from a cast of mind that regards being for the other and "being-for-us" as paramount, that other related moral values such as accountability to one's teammates, like not letting them down, and to opposing players, the importance of fair play, and generating "courage in the clinch" and "strength in adversity" (Gould, 2003, p. 177) probably emanate. As Will noted, to play baseball skilfully, "[A] remarkable degree of mental and moral discipline is required" (1990, p. 226). Indeed, this other-directed, other-regarding, other-serving moral vision that baseball personifies at its best has been suggested by some of baseball's heroes, Joe DiMaggio and Tom Seaver. Tellingly, both of these greats referred to one of the paradigms of selfless giving, namely, the love a parent gives a child. Moreover, both express a wish for symbolic immortality in terms of the legacy of excellence that is passed on to the next generation. Joe DiMaggio said, "There is always some kid who may be seeing me for the first time. I owe him my best" (Rosen, with Bruton, 2012, p. 125); Tom Seaver quoted, "My children will be able to take their children to the Hall of Fame and say, 'There's your grandfather. He was pretty good at what he did.' It's something that solidifies a family" (Dickson, 2008, p. 486).[46] Finally, there are the uplifting words from the master of the "cutter" pitch, the extraordinary Mariano Rivera, a fervent religious believer, who said, "Everything I have and everything I became is because of the strength of the Lord, and through him I have accomplished everything. Not because of my strength. Only by his love, his mercy and his truth." Most important for this chapter, Rivera said, "He put it in me, for me to use it. To bring glory, not to Mariano Rivera, but to the Lord" (Miller, 2013, p. 22). Sometimes when a person is being for the other before oneself, the "other" is highly abstract, that is, "unthematiseable" and unrepresentable using ordinary language. That "other" is literally and metaphorically beyond oneself, or at least it feels that way, and yet the "other" positively animates one's everyday outlook and behaviour. The "other" is thus both transcendent and immanent. In religious parlance, this feeling of being "beyond oneself", a feeling that points to an inexplicable "something more", has been described by theologians and others as calling to mind God, the Ineffable, the Eternal, the Infinite, or as I have called it, the sense that one is glimpsing immortality. It is on this topic that I will conclude this chapter.

IV. Baseball and immortality

In Chapter One I described, following Robert Jay Lifton, the personal encounter of glimpsing immortality in everyday life as a form of experiential transcendence, a moment when time and death seem to vanish. Such profoundly transformational and pleasing moments reflect what psychoanalyst Margaret Mahler characterised as emblematic for the well-taken-care-of child beginning to walk, a toddler's "love affair with the world". Such adult analogies of being charmed, if not in love with life, always involve an "unselving" or self-emptying, that is, a "losing oneself" and entering into what feels like a different dimension of the spirit, a higher plane of existence. In baseball, there are at least two modes of glimpsing immortality. The first is a more familiar and accessible experience, those moments when one witnesses a brilliant flash of astonishing excellence in baseball craftsmanship, like Willie Mays's famous on-the-run, over-the-shoulder catch on the warning track during the first game of the 1954 World Series between the Cleveland Indians and the New York Giants at New York's Polo Grounds. The second mode of glimpsing immortality is less brilliant but no less elevating and transformational—the dreamy, mystical-like experience of going to a ball game, that sacred place[47] where freedom is the condition of possibility for an upsurge of faith and hope as it longs for fulfilment.

"Peak" moments in baseball

Like any sport, baseball loves its moments of pure perfection, when an individual player or team achieves something so extraordinary that it feels nearly god- or divine-like. These perfect moments become the stuff of legend, "canonical stories" (Gould, 2003, p. 237) that are told and retold and provide the meaning and pleasure associated with a retrospective consciousness. Such memories are often textured with nostalgia, reminding us of "the most poignant fact" about the game, and indeed of any sport—the fleeting nature of an accomplishment (Sexton, 2013, p. 39). Nostalgia is one of baseball's most distinctive aspects. "The game's past shadows its present, to prod memories, and to revive dormant emotions. Nostalgia is the tribute the present pays to the past" (ibid., p. 198). As Gould reflects:

> As a pure contingency of my own life, I happened to
> come of baseball fandom's age in the greatest conjunction

of time and place that the game has ever known: in New York City during the late 1940s and early 1950s [Gould was born in 1941]. The situation was entirely unfair to the rest of the country—hey—you can't possibly cast any blame on me, so I owe no one any apology. From 1947 to 1957 New York City had the three greatest teams in major league baseball [the Dodgers, the Yankees, and the Giants] ... All New York City boys of the late 1940s and early 1950s were baseball nuts, barring mental deficiency or incomprehensible idiosyncrasy. How could one not be? (2003, p. 32)

Central to this part of baseball history was the hundred-year Brooklyn Dodger rivalry with the Manhattan-based New York Giants, what many baseball scholars have called the greatest rivalry in baseball history. Most noteworthy was the 1951 legendary game-winning ninth inning home run— "the shot heard 'round the world"—hit by Giant outfielder Bobby Thomson off the Dodgers pitcher Ralph Branca at the Polo Grounds, a celebrated hit that led the Giants to win the National League pennant and go to the World Series against the Yankees (the Yankees won). Thomson's remarkable home run, and the Giants' win after surmounting a double-digit deficit in the standings during the weeks before the show-down, made the Giants' victory that much more magnificent. Thomson described the exhilaration of that moment that was shared with thousands of fans and spectators:

> Cloud nine. How else can I describe the feeling? We beat the Dodgers. We won the pennant. I hit a home run. Everybody went nuts. Storybook stuff, the whole thing. I still don't know why I was hyperventilating as I ran around the bases. It must have been the excitement, the pure joy, all those amazing feelings just coming together ... I didn't run around the bases—I rode around 'em on a cloud.

Wow, I still don't know what time it is or where I am. Frankly, I don't care. (Dickson, 2008, p. 553)

The great sportswriter for the *New York Herald Tribune*, Red Smith, famously wrote about the Giants' victory: "Now it is done. Now the story ends. And there is no way to tell it. The art of fiction is dead. Reality has strangled invention. Only the utterly impossible, the inexpressibly fantastic, can ever be plausible again" (1951, n.p.).

As Sexton correctly pointed out, Thomson's home run and the Giants' victory has become part of baseball mythology. Similar to liturgical stories, such moments are "forever remembered and repeated with the solemnity of the most beloved sacred stories". In baseball there are hundreds of such stories, and as the quotation from Thomson indicates, such moments involve "heightened awareness—divergent from ordinary time and place—in which some discover a connection to something deeper than the ordinary". Such moments are not only remembered for what they were, but more important, for "what they have evoked in those who experienced them" (Sexton, 2013, pp. 15, 195), namely, a sense of wonder and awe, of the miraculous. And like observing a miracle, they are thoroughly elevating and inspiring to those who engage the experience with the fullness of their being. As Gould noted about the Thomson home run,

> Nothing can explain the meaning and excitement of all this to nonfans. No sensible person would even try. This is church—and nonbelievers cannot know the spirit. One can only recall Louis Armstrong's famous statement about the nature of jazz: "Man, if you gotta ask, you'll never know." (2003, p. 74)

My point is simple: To glimpse immortality in everyday life, one must be radically welcoming of the transcendent, the willingness and ability to be receptive and responsive to the "other". This includes embracing the otherness of the subtle, nuanced, and complex game of baseball that skilful and heart-felt spectatorship at its best demands. To fully engage the tapestry of life-affirming, numinous presences, events of "pure disclosure", like the "sudden epiphany" (O'Donohue, 2004, p. 12) of Thomson's home run and the Giants' victory, is to be actively receptive to what can be described as a moment of "grace". Indeed, the sublime, spontaneous baseball moments have the hallmarks of a grace experience, including the gratitude that one feels for having been given a "gift" of witnessing baseball perfection, and of course, of one's loved team achieving victory. Moreover, in a game that involves so many inexplicable changes of fortune, accident, and lucky breaks, like in all grace experiences, there is a felt sense of the "gift" being unmerited, an aspect of the grace experience that makes it feel that much more uplifting and gratitude-inducing. As Joe DiMaggio famously said in 1949 at Yankee Stadium, "I'd like to thank the Good Lord for making me a Yankee" (Dickson, 2008, p. 142).

The "beautiful infinitude" of baseball

Glimpsing immortality can also take place amid less dramatic moments than witnessing, say, a clutch home run by Bobby Thomson, a triple play, or a runner stealing home (a lost art these days). Unlike football, basketball, and soccer, baseball is a game that has no time limitations, and this is perhaps one of the reasons why it tends to display a more subtle "beautiful infinitude" (Sexton, 2013, p. 217), at least to those who can appreciate not only the nuances of the game, but the overall ambience of the stadium, the place that holds "paradise, the public place for public pleasure" (Giamatti, 1998b, p. 78), and spiritual enlightenment within the context of a community. Baseball has no clock; it moves counterclockwise and therefore has its own unique rhythms, tempos, and patterns (Will, 1998,

p. 219),[48] most notably, the long season that begins in spring and gradually builds up to its thrilling culmination points in autumn, playing for the pennant and in the World Series. Thus, baseball beckons us to live more slowly, mindfully, and seasonally, to view the world "differently and more intensely" (Sexton, 2013, p. 217)[49] than we usually do. When we take time to notice, we are able to perceive and appreciate some of the quieter lovely moments, the "fragile intangibles" (Will, 1998, p. 47)[50] that are taking place throughout the typical baseball experience, moments of perception that constitute some of its more subtle "ineffable joys" (Sexton, 2013, p. 220).

To begin with, there is the zany world of baseball fandom, a world that is forever amusing in its extremism about something that has no serious implication for everyday life. Indeed, as Will aptly noted, "Americans, myself emphatically included, are prone to forget that sports are only serious in a funny way. Part of the fun of having flaming passions about our favorite teams—the fun of being a 'fan,' short for *fanatic*—is the comic lack of proportion in it" (1998, p. 25).[51] As the anonymous saying goes, "A baseball fan is a spectator sitting 500 feet from home plate who [actually believes he] can see better than an umpire standing five feet away!"

Baseball's zany fans are also uniquely obsessed with statistics. I am reminded of a billionaire (not millionaire, a billionaire) businessman patient I saw in psychotherapy who told me that the first thing he does when he comes down for breakfast is check the baseball statistics from the previous night. Only after digesting these numbers does he then review what happened in the European and Asian financial markets![52] The charm of baseball, especially for us ordinary beleaguered adults, is the illusion it provides that life can be controlled, if not mastered, if it is reduced to numbers. That is, just as managers and coaches rely on performance averages, like batting averages, sacrifices, stolen bases and the like, to try to predict future player performance, the typical fan unconsciously believes that if he studies the numbers associated with baseball, and this becomes a cast of mind that he applies to everyday life, he will never be surprised, let alone overwhelmed or defeated. Of course, this is pure nonsense because like baseball, said Will, life is a "magical mix of science and serendipity". There is an "irreducible indeterminacy" to baseball statistics that makes the quest for perfect control an absurd undertaking (1990, p. 298). Listening to two baseball fans talk baseball statistics and what they allegedly mean for the future, especially if they root for different teams, is almost as much fun as watching a lively presidential debate. As Will further notes, fans' love of statistics has childhood origins—"baseball statistics gave many of us our first sense of mastery, our first (and for some of us our last) sense of what it feels like to really understand something, and to know more about something than our parents do" (1998, pp. 55, 66).

The fan's obsession with baseball statistics often also involves the accumulation of other interesting information about the game, anecdotes that demonstrate that deeply caring about the game for its own sake is a worthwhile endeavour. This caring mirrors baseball players at their best. Baseball heroism, John Updike wrote, "comes not from flashes of brilliance, but … from 'the players who always care' about themselves and their craft" (ibid., pp. 159–160). Thus, fans have a great sense of baseball history and tradition involving comparisons between current and past players, teams, and eras. In fact, as Giametti pointed out, "Baseball is in a sense, the conversation about it" (ibid., p. 192). It is such baseball talk that provides a sense of historical continuity, a form of "institutional memory", that strengthens a fan's (and player's) attachment and loyalty to the national pastime. Will makes this point just right: baseball "… has had an ambience of ritual matured through long, steady seasons. It has conveyed a marvelous sense of cumulativeness of life, captured in the richness of baseball statistics" (ibid., p. 48) and conversation.

Baseball players and fans also provide a powerful context for observing the dynamics of faith and hope (and their opposites),[53] which can be uplifting to observe. One only has to recall the great relief pitcher Tug McGraw's immortal words spoken in late July 1973, words that became the motto and exhortation that was used by the underdog New York Mets as they advanced from sixth place to the National League pennant, "Ya gotta believe" (Dickson, 2008, p. 363). McGraw's motto personifies the faith that the improbable is possible, if one is hugely motivated to prevail. In this sense, baseball provided what faith at its best does, the consolation, incentive, comprehension, and most of all, a "meaning and ultimate purpose" that transports a player and fan to a different dimension of the spirit, to what feels like a higher plane of existence (Sexton, 2013, pp. 36, 45). Even when one's team loses, when one's aspirations have been crushed, hope springs eternal. Just think of the vanquished fan's heartfelt cry, "Wait 'til next year!"

Likewise, every time a batter comes to the plate, it evokes an upsurge of hope in the spectator. When the batter gets a hit, especially in the clutch, the experience becomes etched in our memory, "memories of our best hopes". Giamatti further clarified,

> They are memories of a time when all that would be better was before us, as a hope, and the hope was fastened to a game. One hoped not so much to be the best who ever played as simply to stay in the game and ride it wherever it would go, culling its rhythms and realizing its promises. That is, I think, what it means to remember one's best hopes, and to remember them in a game, and revive them whenever one sees the game played, long after playing is over. (1998a, p. 88)

What is noteworthy about this hope/memory dynamic is that it is linked to our deepest individual and collective aspirations for self-transformation, the wish to be all we can be as we honourably strive for real or imagined excellence. This emotional cluster is part of what makes baseball so lovely and lovable. As Morgan aptly noted, baseball invokes a moral image of America at its best, one that as individuals and a nation we want to passionately identify with: "a nation of strivers moved not so much by greed and crass self-interest as by a larger vision of excellence, one obtained by arduous effort, social cooperation, and an abiding sense of fair play" (2004, p. 157). For those fans who love the game around the world, the universal spirit of this moral image also deeply resonates.

V. Final reflection

I have argued that baseball, when skilfully and passionately played and observed, is "a form and object of love", and because it is, it touches, sometimes only marginally, on many of "life's great themes" (Will, 1998, p. 100). Most important, baseball teaches us something about what is a critical psychological achievement in terms of human growth and development, and what it takes to live the "good life". A flourishing life requires effectively negotiating separation and individuation, that daunting process that begins in childhood, of "becoming a person", of actualising inner autonomy, integration, and humanity. Giamatti has noted that in baseball the batter's Odyssey-like goal is "to arrive at the same place, which is where they start", home plate, though reaching home is less a place than a state of mind. As I have emphasised, this state of mind is very different from when one began one's odyssey, whether on or off the baseball field. Such an altered state of mind personifies the actualisation of inner freedom and responsibility as one confronts the challenges that leaving one's home entails. As Ted Williams said, "God gets you to the plate, but from then on, you're on your own" (Gould, 2003, p. 17).[54] Most important, unlike Odysseus, who nostalgically longs for the return to an existence that he has always lived, baseball also calls to mind the biblical image of Abraham, who is uprooted from his country and never looks back, having no hope of returning home. That is, as Levinas has noted, it is the estrangement of the uprooted, the engagement with the unfamiliar and foreign, both externally and internally, on and off the baseball field, which brings about one's individuation, integrity, and humanity (Marcus, 2008, p. 200). Indeed, this is one of the important insights that baseball teaches us—there is no such thing as "going home again" in an absolute way. By resigning oneself without despair to this existential truth, by never making one's home in a place, one learns to reside in the imaginative realm of the mind, in that "internal stadium"[55] of cherished memories and dreamy hopes. It is these inspiring and nurturing memories and hopes which we safely preserve deep within us that provide the emotional staging ground for appreciating, if not celebrating, the loveliness and profundity of baseball. Such a "reverential mind" allows the possibility for transcendence, for we graciously let a thing simply be, and celebrate its beauty without wanting something tangible from it (O'Donohue, 1998, p. 111). As the immortal "Sultan of Swat", Babe Ruth, said on Babe Ruth Day at Yankee Stadium in 1947, "I thank heaven we have had baseball in this world" (Dickson, 2008, p. 475).[56]

Notes

1. Galeano further noted, "Sometimes soccer is a pleasure that hurts" (p. 270).
2. While it is beyond the scope of this chapter to discuss other sports in detail, I will from time to time reference soccer and other sports in the body of the text, though mainly in the foot-notes. This being said, it must never be forgotten that each sport has its unique aura.
3. Soccer has even more impressive statistics. As Philip Moore pointed out, "No other game is played by as many people, and no other sport has the numbers of spectators that this sport

attracts" (2000, p. 117). For example, Juventus Football Club, based in Turin, Piedmont, the most successful Italian team, has about 12 million fans in Italy and 173 million worldwide (Borghini & Baldini, 2010, p. 306). While most spectators by far are men, it has been estimated that about 10% to 20% of worldwide soccer spectators are female and the numbers are rapidly increasing (Hoyningen-Huene, 2010, p. 9).

4. Soccer, too, appeals to famous intellectuals. Consider, for example, the great rhapsodist of soccer, the Uruguayan journalist and novelist, Eduardo Galeano, who wrote his highly regarded ode to soccer's immortality, *Soccer in Sun and Shadow*. Jean-Paul Sartre was also a devotee of soccer, and even wrote a complicated passage about relationships between soccer players in his *Critique of Dialectical Reason*, while he also discussed the nature of refereeing in other works (Crowe, 2010, p. 347). Finally, the former prime minister of the UK, Harold Wilson, quipped, "I know more about soccer than about politics" (Pepple, 2010, p. 201). For more reflections about soccer by intellectuals, see Turnbull, Satterlee, and Raab (2008).

5. As the former American League baseball pitcher, Jim Bouton, quipped, "Baseball players are smarter than football players. How often do you see a baseball team penalized for too many men on the field?" (Burman, 2012, p. 116). This being said, as national TV ratings have repeatedly shown, football and basketball have become more popular than baseball in American society. Why this is the case has to do with broader cultural trends that have fashioned America. For example, football is "louder, faster and more violent", and this facilitates more excitement, compared to baseball which is "quiet" and "slow" with flashes of excitement. In our current cultural moment such considerations appear to be more psychologically in tune with sports fans (see Mahler, 2013). However, some baseball scholars have claimed that basketball is not a more popular sport than baseball by most measures such as viewership, attendance, and revenue/team value (Peter Schwartz, personal communication, 20 December 2013).

6. George Orwell made a similar point when he wrote, "International football is the continuation of war by other means."

(In fact, Orwell further noted, "Serious sport is war minus the shooting.") Galeano also described soccer as "choreographed war" and as a "metaphor for war" (2009, pp. 18, 149). These observations are supported by the fact that in baseball and international soccer matches the national anthems are played before a game begins, which amplifies the fan's sense of solidarity and patriotism (see www.hdfootballwallpaper.com/quotes.php). The American writer, Chad Harbach, highlighted another interesting difference between baseball and soccer: "Baseball is a team game but, at the same time, it is a very lonely game: unlike in soccer or basketball, where players roam around, in baseball everyone has their little plot of the field to tend. When the action comes to you, the spotlight is on you but no one can help you" (*Sydney Morning Herald*, www.smh.com.au/.../interview-chad-harb).

7. Will was quoting from Sandy Alderson, the Harvard lawyer who was the general manager of the Mets.

8. Soccer has also been written about in a similar manner. For example, one author claims that "Football re-enacts the drama of life," in particular the mixture of "ability" and "chance", that often ends in terrible injustices on the pitch. Thus, "The secret of the beautiful game is its variability in the mixture of these two elements" (Hoyningen-Huene, 2010, pp. 12, 15). Similar to baseball, soccer allows the spectator to find consolation in the beauty of the game; it provides a sense of belonging, and it allows for emotional catharsis among other psychological functions (Lambert, 2010, pp. 218–219). As one author put it, through soccer "... we learn how short and long a minute can be. We learn to suffer. We learn to rejoice. All of this happens because football is an emotional compromise" (Olaya, Lammoglia, & Zarama, 2010, p. 285). Soccer is also frequently "used to interpret life's good and bad fortune, ethical virtue, creativity, loyalty, and honor" among other valuative attachments (Borghini & Baldini, 2010, p. 316). And finally, as the great Liverpool manager Bill Shankly famously remarked, "Some people believe football [soccer] is a matter of life and death. I'm very disappointed with that attitude. I can assure

you it is much, much more important than that" (see www.shankly.com/article/2517).

9. Soccer also requires considerable literacy to fully grasp and enjoy it. As English novelist J. B. Priestly noted, "To say that these men paid their shillings to watch twenty-two hirelings kick a ball is merely to say that a violin is wood and catgut, and that Hamlet is so much paper and ink" (Hutchinson, 2000, p. 3).

10. The great powerhouse Ted Williams noted about the art of hitting, "Wait-wait-wait and then quick-quick-quick." As Will noted, "Quickness is the quality most rewarded in baseball," whether when one is batting or on the field (1990, p. 281). Wade Boggs was less clear about the art of hitting, though his words are probably more typical for the geniuses of the game: "Everyone asks me 'why' about everything. I have no idea. I see it. I swing, I hit it" (Dickson, 2008, p. 65). Cristiano Ronaldo, the great Portuguese soccer player known for his offensive brilliance, had a similar view: "I don't think about one trick or the other, they just happen" (www.ronaldo7.net/extra/quotes/cristiano-ronaldo-quotes.html). Lionel Messi, the spectacular Argentine forward, also noted, "I never think about the play or visualize anything. I do what comes to me at that moment. Instinct. It has always been that way" (see www.lushquotes.com/author/lionel-messi/).

11. The Brazilian soccer legend Pelé, arguably the greatest soccer player of all time, noted, "Pelé doesn't die [that is, his accomplishments]. Pelé will never die. Pelé is going to go on for ever" (see www.theguardian.com:Sport:Football). A headline in *The Sunday Times* after Brazil's World Cup victory read, "How do you spell Pelé? G-O-D" (see www.fifa.com/.../players/player=63869/).

12. The great outfielder Willie Mays noted, "I remember the last season I played. I went home after a ball game one day, lay down on my bed, and tears came to my eyes. How can you explain that? It's like crying for your mother after she's gone. You cry because you love her. I cried, I guess, because I loved baseball and I knew I had to leave her" (Dickson, 2008, p. 356).

13. In soccer, the theme of father/son bonding is poignantly expressed by Cristiano Ronaldo, who said, "When I win awards, I think of my father" (www.ronaldo7.net/extra/quotes/cristiano-ronaldo-quotes.html). Pelé recalled, "I always had a philosophy which I got from my father. He used to say, 'Listen, God gave to you the gift to play football. This is your gift from God. If you take care of your health, if you are in good shape all the time, with your gift from God no one will stop you, but you must be prepared" (see thegoaldiggers.weebly.com/legends-of-the-game.html). Also worth mentioning is that Hope Solo, American soccer goalkeeper who won two Olympic gold medals, noted, "My father was never around. But I glorified my father, and I was always daddy's little girl. He was my first soccer coach" (see www.npr.org › Arts & Life› Books› Author Interviews).

14. A home run is also a symbolic "gift" to the adoring fans.

15. I am indebted to Joe Kraus's essay, "There's No Place Like Home!" for drawing my attention to the applicability of Freud's "uncanny" to baseball (Bronson, 2004, p. 12).

16. In soccer, the referee has been aptly described in terms of his "loneliness" (as has the goalkeeper who watches the game alone, from a distance). As in other sports, some referees are sticklers, others dodge making tough decisions, some are frustrated players and others are "poseurs" or "tough guys" (Crowe, 2010, p. 347). In one recent instance, a referee in Santa Ines, Brazil got horribly swept into the usually beautifully sublimated violence associated with soccer. Referee Octavio da Silva "told player Josenir dos Santos Abreu ... that he was out of the game. The two began to scuffle, and da Silva pulled a knife and stabbed the player to death. Fans armed with rocks poured onto the field, stoned da Silva to death, and tore his body into quarters. Local media reported that the spectators then decapitated da Silva and stuck his head on the pike in the field" (*The Week*, 19 July 2013, p. 6). This grotesque anecdote calls to mind the fact that soccer, as we know the game, "purportedly began somewhere in medieval England with the severed head of an opposing army's leader being kicked

around" (Ilundain-Argurruza & Torres, 2010, p. 196). Indeed, the socio-biological roots of soccer, of our "soccer tribe," are lodged deep within our primeval past.

17. Italy defender Tarcisio Burgnich, who marked Pelé in the Mexico 1970 final, noted that intimidation is an operative dynamic in soccer: "I told myself before the game, 'He's made of skin and bones just like everyone else.' But I was wrong" (see www.fifa.com/world-match-centre/.../7/).

18. As Jim Bouton approvingly noted, "My wife says there is that sexy moment in baseball when the pitcher and the batter size each other up. She says football is just herds of buffalo running together into head-on collisions for no good reason" (Dickson, 2008, p. 69). One cannot but also remember the famous "man-to-man" duel between the legendary Italian forward, Roberto Baggio, and the goalie in the 1994 World Cup final against Brazil, in front of over 90,000 spectators. Baggio, a great penalty kicker, unbelievably and heartrendingly, missed the goal (the ball sailed over the bar) and Italy lost the championship. Said Baggio, "It affected me for years. It is the worst moment of my career. I still dream about it. If I could erase a moment, it would be that one" (see www.thedivineponytail.com/.../roberto-baggio-and-the-moment-that-def...).

19. Babe has made a number of comments, sometimes contradictory, about this home run. The following quote seems to be closest to the "truth": "Aw, everybody knows that game, the day I hit the homer off Charlie Root there in Wrigley Field, the day, October 1, the third game of that 1932 World Series. But right now I want to settle all arguments. I didn't exactly point to any spot, like the flagpole. Anyway, I didn't mean to, I just sorta waved at the whole fence, but that was foolish enough. All I wanted to do was give the thing a ride ... outa the park ... anywhere" (Dickson, 2008, p. 473).

20. Soccer, too, has its seemingly "other-worldly" moments of offensive genius. For example, the "Goal of the Century", in which during the 1986 quarter finals of the World Cup, Argentine attacking midfielder, Diego Armando Maradona, seized the ball inside his own half of the pitch and made a

sixty-metre (about 197 feet), ten-second dash, and dodging five English opponents dribbled around the goalie to score a goal. Maradona is also known for his "Hand of God" goal that he got in the same game before the goal just described, in which he deceptively used his hand to get a goal while the referee ruled it was not an infringement. In an interview, Maradona, known to be a "rascal" in his style of play, famously accounted for his goal as "a little with the head of Maradona and a little with the hand of God". Of course, deception of various types has a long and quasi-accepted history in soccer; for example, the dive to draw a penalty, faking fouls, and stalling to main-tain a one-goal lead (Dura-Vila, 2010, pp. 142, 147). Portuguese goalkeeper Costa Pereira pointed to the seemingly "other-worldly" nature of the incomparable Pelé: "I arrived hoping to stop a great man, but I went away convinced I had been undone by someone who was not born on the same planet as the rest of us" (www.fifa.com/world-match-centre/.../7/). Finally, another English centre-half, Sidney Owen, described playing a Hungarian team that beat them 7 to 1 (the worst international defeat in English soccer) in decidedly "other-worldly" terms: "It was like playing people from outer space" (Imre, 2010, p. 290), while one newspaper editorialist described the play of Xavi, Iniesta, and Messi during a game as, "Only in paradise can you see soccer like this" (Nguyen, 2010, p. 274).

21. I am aware that my oedipally based formulation is focused on the psychology of the typical boy, leaving the question of the appeal of baseball to the typical girl unanswered. While this subject deserves its own study, my sense is that women who find baseball appealing are probably also identified with the "home/mother" symbolism and the phallic strivings that permeate hitting and pitching. The "castrating" father/pitcher may also hit her nerve, though this is probably a displacement from the girl's rivalry with the dominating mother for her father's love.

22. Actor/comedian Billy Crystal has further noted, "I've been all over the world, and the sight of Yankee Stadium for the first time on May 30, 1956, is still the most vivid in my memory.

I love Dodger Stadium, but it doesn't smell like there's going to be a game that day. You walk into Yankee Stadium, and you just know, the hot dogs have been there for awhile, and even though the ball park looks different, you know there's going to be a game" (Dickson, 2008, p. 125). Second-baseman Roberto Alomar also expressed an olfactory affection for baseball; he spoke of the love of the "smell of the ballpark—hot hogs, grass ... This is what God chose me to do. He sent me here to play baseball" (Will, 1998, p. 284). The sounds of baseball also evoke a similar affection, like the "crack" of the wooden bat hitting the ball and the spectator's thunderous roaring in pure pleasure. Soccer is actually nicknamed the "Beautiful Game", and Pelé even titled his book *My Life and the Beautiful Game*. There are many reasons why soccer is said to be beautiful, for example, "the range of bodily expressions found in the sport", "the interface of body and ball is also a site of skill and grace" (think, for example, of the goalie's "fingertip save"), and "the distinct forms and techniques such as shooting, trapping, dribbling, tackling and passing" (Lambert, 2010, p. 221). Another soccer aficionado noted: "From the daring relentlessness of Lionel Messi, the ball handling wizardry of Ronaldhino, the impenetrableness of Babi Cannavaro's defense, the completeness of Steven Gerrard, the technical mastery of Kaka, and of course, the offensive brilliance of Cristiano Ronaldo [and the rich differences between the European and South American ways of playing], the game's beauty can be spontaneously revealed" (Elcome, 2010, p. 163). Perhaps most important, as the great Russian composer, Dmitri Shostakovich, noted, "Football is the ballet of the masses" (see www.theglobalgame. com/.../shostakovich-football-is-the-ballet-of-the-m...). For more about soccer as cultural expression, specifically as a ritualised and passionate art form, see Turnbull, Satterlee, and Raab, *The Global Game: Writers on Soccer* (2008). Indeed, what Germaine Greer, the Australian academic and journalist said about her country applies to many other countries: "Soccer is an art more central to our culture than anything the Arts Council deigns to recognize" (quoted in Pepple, 2010, p. 201).

23. In soccer, it is said that the "worst blindness" is only seeing the moving ball.

24. Galeano also described soccer using a theatre metaphor: he called it "the great theater of soccer", in which "suddenly, whoosh, up jumps the player and the miracle of the resurrection occurs" (2009, p. 15).

25. This quotation was taken from a June 1974 TV interview. Pelé noted, "I always think that I would have become an actor if I hadn't been a soccer player" (see www.dailymail. co.uk/.../Pele-wants-Escape-Victory-again.ht).   Somewhat similarly, Rod Stewart noted, "I'm a rock star because I couldn't be a soccer star" (see www.pinterest.com/pin/ 508273507916040657/).

26. For a psychoanalytically informed study of acting theory and technique and its application for living the "good life", see Marcus and Marcus, 2011.

27. As Will noted, "Games are won by a combination of informed aggression and prudence based on information" (1998, p. 150).

28. The same is true for soccer players: Said Roy Keane, the former captain of Ireland and Manchester United, "I don't believe skill was, or ever will be, the result of coaches. It is a result of a love affair between the child and the ball" (see www.topend-sports.com/sport/soccer/quotes.htm). Galeano described the players' erotically tinged relationship to the ball in a section called "The Idol": "The ball seeks him out, knows him, needs him. She rests and rocks on the top of the foot. He caresses her and makes her speak and in the tête-à-tête millions of mutes converse"; "Didi," one of the greatest Brazilian midfielders, said in an interview about his relationship with the ball: "I'd treat her with as much affection as I give my own wife. I had tremendous affection for her. Because she's fire. If you treat her badly, she'll break your leg. That's why I say, 'Boys, come on have some respect. This is a girl that has to be treated with a lot of love ...' Depending on the spot where you touch her, she'll choose your fate" (2009, pp. 5, 121). None of this should be surprising, as former German-American soccer defender,

Thomas Dooley noted, "In Europe [compared to America], it's different, you eat soccer, you breathe soccer, you drink soccer. Everything is about soccer" (see izquotes.com/quote/52360). Thus, soccer has been described as a "civil religion" in certain parts of the world, a good substitute for creating a robust social identity and sense of group cohesion, especially among the millions of young fans who are estranged from traditional political and religious forms of affiliation.

29. Speaking of idealisation, soccer player Cristiano Ronaldo noted, "I am living a dream I never want to wake up from" (see www.manchester.com: Sport:United). And one BBC Sports commentator, Alan Parry, said about Ronaldo, "He's a gift from heaven, he is truly a gift from heaven. Whatever he touches turns to gold" (see www.ronaldo7.net/extra/quotes/cristiano-ronaldo-quotes.html).

30. "Through-action/counter-through-action" is "the logic of the sequence of actions, which bind together all the single actions and enables the character to reach his goal" (Benedetti, 1998, p. 154).

31. Lionel Messi made a similar point about soccer: "In football as in watchmaking, talent and elegance mean nothing without rigour and precision" (see geniusrevive.com/en/geniuses.html?pid=142&sid...Football).

32. Acting, said Stanislavski, can be a "painful process", it "requires enormous self-mastery", "physical endurance", and "awareness", among other personal qualities difficult to cultivate (1958, pp. 9, 70). Stella Adler also advocated that actors have to push themselves out of their comfort zone, which can cause anxiety: "You're here to learn to stretch yourself in life, and in so doing on stage as well" (2000, p. 207). This being said, "Acting is happy agony," said Sartre (www.sartre.org/quotes.htm). So is baseball playing and spectatorship.

33. As Gabriel Marcel has indicated, the denial of the transcendent reflects the "brokenness" of the self (e.g., the incapability or unwillingness to imagine and to wonder) and the world (e.g., the overvaluation of functionality, technical reasoning, and so-called objectivity in everyday life). (See Treanor, n.d.)

34. Soccer great David Beckham succinctly made a similar point in an interview: "Soccer is a magical game" (*People Magazine*, 20 March 2008).

35. As Galeano noted, "How is soccer like God? Each inspires devotion among believers and distrust among intellectuals" (2009, p. 36).

36. Ruth had a similar impression of Cobb: "Cobb is a prick. But he sure can hit. God Almighty, that man can hit" (Dickson, 2008, p. 473). Cobb was also a racist; he refused to sleep in the same hunting lodge as Babe Ruth, whom he and others believed was a black American (he was often teased, being called "nigger lips"): "I never slept under the same roof with a nigger, and I'm not going to start here in my own native state of Georgia" (ibid., p. 109).

37. Galeano pointed out that soccer has its dark side, such as the shameful hooliganism of fans yelling contemptuous chants at opponents when the game is supposed to promote human solidarity and sportsmanship. Also troubling is the extreme commercialisation of the game and the crass values it perpetuates among players ("Advertisement[s] in Motion", 2009, p. 108) and fans (e.g., among children, the extreme celebrity-seeking via the game). And then there is the unbridled narcissism among players, for example, the great Brazilian striker, Romario, also known for his womanising, noted, "When I was born, God pointed at me and said 'That's the man'" (see www.pinterest.com/pin/259308891017930436/). Johan Cruyff, the Dutch legend and advocate of "total football" (which emphasises player ball control and tactical inventiveness) said of himself, "In a way I'm probably immortal." It is the word "probably" that betrays his false modesty (see isleofholland.com/read/sports/14-classic-johan-cruyff-quotes-explained). As with most narcissistically compromised sports celebrities, their need for affirmation has a pained aspect to it: Physically battered by years of playing and when asked about retirement, Maradona confessed: "I need them [the fans] to need me" (Galeano, 2009, p. 233). Galeano and others have noted that soccer has become a game that is coldly efficient, "staid and

standardized", full of "mechanical repetition" in how it is played, emphasising "lightning speed and brute strength" at the expense of joy, fantasy, creative spontaneity and risk and daring. Moreover, this "efficiency of mediocrity" is motivated by the "bottom line" industry demands of the coaches, owners and gamblers who want victory at any price, including at the expense of the aesthetics of the game (ibid., pp. 2, 199, 157; Winters, 2010, p. 162). As Galeano elegiacally wrote, "I go about the world, hand outstretched, and into the stadiums I plead: 'A pretty move, for the love of God'" (2009, p. 1). Soccer, "a primordial symbol of collective identity" (ibid., p. 243) as Galeano describes it, has also been exploited by dictators like Franco and Mussolini and by South American politicians to perpetuate their authoritarian rule as well as stir up destructive ethnocentrism and nationalism (see Lever, 1983).

38. Camus explained what life lessons he learned playing goalie: "That the ball never comes where you expect it, that helped me a lot in life, especially in large cities where people don't tend to be what they claim." In addition, he "learned to win without feeling like God and to lose without feeling like rubbish, skills not easily acquired" (Galeano, 2009, p. 66). Goalies are an unusual group, often unfairly taking the blame for a lost game. As the great English goalkeeper Gordon Banks noted, "At that level, every goal is like a knife in the ribs" (see www.ifhof.com/hof/banks.asp). The Russian goalkeeper, Lev Yashin, nicknamed "The Black Spider", who is considered the greatest goalkeeper of the century, explained the secret to his defensive genius: "The trick was to have a smoke to calm your nerves, then toss back a strong drink to tone your muscles" (Galeano, 2009, p. 134).

39. So-called "soccer values" include "creativity, the emphasis on skill over brute force, on technique over physical strength or the use of intelligence and vision instead of unthinking discipline" (Dura-Vila, 2010, p. 143). Soccer also perpetuates many of the familiar values associated with any sports excellence, like self-discipline and dedication, and on the pitch, the ability to adapt to change and possess inventive improvisation, as well

as embrace the idea that above all else, it is the "mind" that matters (along with luck) to attain victory. In an interview, Pelé made the point that success in soccer is no accident—it is lodged in wholesome moral values: "It is hard work, perseverance, learning, studying, sacrifice and most of all, love of what you are doing or learning to do." This being said, Pelé responded to those who accounted for his playing excellence in terms of his "uncommon peripheral vision and well-placed center of gravity" by affirming that "his talents were the gift of God" (Lever, 1983, p. 141) (see www.360soccer.com/pele/peleplay.html).

40. As Hamilton noted, baseball has had its fair amount of cheating over the years, like "using corked bats, pitchers who doctor baseballs, or coaches who teach players to break the rules", and of course, most recently, the use of performance-enhancing drugs. Many believe that it has been institutionally tolerant of a degree of cheating (Hamilton, 2004, p. 127).

41. The Dutch manager and former soccer player, Ruud Gullit, explained the "rough justice" after a defeat: "We must have had 99 percent of the game. It was the other three percent [sic] that cost us the match" (see www.backpagefootball.com/clean-sheet-grand-final-countdown/56929/).

42. In his book *God is Round* (2010), Mexican writer Juan Antonio Villoro Ruiz has discussed soccer as representing the wish to form an emotional community, one that both celebrates the game and themselves.

43. Soccer player Lionel Messi noted, for example, "Like I've said many times before, I'm always more likely to remember goals for their importance [to the team] rather than if they're beautiful or not [i.e., self-aggrandising]. Goals scored in finals, for example"; "When the year starts the objective is to win it all with the team, personal records are secondary" (see www.vanguardngr.com/2013/01/messi-ive-changed-so-much/). Ronaldo had a similar sentiment: "What I do as an individual player is only important if it helps the team to win. That is the most important thing" (see www.ronaldo7.net/extra/quotes/cristiano-ronaldo-quotes.html). Like any team sport, soccer

highly values individual accomplishment, but never above team victory.

44. I am indebted to Young for drawing my attention to the philosophical notion of sacrifice and its relationship to baseball.

45. I am aware that being for the other before oneself, which is often discussed in terms of altruism in psychological literature, always has a narcissistic motive to it. Such conduct engenders the narcissistic gratification associated with behaving in a manner that is congruent with one's "higher" values that are self-esteem boosting and self-concept enhancing. This being said, what makes radically altruistic behaviour so unusual, if not compelling, is that the narcissistic gratification appears to be deep in the individual's unconscious motivational background as opposed to being in the conscious foreground.

46. Pelé felt a similar responsibility to the next generation: "Every kid around the world who plays soccer wants to be Pelé. I have a great responsibility to show them not just how to be like a soccer player, but how to be like a man" (see sportsillustrated. cnn.com/.../siflashback_p...). Even more emotionally demonstrative, after Pelé scored his historic thousandth goal, the former shoeshine boy, peanut vendor, and fourth grade dropout (though he did eventually get a university degree), called by the Brazilian Congress the "nonexportable national treasure", wept, "Remember the children, remember the poor children" (Lever, 1983, pp. 141–142).

47. Galeano described the soccer pitch as "that sacred green space where the ball floats and glides" (2009, p. 11).

48. Unlike most other sports, baseball has a frequent sense of stillness, such as when the pitcher winds up before he releases the ball. During those few seconds, the batter, fielders, and umpire are all poised like cats ready to pounce. Also worth noting is that the average 180-minute baseball game contains only seventeen minutes and fifty-eight seconds of action, such as pitches, balls in play, running, and throws. The average football game contains much less, only eleven minutes of action time (*The Week*, 26 July 2013, p. 16). Soccer requires the longest period of uninterrupted action of any sport, typically two

halves of forty-five minutes each, and the clock never stops (Kent, 2010, p. 54).

49. Baseball, said Gould, satisfies our need for cyclical repetition, that is, to "forge time into stories" and to "grant stability, predictability and place". To the baseball fan, "[O]pening day marks our annual renewal after a winter of discontent"; it both calls to the mind the bittersweet past and the passage of time, and the promises of the beckoning future (2003, p. 55). These are the "seasonal ceremonies of birth and renewal" that humans seem to need (Sexton, 2013, p. xii).

50. Will was paraphrasing Giamatti.

51. Gould also noted, "I don't know why grown men care so deeply about something that neither kills, nor starves, nor maims, nor even scratches, but I'm mighty glad that we do" (2003, p. 53).

52. Soccer has its fair share of zany fans too. Galeano told the story of how a Boca Juniors fan on his deathbed declared his last wish—he wanted to be draped in a flag of an enemy club River Plate so that when he died, "[H]e could celebrate with his final breath the death of 'one of them'" (2009, p. 125). In another tragicomic moment, a referee begins the match with the fans mourning the death of his mother. He is shortly thereafter cursed and jeered by them when a decision opposes their club (www.betweenthelines.in/2014/01/book-review-s0ccer-sun-sha...).

53. Doubt, said Sexton, "is at the core of baseball", and I would add, of life; it is what Freud called ambivalence, a feeling that is often evoked when one is faced with ambiguous circumstances that require a decision (2013, p. 55).

54. Baseball wisdom, as in real life, asserts that while "natural" talent is important, it is how hard you work at mastering the skills of this most challenging of games that ultimately distinguishes the great player from the good one. Though there have been exceptions, such as Babe Ruth, who was hardly a disciplined athlete, he did "more than his share of drinking and whoring", though "his play didn't seem to suffer" (Gould, 2003, p. 139).

55. Roger Angell used the phrase, "the interior stadium" (Will, 1998, p. 311).

56. Former Vice President Al Gore is probably right when he noted that at least three baseball players have transcended the game to become a constituent part of American legend: "Where Babe Ruth was known for his power and Jackie Robinson was known for his courage, Joe DiMaggio was known for dignity and grace" (ibid., p. 215).

CHAPTER FOUR

"Wake up and smell the coffee"
The pleasures of drinking coffee

Creating Heaven on Earth

> "A cup of coffee—real coffee—home-browned, home ground, homemade, that comes to you dark as a hazel-eye, but changes to a golden bronze as you temper it with cream that never cheated, but was real cream from its birth, thick, tenderly yellow, perfectly sweet, neither lumpy nor frothing on the Java: such a cup of coffee is a match for twenty blue devils and will exorcise them all."
>
> —*Henry Ward Beecher* (Kolpass, 2005, p. 109)

Should I kill myself," asked Albert Camus, "or have a cup of coffee?" (Schwartz, 2004, p. 42). Indeed, as the Beecher and Camus quotes strongly suggest, drinking coffee is an experience that can have profound existential significance for the average person. "Coffee is not a matter of life and death," the unknown saying goes, "it's much more important than that" (Phillips, 2011, p. 34). The commonly heard refrain in the typical coffee-drinking household—"Please don't even talk to me until I've had my coffee" (Austin, 2011, p. 25)—further suggests that coffee drinking has become a vitally important aspect of millions of people's daily lives. Survey research has found 83% of Americans say they drink coffee on a "past year basis", while it is estimated that 1.6 billion cups of coffee are drunk worldwide, daily. That's a whopping 584 billion cups in a year ("National Coffee Drinking Trends", 2013)![1] While no doubt caffeine addiction and slick marketing helps explain why so many people all over the world drink coffee, there is a lot more to understanding the passionate nature of coffee drinking.[2] That is, as the quip suggests—"Coffee smells like freshly ground heaven"—the experience of drinking coffee alone and/or with others can be an activity that makes us feel very happy, at least for a while, especially if we take the time to notice what we are feeling. The "perfect cup", say the aficionados, beautifully blends four elements: aroma, body, acidity, and flavour. The last of these can be sweet, sour, salty, bitter, or savoury (Pendergrast, 2010, p. xvi). As Don Holly, the director of roasting and quality for Vermont's Green Mountain Coffee® noted after tasting eight coffees at a world-class specialty coffee competition, "When I tasted this coffee I saw the face of god in a cup" (Weissman, 2008, pp. 36, 56). In fact, it is often while drinking coffee alone, for example, in the morning while staring out of the window at the falling snowflakes or while doing a crossword puzzle, or, alternately, while engaging in lively conversation with a good friend at a favourite café, that we find ourselves having some of the most subtly pleasurable, joyful moments that help us to optimistically "press on" in an ordinary day.

In this chapter, I argue that the experience of coffee drinking, both alone and with others, can be a creative activity that helps us to engage ourselves and others in a particularly meaningful and pleasing manner. Such moments can point to something that feels both beyond, and better than, our usual sense of ourselves, a moment of flourishing that gives us an uplifting inkling of having a hopeful future amid our humdrum and burdensome lives. Such inspired and inspiring instances give us a sense of what I have called a glimpse of immortality. As the Icelandic Nobel Prize-winning author, Halldór Laxness, wrote in his masterpiece, *Independent People*, "Presently the smell of coffee began to fill the room. This was morning's hallowed moment. In such a fragrance the perversity of the world is forgotten, and the soul is inspired with faith in the future ..." (Laxness, 1996, p. 151). Coffee drinking has the potential to summon us to the "mystery of awakening" (O'Donohue, 2004, p. 42), an invitation to live life with the fullness of our whole being. Put simply, coffee drinking is "chock-full" of longing for "enhanced and enchanted significances" (Stilgoe, 1969, p. 10). Before we begin our journey into the intriguing world of this appealing beverage, I want to make a few brief contextualising comments about the history of the coffee specialty industry, research findings on what particular types of coffee drinking may reveal about the personality of the consumer, and my angle of vision to my subject.

I. Coffee drinking in context

Coffee was first discovered in Ethiopia about a millennium ago. It has had a fascinating "ideologically-freighted" (Schivelbusch, 1993, p. 38) history which has been explicated by a number of social historians, including the story of the modern specialty coffee industry which has gripped the imagination and tastes of billions of people worldwide.[3] The "First Wave" of the coffee industry, said Trish Rothgeb (formerly Skeie) who popularised the "wave" notion, refers to those people who prior to and after the Second World War "… made coffee commonplace … who created low quality instant solubles … who blended away the nuance [in coffee] … and forced prices to an all time low." The "Second Wave" began in about the late 1960s and continued into about the mid-1990s. The "Second Wave" included many northern European immigrants who made their lives in California after the Second World War. As Michaele Weissman further noted, "These transplants carried with them old-world knowledge of coffee roasting, tasting, and sourcing." Such entrepreneurs included Alfred Peet of Peet's Coffee & Tea® and Erna Knutsen of Knutsen Coffees, Ltd., the latter of whom first used the term "specialty coffee", those coffees that are grown and harvested in distinctive "geographic microclimates and they have unique flavor profiles". Starbucks® emerged during the "Second Wave". The "Third Wave" came about in the mid-1990s, in part due to the powerful negative influence of Starbucks® (in the "Third Wave's" view), with its industrialisation, automation, and homogenisation of gourmet coffee production and consumption. The "Third Wave" specialty coffee pundits have been called the "first global generation". They are fiercely competitive "rebels" who may not look like typical corporate executives with their casual dress, but they are bent on outperforming Starbucks® and making billions of dollars in the process. These "Third Wave" entrepreneurs have taken advantage of sophisticated technology and comparatively inexpensive overseas travel that has radically changed the specialty coffee industry, and thus, they focus on the productive end of coffee development and manufacturing, that is, the farmers, and their intimate connection to "the consumer ends of the coffee chain". As Weissman comments, the "Third Wave" …

> … are not the first coffee guys to realize farmers matter— far from it. But they are the first to travel constantly and communicate readily with farmers in remote locales. You have to go where the coffee is grown, and you have to help farmers improve their product to meet specialty standards, say Third Wave coffee guys. And that is what they do. (2008, pp. 4–6)

While I am not going to further delve into the history of the specialty coffee industry in this chapter, it is important to be mindful of the fact that the cup of coffee you drink is the end product of a long, complex, meticulously thought-out production chain that is geared to seduce you into loving it. As Howard Schultz, the CEO of Starbucks®, put it:

> For more than three decades, coffee has captured my imagination because it is a beverage about individuals as well as community. A Rwandan farmer. Eighty roast masters at six Starbucks plants on two continents. Thousands of baristas in 54 countries. Like a symphony, coffee's power rests in the hands of a few individuals who orchestrate its appeal. So much can go wrong during the journey from soil to cup that when everything goes right, it is nothing short of brilliant! After all, coffee doesn't lie. It can't. Every sip is proof of the artistry—technical as well as human—that went into its creation. (Schultz, with Gordon, 2011, p. 4)

Schultz's comments remind us how an individual can deeply dedicate himself to ordinary and small things and thereby "make them his own by perfecting their beauty" (Bachelard, 1969, p. 69). Humans are magnifying entities. Just by making something ordinary and small "a little more beautiful" (ibid.), we have created something very different, which has significance in the "real" world. This is because transcendent values are often invoked in ordinary, small things, if only we are able to reside in a more "poetic immensity" (ibid., p. 210). Something miniature, like a cup of coffee, "stimulates profound values" (ibid., p. 151) and imaginings, it "causes men to dream" (ibid., p. 152), especially about things with which they ultimately fall in love.

And fall in love we have. In the West and elsewhere around the world, we are a coffee-crazed society. Research has suggested that the coffee specialty industry has figured out how to appeal to the spectrum of personalities that drink coffee. While this research is mainly based on survey interviews and therefore has marked methodological limitations, it is interesting to reflect on some of these findings to further contextualise the main thrust of this chapter, that coffee drinking is a way to glimpse immortality.

In her engaging book, *You Are WHY You Eat: Change Your Food Attitude, Change Your Life*, psychologist Ramani Durvasula (2013) suggests that the type of coffee you consume can indicate something pertinent and meaningful about your personality and outlook on life. For example, the black coffee drinker tends to be an "old school type" or "purist" who has considerable forbearance and desires to keep things simple. Coffee drinkers who prefer a "dark" cup can be moody, abrupt, and flippant with others, and rigid when it comes to required change. Latte coffee drinkers add milk, cream, and sugar to their black coffee; hence, said Durvasula, they are probably in search of comfort and pleasing others. One might say that their desire to make their black coffee less bitter reflects their wish to make their life feel easier. Though coffee drinkers on the "dark" side tend to be generous with their time and are inclined to go the extra mile for a friend, they often do so at an unreasonable cost to themselves. The frozen/blended coffee drinker tends to attract young people and older folk who have a child within that seeks immediate gratification. Durvasula said that these consumers are often audacious trendsetters who desire new experiences. On the "dark" side, frozen/blended coffee drinkers can be immature in their decisions, even irresponsible as they are inclined to look for quick fixes to complex problems. The decaf/soy/very specifically ordered coffee drinkers tend to be annoying control freaks. They can be obsessive perfectionists, too rule- and order-bound, on the selfish side, and they are often worriers and narcissistically vulnerable to criticism. On the positive side, these coffee drinkers are health conscious, which can lead to making good decisions about their body care. Finally, we come to the instant coffee drinkers. These are the "laid back" slackers, loafers, and procrastinators. They tend to "take life as it comes" without getting overwhelmed with the details of everyday life. They also tend to be poor planners and they can be neglectful of their bodily care and health.

Obviously, the above findings are ideal types and typically the coffee drinker can be a combination of these categories. However, what is most important from my point of view is the attempt to quasi-scientifically delineate in what way a person's choice of coffee reflects his personality, especially the way he constructs his world and behaves in everyday life. In other words, coffee drinking is usefully understood as part of what philosopher Gaston Bachelard called in his brilliant book, *The Poetics of Space*, "topoanalysis": "the systematic psychological study of the sites of our intimate lives" (1969, p. 8). As Bachelard noted, our soul is a place of residing, of dwelling, whether this is having morning coffee in our kitchen or coffee during lunch at a favourite café haunt. In both instances these spaces reflect the intimacy of our internal mental space. We do not just envisage our kitchen or café table, we intimately and palpably live in them, and they provide us with a sense of predictability, safety, and protection. Bachelard further noted,

> In the theater of the past that is constituted by memory, the stage setting maintains the characters in their dominant roles. At times we think we know ourselves in time, when all we know is a sequence of fixations in the spaces of the being's stability—a being who does not want to melt away, and who, even in the past, when he sets out in search of things past, wants time to "suspend" its flight. In its countless alveoli space contains compressed time. That is what space is for. (ibid.)

My point, following Bachelard, is that the kitchen and café are not to be viewed only literally, but in addition they are the "dreamed, imagined, remembered, read" and most important, felt places which permit us to come nearer to the centre of our psychological experience ("The Cultural Studies Reader", n.d.). At these moments, we feel the existential grounding, the peacefulness and delight associated with our real and imagined "home world". The atmosphere in which we consume coffee is an experience that engenders this love of literal and figurative space, that is, of the life-affirming experience of being washed over by the loveliness of a "nostalgia-dredged" nook or corner (Bachelard, 1969, p. 141). As the French diplomat Charles Maurice de Talleyrand-Périgord once said about coffee, "Black as the devil, Hot as Hell, Pure as an angel, Sweet as love" (Maberry & Kramer, 2007, p. 44).

II. The splendid solitude of morning coffee

"I don't have a problem with caffeine," it was once said, "I have a problem without caffeine." Indeed, caffeine is the most pervasively used psychoactive drug on the planet and its leading delivery system is coffee drinking (Pendergrast, 2010, p. 19). In 1803, the well-known homeopath, Samuel Hahnemann, wrote a very good description of the effects of coffee on the person who has just awoken from a night's sleep:

> In the first moments or first quarter hour of waking, especially when waking occurs earlier than usual, probably everyone who does not live in an entirely primitive state of nature experiences an unpleasant sensation of less than fully roused consciousness, gloominess, a sluggishness and stiffness in the limbs; quick movements are difficult and thinking is hard. But lo and behold, coffee dispels this natural but unpleasant feeling, this discomfort of mind and body, almost immediately. (Schivelbusch, 1993, p. 43)

The American physician and poet, Oliver Wendell Holmes, Sr., also noted in his 1891 book, *Over the Teacups*, "The morning cup of coffee has an exhilaration about it which the cheering influence of the afternoon or evening cup of tea cannot be expected to reproduce" (Rattiner, 2004, p. 7).

While we will compare coffee and tea drinkers later, for now what I want to emphasise is that after a night of sleep, upon waking, coffee drinking devotees have a powerful longing for their morning coffee. While this powerful longing has its physiological anchoring in the bodily effects of caffeine consumption—the so-called caffeine buzz—I believe that morning coffee often represents something much more profound than simply a wish to get turbocharged to face the day's challenges. After all, one can simply drink the most popular energy drink in the world, the Austrian manufactured Red Bull®, whose slogan says it all: "Red Bull gives you wings." The meaning of the yearning for morning coffee must be understood as something other than simply a "mind-racing, jump-start" (Pendergrast, 2010, p. xv) caffeine craving. What

115

may hold the most meaning in terms of longing, morning coffee follows either a night of more or less uninterrupted, restorative sleep or a night of varying degrees of insomnia.

The ambiguous and ambivalent nature of morning awakening, with its unpleasant sense that "I am not yet myself", the surreal twilight zone between waking and waiting for the coffee to be ready to drink—requires what feels like infinite patience. Most important, when the coffee is drunk and quickly works its way into one's system, there is a lovely revival and renewal, the inner realisation of happily waking to the "daytime me" (Geisz, 2011, p. 46).[4] This is a gently uplifting return to the self that one knows and feels more or less comfortable with, a form of existential "homecoming". Sometimes after a few moments of drinking one's coffee, this pleasant sense of the "normal me" or "daytime me" is not so pleasurable, for as with real life, homecomings reconnect us to the world of "deadlines, dirty dishes, day care drop-offs" (ibid., p. 47) and other mundane— though for a fully engaged person embedded in a web of relationships and responsibilities—essential tasks of everyday life. This morphing from the pleasant to the unpleasant feelings associated with morning coffee can also reconnect us to something much more hard-going than our daily responsibilities; it can insert us back into our worries and troubles that were temporarily obliterated during our sleep.

Thus, awakening and consuming one's coffee has a duality of structure to it. On one hand, it reminds us that there is a comfortable continuity to our sense of who we are. We reclaim our familiar self, our routine "situatedness" in our "home world", and our relief that the world feels like it "hangs together" the way we remembered it from yesterday. Playing off Ecclesiastes' pessimistic observation, but giving it a positive meaning, "There is nothing new under the sun." And yet, as the great Torah scholar and Kabbalist, Rabbi Abraham Isaac Kook noted, coffee reminds us of the opposite: we and the world are not the same as yesterday, there is a newness and possibility to each day if we are creatively receptive to what we encounter—"There is nothing old under the sun,"said the wise rabbi. Such a totality of interrelated, interdependent, and interactive external and internal circumstances associated with drinking early morning coffee is thus analogous to a "slow rebirth" (ibid.), one that propels us forward to face the day with a modicum of self-confidence, anticipation, and hope.

I mentioned that sometimes we have trouble falling asleep or staying asleep through the night. In the context of insomnia, morning coffee can take on an additional meaning to what I have already said. While insomnia has many causes and manifestations, what I want to focus on is the relationship between insomnia and what is consciously or unconsciously driving it, namely, a certain form of existential anxiety that ethical philosopher Emmanuel Levinas has evocatively called the "there is", the deeply disturbing experience of anonymous being. To some extent we are all vulnerable to feeling the "there is", that horrifying feeling of impersonal being, but the insomniac is inescapably "thrown" into it when his head hits the pillow. It is the "there is" that keeps the insomniac twisting and turning in his bed like a man with a fever who cannot get comfortable. It is this fear of entrapment within oneself, without an avenue of flight, that points to what Levinas is getting at. Before I suggest where morning coffee "comes to the rescue" of the insomniac's experience of the "there is", we need to get a better phenomenological sense of the "there is". To do this, we need to take a short excursion into rather dense and abstract Continental philosophy, in particular, delineating the difference between Levinas and his teacher, Martin Heidegger, on the subject of existential anxiety, as I am calling it.

Let us begin with Levinas's evocative descriptions of the "there is":

> My reflection on this subject starts with childhood memories. One sleeps alone, the adults continue life; the child

feels the silence of his bedroom as "rumbling." It is something resembling what one hears when one puts an empty shell close to the ear, as if the emptiness were full, as if the silence were a noise. It is something one can also feel when one thinks that even if there were nothing, the fact that "there is" is undeniable. Not that there is this or that; but the very scene of being is open: there is. In the absolute emptiness that one can imagine before creation—there is ... neither nothingness nor being. I sometimes use the expression: the excluded middle. One cannot neither say of this "there is" which persists that it is an event of being. One can say that it is nothingness, even though there is nothing. *Existence and Existents* tries to describe this horrible thing, and moreover describes it as horror and panic. (1985, pp. 48–49)

Elsewhere Levinas further describes the "there is", again reminiscing about his childhood:

The "there is" is unbearable in its indifference. Not anguish [as in Heidegger's *es gibt*, "there is"], but horror, the horror of the unceasing, of a monotony deprived of meaning. Horrible insomnia. When you were a child and someone tore you away from the life of the adults and put you to bed a bit too early, isolated in the silence, you heard the absurd tie in its monotony as if the curtains rustled without moving. My efforts ... consist in investigating the experience of the exit from this anonymous "nonsense." (2001, pp. 45–46)

Finally, Levinas draws from the French writer and philosopher Maurice Blanchot, to describe the "there is":

He has a number of very suggestive formulas; he speaks of the "hustle-bustle" of being, of its "clamor," its

> "murmur," of a night in a hotel room where, behind the
> partition, "it does not stop stirring"; "one does not know
> what they are doing next door." This is something very
> close to the "there is." (1985, p. 50)

For now, I want to emphasise what is striking about Levinas's
descriptions. In two of three instances, he refers to experiences
of separation from adults, probably his parents, and the lonely
and pained experience of being excluded from their palpably bountiful, pleasurable, and meaningful lives. The third
instance also speaks to being excluded from the stirrings of life
and pleasure that Levinas fantasises are occurring behind the
partition, next door. Thus, according to Levinas's descriptions,
the "there is" emerges within the psychological context of felt
radical disconnection, distance, and loneliness, the opposite of
the phenomenology of love, with its strong feelings of connection, closeness, and togetherness.

The "there is", says Levinas, pre-exists nothingness; it is
evoked in the terrifying silence facing the "vigilant insomniac"
(Hand, 1987, p. 29). The vigilant insomniac "is and is not an I"
who cannot fall asleep (ibid.). As we have seen, for Levinas,
the child who in his bed senses the night dragging on has an
experience of horror that "is not an anxiety" (1985, p. 49), at
least not as conceived by psychoanalysts. Rather, it is something even more terrifying and menacing, though Levinas only
hints at this difference:

> The impossibility of escaping wakefulness is something
> "objective," independent of my initiative. This imperson-
> ality absorbs my consciousness; consciousness is deper-
> sonalized. I do not stay awake; "it" stays awake. Perhaps
> death is an absolute negation wherein "the music ends …
> But in the maddening 'experience' of the 'there is' one
> has the impression of a total impossibility of escaping, of
> 'stopping the music.'" (ibid.)

For Levinas, the "there is" is not a psychological experience as usually construed, because "it is subjectivity itself which has fled". This is because all that constitutes an experience as psychological, that is subjectively knowable and intelligible, is besieged with the horror and panic of mere existence. Consciousness, in other words, has been objectified, it has become a thing, an it, and personal identity has become swamped, swallowed up by it (Alford, 2002, pp. 57–58).

What Levinas is getting at is a reversal of the way in which Heidegger conceptualises this type of subjective experience, the "*es gibt*" ("there is"). The Heideggerian "*es gibt*" is generosity and abundance. It refers to "the donation by Being to beings of light, freedom and truth" (Davis, 1996, p. 129; Levinas, 1985, pp. 4–48; Levinas, 2001, p. 45). In contrast to the "there is" as abundance and diffuse goodness, says Levinas, the "there is" is unbearable in its indifference. Before the generosity of Being there is a "chaotic indeterminacy" to being that comes before all giving, "creativity and goodness" (Peperzack, 1997, p. 3). Heidegger's "*es gibt*" is mainly rooted in the fear of pure nothingness, of death. In contrast, for Levinas the experience of the "there is" is a terrifying feeling that there is no way of escaping from mere being, there is "no exit" from existence, not even suicide. In other words, says Levinas, in contrast to Heidegger's use of the term "there is", the horror of the night of the vigilant insomniac is not merely anxiety about nothingness and the fear of death. Rather, "There is horror of ... the fact that tomorrow one still has to live, a tomorrow contained in the infinity of today. There is horror of immortality, perpetuity of the drama of existence, necessity of forever taking on this burden" (Levinas, 1987a, pp. 34–35). Levinas succinctly notes elsewhere, "Anxiety, according to Heidegger, is the experience of nothingness. Is it not, on the contrary—if by death one means nothingness—the fact that it is impossible to die?" (Levinas, 1987b, p. 51).

What Levinas is contrasting is the horror of the night to Heideggerian anxiety, fear of being to Heideggerian fear of nothingness. The primordial anxiety and fear for Levinas is mere being, existing forever, with no escape, trapped in the nocturnal horror of existence that is prior to the emergence of consciousness. This is striving for immortality gone bad. Psychoanalytically speaking, such a moment is perhaps a kind of terrifying, persecutory psychotic-like regression into a preverbal autistic-like primary narcissism.

Where does morning coffee fit into all of this heady talk about different ways of conceptualising the dreaded existential anxiety called the "there is"? The television host and comedian David Letterman hinted at the redemptive value of coffee in its ability to help foster a stabilising sense of individuation and personal identity amid the anonymous being that is the heart of the "there is": "[I]f it weren't for the coffee, I'd have no identifiable personality whatsoever" (Burroughs, 1994, p. 98). Likewise, a patient of mine who had an agitated depression that was particularly fierce in the morning told me that more than taking Klonopin® (clonazepam) to reduce his anxiety, it was a double espresso and a hot shower that released him from his awful state of mind. It is the totality of external and internal circumstances, the entire ambience that constitutes morning coffee that arrests, if not transforms, the panic and horror-filled wakefulness of the insomniac's utterly self-encapsulated existence into a "gracious self-forgetting" that is "full of invitation, possibility and depth" (O'Donohue, 1997, pp. 7, 65). Such self-forgetting is a form of wakefulness that points to the need and desire to engage the otherness of the world in all of its unique Beauty, Truth and, perhaps most important, its Goodness. For Levinas, what is crucial to his conceptualisation of the "there is", and I would add, to the longing associated with morning coffee, the possibility of escape from the horror of the "there is", means embracing a different mode of being in the world, what he calls "otherwise than being".[5] "Otherwise than being" is Levinas's way of describing love, understood as "responsibility for the Other", "being-for-the-Other". It is through love, "in the form of such a relation that the deliverance from 'there is' appeared to me" (Levinas, 1985, p. 52). "The true bearer of being," said Levinas, "the true exit from the 'there is' is in obligation, in the 'for the Other,' which introduces a meaning into the nonsense of the 'there is.'" This moment, Levinas continued, is "the I subordinated to the other. In the ethical event, someone appears who is the subject par excellence" (2001, pp. 45–46). Indeed, morning coffee as I have described it can facilitate the willingness and ability to cross a threshold from mainly being for oneself to being for the other, to engage the world in a manner that embraces its lovely otherness and numinous presences. Writer/performer Nicole Johnson aptly captured the other-directed, other-regarding, and other-serving nature of such a coffee-inspired, threshold-crossing comportment:

> Coffee is far more than a beverage. It is an invitation to life, disguised as a cup of warm liquid. It's a trumpet wakeup call or a gentle rousing hand on your shoulder. Coffee is a lingering scent, better than any potpourri. Coffee is an experience, an offer, a rite of passage, a good excuse to get together. When someone invites you to get a coffee, it isn't because they are thirsty. It might be because they're cold, but more likely it is because they want to spend time with you. Coffee makes a promise. (Johnson, 1999, pp. ix–x)

While morning coffee at its best can invoke much of what Johnson is describing, it is coffee drunk with a good friend in a café, restaurant, or even at home where the meaning of coffee drinking as a signifier of strong affiliation, social bonding, if not Levinasian love is best realised. It is to this subject that I now turn.

III. Drinking coffee with a good friend

A rather astute social commentator noted in 1902, "The best stories [are told] over coffee, as the aroma of the coffee opens the portals of [the] soul, and the story, long hidden, is winged for posterity" (Pendergrast, 2010, p. 381). Indeed, coffee, a beverage that lends itself to slow consumption, tends to slow down the hustle and bustle of our frantic everyday lives and give us an occasion to talk, think, and read more deeply (Parker & Austin, 2011, p. 2). Culturally and historically speaking, the coffeehouse was a central place to gather together, to have lively conversation, to amuse one another, write, read, or simply while away time, either individually or in small assemblages. Think, for example, of the *Café de Flore* in Paris which Jean-Paul Sartre, Simone de Beauvoir, and other famous intellectuals frequented.

As Brook J. Sadler further noted, our current collective obsession with coffee refers to a more profound "need to peer into the dark, bitter cup of our modern anxiety, of our experience of isolation, and ultimately, our confrontation with death" (2011, p. 100). In short, we are drawn to the coffeehouse and its derivative public spaces because we feel forlorn and crave a place where real conversation can occur. However, the "dull corporate uniformity" (ibid., p. 110) of contemporary American chain coffeehouses like Starbucks® hosts self-isolated and disengaged people who seemingly have no interest in co-producing a community of others. In his *Nine Talmudic Readings*, Levinas comments on the ill-conceived, ill-fated decision to spend one's Monday afternoon hanging out in a coffee shop:

> The café is a place of casual social intercourse, without mutual responsibility. One goes in not needing to. One sits down without being tired. One drinks without being thirsty. All because one does not want to stay in one's room. You know that all evils occur as a result of

our incapacity to stay alone in our room. The café is not a place. It is a non-place for a non-society, for a society without solidarity, without tomorrow, without commitment, without common interests, a game society. The café, house of games, is the point through which game penetrates life and dissolves it. Society without yesterday or tomorrow, without responsibility, without seriousness—distraction, dissolution. (1994, p. 111)

Levinas further comments,

At the movies, a common theme is presented on the screen; in the theatre a common theme is presented on the stage. In the café, there are no themes. Here you are, each at your own little table with your cup or your glass. You relax completely to the point of not being obligated to anyone or anything; and it is because it is possible to go and relax in a café that one tolerates the horrors and injustices of a world without soul. The world as a game from which everyone can pull out and exist only for himself, a place of forgetfulness—of the forgetfulness of the other—that is the café. (ibid., p. 112)[6]

Levinas, always the ethical extremist, is making a rather severe and sweeping judgment about the cultural meaning of the café, especially applicable during the time when intellectual celebrities like Sartre and company frequented trendy Parisian cafés as if they were rock stars. What Levinas is not appreciating is that participating in café culture can be part of the life-long process of socialisation, that is, a way that the individual creates a social self and a sense of connection to social systems. This process is a basis of shared identity, social order, and, sometimes, positive social change.

The troubling scenario that Levinas describes is not how it always goes when one visits a Starbucks®, a place we are drawn to because it calls to mind the life-affirming coffeehouse experience of the past. That is, it invites us to enter into a public space that promises authentic "sociality", a place where people can engage in "real, embodied, face-to-face social intercourse and the enlarged sense of aesthetic, intellectual, political, and creative possibility it brings" (Sadler, 2011, p. 110). This is especially true if one visits a less homogenised, corporate-looking café to meet a good friend, a cafe that one often frequents and where one is greeted in a friendly manner by the servers and owner. In contrast to Levinas's grim portrait of a café experience, a café can be a place where one engages the other face-to-face in authentic dialogue, including mainly as a creatively engaged listener, this being a form of giving to the other before oneself. Coffee is part of the ambience that both literally and figuratively can play an important role in fostering such dialogue.

How does drinking coffee with a good friend in a café help foster authentic face-to-face dialogue, including one that engenders giving to the other before oneself? To suggest a plausible answer to this question, we can usefully compare the ambience of English afternoon or high tea versus coffee drinking in different contexts. The late afternoon, roughly between 4pm and 6pm, is the traditional time for serving afternoon tea. It is characteristically a light meal of tea and sandwiches or cakes. It has been said that "An Englishman would interrupt a war to have his afternoon tea". High tea, served somewhere between 5pm and 7pm, is the evening meal or dinner of the working class. Whether afternoon or high tea, such assemblages feel like mini indoor picnics where the focus is to eat, drink, and have a pleasant time. As Henry James said in *The Portrait of a Lady*, "There are few hours in life more agreeable than the hour dedicated to the ceremony known as afternoon tea" (1881, p. 21).

In contrast, ordering coffee can a have a dark, if not tragicomic side to it, such as is personified in the question a waiter or host asks: "How do you take it?"—as if coffee were a bitter, unpleasant medicine or a test of character, something to be endured: "Will you take it hard? Take it like a man? Take it standing up?" In fact, Sadler noted, "There is even a faint suspicion ... too much sugar and cream and you are not a real coffee drinker. Coffee black: There is a realism in that" (2011, p. 102).

As I suggested earlier, how one engages the other in face-to-face dialogue in a café is suggested by what the person orders. It can sometimes be a portal into a person's existential comportment to the meeting. The great comedian George Carlin quipped, "The more complicated the Starbucks order, the bigger the asshole. If you walk into a Starbucks and order a 'decaf Grande half-soy, half-low fat, iced vanilla, double-shot, gingerbread cappuccino, extra dry, light ice, with one Sweet-n' Low and one NutraSweet,' ooh, you're a huge asshole" (Redmon, n.d.). In another instance, ordering a "'half-double decaffeinated half-caf, with a twist of lemon' can be seen as an amalgam of courage ('a double'), restraint ('decaffeinated'), and enigmatic edginess ('a twist of lemon') within a cup of coffee" (Wear, 2011, p. 160). I am always suspicious when a friend I meet for coffee orders it decaffeinated; it usually means he is not geared up for a lively and engaged encounter with me. As Robin Williams wisecracked, "Decaf is like masturbating with an oven mitt!" (http://www.izquotes.com/quote/293033, retrieved 29 October 2013).

Compared to alcohol consumption, which clouds the mind and loosens inhibitions and thereby encourages drinkers to say things without adequately considering the impact of their words, coffee is a drink for people who want to "take life straight", as it were (Romaya, 2011, p. 114). As the Anglo-Irish satirist Jonathan Swift noted, "Coffee makes us severe, and grave, and philosophical" (Ukers, 1922, p. 562). That is, in part because eating and emotional frolicking is not the main focus of the coffee experience as it is with traditional tea, it tends to foster more direct and honest communication.

There are other differences between coffee and tea. In contrast to the dark meaning of coffee discussed above, tea often "reflects decorum, calm, health, order and prosperity". That is, "Tea is a beverage of well-being" (Sadler, 2011, p. 101). Its origins are in ancient China when it was used for medicinal purposes, and it is still aggressively marketed as having a wide range of health benefits. As Sadler aptly noted,

> Where there is *tea time*—connoting the luxury of reserved time—there are *coffee breaks*, mere interruptions of work. Coffee goes to work, whether in a steel-handled thermos to the construction site or in a paper cup from McDonald's to the drone's cubicle or in the ubiquitous cardboard sleeved Starbucks cup to, well, any job at all. Despite the fancified coffee menu—flavored syrups, whipped cream, this-u-*ccino* and that-a-*latte*—the proliferation of Starbucks speaks to our bourgeois dissatisfactions: How can we make it through the wearying workday? (ibid.)

Thus, compared to the agreeableness and relaxation of tea and the anaesthesia and rowdiness of alcohol consumption, coffee drinking points to something more, something deeper. It literally and psychologically "quickens our hearts" (O'Donohue, 2004, p. 21), both with yearning for the lovely intimacy of self-belonging in solitude *and* close connection with another person and with community, this being what constitutes the "good life", or the "fresh brewed life", as it has been called. Drinking coffee presents a glorious moment when we feel awakened to the concealed vitality and hope that is embedded in longing (O'Donohue, 1997, p. 22) for the perfect cup with the perfect friend. Put simply, this is the longing for "the source and horizon", the "awakening and surrender" (O'Donohue, 2004, p. 9) to immortality.

IV. Final thoughts

I have suggested that morning coffee in one's kitchen can be an experience of joyful solitude, a moment of passionate longing for reawakening, resurrection, and renewal, that helps us individualise, personalise, and endure our ordinary day (Bachelard, 1969, p. 117). Similarly, having coffee with a friend can be the context for engaging in a particularly open, honest, and direct manner. Taken together, these two coffee drinking contexts can point to something beyond the literal act of drinking coffee. That is, provided one approaches coffee drinking in a phenomenologically open and astute manner, we are able to invest an object, even a two-dollar cup of coffee, with a "poetic immensity". This is living life in a "higher key", as Bachelard called it. At this moment our mug of coffee becomes like a "sacred goblet", for we have used our poetic imagination to visualise and experience a fresh nuance, a concealed presence, depth, and grandeur in the context of surface circumstances of ordinariness and uniformity. What I am arguing for is the cultivation of a way of being that more frequently and comfortably resides in the world of the imagination, an imagination that especially values the creative capacity for artful exaggeration and transfiguration, for as Bachelard noted, exaggeration is the "surest sign of wonder". Put simply, "An artist"—and we are all potentially great artists of our own lives—"does not create the way he lives, he lives the way he creates" (ibid., pp. 107, 194, 204, 209–210). At these beautiful, lyrical moments of radical attunement to drinking coffee, quite simply, it is as if we are taking immortality into our mouth. As romance writer Cherise Sinclair quipped in *Hour of the Lion*, "Coffee and chocolate, the inventor of mocha should be sainted!" (www.goodreads.com/.../537494-coffee-and-chocolate-the-inventor-of-m...).

Postscript

As is my custom, I send my writings to experts in the field and to non-specialists to read and critique. Most recently, I sent this chapter to a good friend, herself an author, Helaine Helmreich, who wrote to me in an e-mail that she felt "inspired" by the chapter. After finishing reading it she wrote a poem in a mere fifteen minutes. I present the poem in its entirety not only because it is a lovely poem about coffee drinking, but more important, Helaine's poem personifies the mode of engagement with the world that I have advocated throughout this book. That is, to be creatively receptive, to be open to the "absolute presence" of the other, as Gabriel Marcel calls it. It is such "porosity", a way of being that is easy to cross, infiltrate, and penetrate, that points to the inner state of readiness that makes an experience of something as trivial as a chapter on coffee feel like a gift, a moment of grace.

Coffee
by Helaine Helmreich

Morning coffee wakes us up
There's love and comfort in the cup,
It's going back to Mommy's breast,
As warmth and sweetness we ingest,
Plus caffeine for an added jolt
Till into life we're forced to bolt
Headlong to our set routine
Humdrum, wild or in-between.
If things are rotten they'll seem less so
After downing strong espresso.
Pour it down like molten lava,
Warm your soul with good, hot java.
Drink alone or with a friend
Your night-time angst is soon to end,
Say goodbye to anomie,
A cup of Joe's good company.
Imbibe at home or at the office,
Or make Starbucks your new "coffice,"
Have a little demitasse
While brushing up on Levinas.

129

Creating Heaven on Earth

Have some with your scrambled eggs,
Drink it down right to the dregs.
Add milk or cream or leave it blacker,
Have it instant (lazy slacker!!)
Have it decaf if you must,
The waiters sneer, but they'll adjust.
Life is often hard to take,
So give yourself a coffee break!

Notes

1. Recent research indicates that the world's biggest coffee drinker, with each person drinking on average 2.414 cups a day, is Holland. Finland is second (1.848), Sweden third (1.357) and Denmark fourth (1.237). The United States comes in at sixteenth, with a per capita average of a little less than a cup a day (0.931). (See *The Week*, 20 June 2014, p. 16.)
2. Voltaire allegedly had about fifty-five cups of coffee a day and he claimed he consumed as many as seventy-two when he wrote his masterpiece, *Candide*. In fact, Voltaire credited coffee for his writing of *Candide* (Kirkwood, 2011, p. 207).
3. Pendergrast's *Uncommon Grounds: The History of Coffee and How It Transformed Our World* and Antony Wild's *Coffee: A Dark History* are probably the two best available histories of coffee.
4. Geisz's essay on Buddhism and coffee consumption has been very helpful in this part of my chapter.
5. In this context, embracing otherwise than being implies that it is something that one can choose. However, for Levinas, any "choice" is a "second order" choice, as we are all subject to the otherwise (*autrement*); it is a condition of possibility for any encounter with another.
6. I am grateful to Will Buckingham who drew my attention to this passage in Levinas ("Three Cups: The Anatomy of a Wasted Afternoon," in Parker and Austin, *Coffee: Philosophy for Everyone: Grounds for Debate*, 2011).

CHAPTER FIVE

"The shorthand of strong emotion"
Listening to great music

Creating Heaven on Earth

> "The aim and final end of all music should be none other than the glory of God and the refreshment of the soul."
>
> —*Johann Sebastian Bach* (Wilbur, 2005, p. 1)

I can't listen to that much Wagner," said Woody Allen, "I start getting the urge to conquer Poland" (*Manhattan Murder Mystery*, 1993). Indeed, whether one is listening to Beethoven or Jay-Z, music has the evocative power to stir up very strong feelings. As philosopher Gabriel Marcel noted, music is a "pure erotic" (Marcel, 2005, p. 121); at its best it illuminates the realm of primordial experience that is not emotional as the term is conventionally formulated, as a private, personal feeling. Rather, great music engages the totality of who one is, as it invokes the sense of wonder and delight, spontaneity and enchantment of childhood, a time when we were not weighed down by oppressive routines (ibid., p. 120; Wood, 2005, p. 27) and responsibilities, but lived much of the time in our free, flowing, and unrestrained imaginations. The "father of modern aesthetics", as Immanuel Kant has been called, concurred that music accesses the "harmonious free play of the imagination and understanding" (Kivy, 2002, p. 57). Learning how better to listen and appreciate music, to enter into meaningful dialogue with it and let it touch, move, and transform us, is what this chapter is mainly about. As I am not a musicologist, I will not discuss in detail musical theory, composition, and the like, but rather I will focus on the art of thinking and most important, "feeling" musically, in terms of fashioning the existential comportment that is most likely to bring about the great pleasures associated with fluidly "living" (Bruscia, 2000, pp. 89–90) in great music. By music I mean not only listening to, for example, Bach or the Beatles, but also to the variety of "soundscapes", the mélange of unmusical sounds that usually go unnoticed in everyday life, like birds tweeting, the sound of the wind, or the melody in a person's voice (Ortiz, 1997,

p. xvi).[1] Every sound has its unique character or personality, whether it is the howling dog in E-flat, an air conditioner chanting in F-sharp minor, or a car tyre singing at a precise speed (Jourdain, 1997, p. 113).[2] As Marcel said, "A musical idea is, precisely, a being," an incarnate "pure being" (2005, p. 101). Most important, I will be suggesting that the capacity to carefully listen to and appreciate beautiful music in the "outside" world is correlated with the capacity to listen to beautiful music in one's "inside" world. As inside and outside are artificial categories, though useful conceptual metaphors, I will use them, though I want to emphasise from the onset that inside and outside are always an integrated, dynamic whole that constitute being-in-the-world. I am thus suggesting a plausible analogy: to the extent that one can learn to better tune in to the music in our external world, we are better able to tune in to the music in our internal world, and by doing so, achieve greater harmony, balance, and pleasure in our lives (Ortiz, 1997, p. xix). As former Conservative prime minister of England Benjamin Disraeli said, "Most people die with their music still locked up inside them" (Moeller, 2001, p. 257).

Thus, I am suggesting that the art of living the "good life" involves cultivating a way of being in the world, a mode of attunement that makes greater participation in the pleasures of music more likely. As O'Donohue has noted, "Music echoes the deepest grandeur of the most sublime intimacy of the soul" (2004, p. 61). It does so in part because it does not "push from behind, but rather it pull[s] forward" (Ortiz, 1997, p. xvi) into something that we believe, and intensely feel, is both more beautiful and better. Thus, music is an exalting way to participate with the fullness of our whole selves in the all-pervasive "mystery of being", as Marcel described it. Engaging the "mystery of being" is identified with apprehending what is divine, what is eternal in others and in the world at large. That is, music "is our incredible gift to creation, for there is no sound on earth to compare with the beauty and depth of music. It has an eternal resonance" (O'Donohue, 2004, pp. 60–61). More specifically, music allows us to participate in the essence of the "mystery of being", in the "Thou" relationship, like a subject-to-subject relation where the other's unity of being is engaged, as in adult-to-adult love (Shakespeare wrote, music is the "food of love"), as opposed to a subject-to-object relation, the "it" relation, and as in the world of ordinary experience where one engages the specific and isolated features of another as if he were a thing, like our relationships to our iPads. Such an "I–Thou" relation evokes, and invokes, an affirming, authenticating "personal Presence" (Wood, 2005, p. 13) that often calls to mind the words "God", "the divine", or their secular equivalents such as "awesome" or "mind blowing", words that connote what I have called glimpsing immortality. Indeed, as Marcel suggested, there is an "ineffable mystery" that characterises the dialogue between music and the receptive listener, a unique mode of joyful communication that points to a human/divine encounter that is at the heart of all great music (2005, p. 77). I now turn to the illumination of some of the conditions of psychological possibility for the artful listener to experience music not only as a "wonder", but, even better, as a "miracle" (Kivy, 2002, p. 65).

I. The meaning of music

In "the best music", said "the Boss", Bruce Springsteen, "you can seek some shelter in it momentarily, but it's essentially there to provide you something to face the world with" (Gentile, 2003, p. 153). Springsteen was hitting on a central reason why the average person listens to music—it is a safe haven and restorative presence that helps us deal with the sham, drudgery, and broken dreams of life.[3] As Marcel noted, we live in a "broken" world, a mass society that is dehumanising if not spiritually degrading, leaving us feeling like "cogs in the enormous machine to which technocrats" and other depersonalising forces run our lives often without us being aware of the subtle forms of control and homogenising normalisation (2005, p. 66). In this context, said Marcel, "Music"—referring to the great classical instrumental canon—"is the very incarnation [the embodiment] of that which, in each one of us, protests against this frightful mutilation" (ibid.). Music thus becomes the "irresistible call of what, in man, surpasses man, but also founds him" (Kivy, 2002, p. 66). In this sense, it has a sacred function, it helps us live better and bring things to life; it is a restorative and "saving light" (Marcel, 2005, pp. 53, 79). Marcel is right in claiming that certain kinds of classical music, like that of Bach, Mozart, and Beethoven, have served this human-ising and integrating function that he alludes to; however, it is also true that so-called great classical music, like Wagner, for example, has been effectively used by anti-Semites to inspire hatred, racism, and Nazi genocide. Musical performances, usu-ally at the request of the Nazi commanders, were even used to cover up the sound of executions, to accompany and inspire marching soldiers, and to entertain the commanders (Shapiro, 2013, p. 14). More recently, certain examples of rap music have also served a racist as well as ultra-narcissistic, hedonistic function. Thus, listening to music always takes place within a socio-intellectual and value-laden context, and as music is a historical and cultural activity, its meaning and effects can be either in the service of life-affirming Eros, or life-denying Thanatos, depending who is making the value judgments.

While music is a universal activity spanning all cultures, music therapists and philosophers of music have identified at least three sources of meaning to music. As Kenneth Bruscia noted, music can be conceptualised as an "implicate order of the universe itself—that fundamental order which holds the uni-verse together in myriad relationships". That is, music reflects "the universal template or foundation for all meaningfulness, both individual and collective" (Bruscia, 2000, p. 85). In this view, music is a realm that is separate from human perception and construction and reflects the a priori "absolute order of the world" (Wigram, Pederson, & Bonde, 2002, p. 38), an order that can never be fully comprehended, and in this sense can be described as ineffable. As Leonard Bernstein noted, "Music, of all the arts, stands in a special region, unlit by a star but its own, and utterly without meaning, except its own." That is, continued Bernstein, music has a meaning only in "musical terms not in terms of words, which inhabit an altogether different mental climate" (2004, p. 33). In this view, the perceptual properties of music essentially include an "objective, universal and metaphysical" meaning (Wigram, Pederson, & Bonde, 2002, p. 39).

A second source of meaning in music, in particular when listening to it, relates to "our own personal encounters with the implicate order", that is, of being radically enlivened, of being transported to a different dimension of the spirit through the music, where one feels in harmony with oneself and the world. Such a relativist view includes the subjective, context-dependent, setting-specific aspects of listening to music. As Bruscia pointed out, "A fundamental characteristic of these [experiences] is that they are ineffable" and they "are not mediated by language". Rather, "They are direct, raw experiences—they are not reflections on the experiences, nor are they attempts to describe or explain the implicate order verbally." Instead, concluded Bruscia, "They are indescribably enlightening encounters that involve our entire being" (2000, p. 86). To the extent that one can expand and deepen one's consciousness one will be more able "to experience the inherent meaningfulness of all existence" (ibid.).

Finally, said Bruscia, there is musical meaning that includes "the various constructions and reconstructions of meaning that we make through thought, language, the arts, or any expressive modality, both alone and with others" (ibid., p. 87). What this boils down to is we critically reflect upon our own specific experiences of the implicate order and connect them to our own personal world and life situation, and by doing so, "[W]e construct [deconstruct] and re-construct the implicate order in terms of our own world—our culture, society, and personal history" (ibid., p. 87). Exactly how this constructing, deconstructing, and reconstructing process is done depends on our personal resources and the totality of our circumstances.

As Wigram, Pederson, and Bonde (2002) have suggested, the upshot of all of this is that music, classical instrumental music, can be best conceptualised as an "ambiguous, presentative symbolic language". That is, while it is a form of language with its unique, perceptive, and syntactical rule and notation system, it is not capable of denoting or representing, let alone in a nuanced, exacting manner, any external or internal experience of the world comparable to the precision of verbal language. In other words, in contradiction to popular notions, "[M]usic cannot express emotions with any degree of success, but rather creates moods to which we respond at an emotional level" (ibid., p. 58) (unlike songs, a representational activity that does convey feelings largely through lyrics; some have argued that the human voice, especially the female soprano, creates the most beautiful music).[4] Music, continued Wigram, Pederson, and Bonde, thus fundamentally expresses qualities of mood to which we project a particular emotional significance. In this sense music seems to "contain and express meaning", powerful and transformative meaning. Such meaning is a co-produced experience, one that is "beyond the pure musical or aesthetic content" (ibid., p. 39), in that it is a function of the complicated relations among the interrelated, interdependent, and interactive musical triangle of composer, performer, and listener. As is common knowledge, music creation can be a straightforward expression of a participant's internal world, whether as an expression of pure feeling, or a symbolic or metaphorical representation of a subtle psychological or spiritual state, or even an analogy to the listener's mode of being-in-the-world. Thus, Wigram, Pederson, and Bonde further claimed that the most useful way of conceptualising the meaning of music is that it has an "ineffable" meaning, one that is apprehended mainly on a preverbal level of understanding that in a certain sense may be more exacting and immediate than communication via words (e.g., we feel the effect of music before we understand it). In these moments, the separation between the listener and the music vanishes and the listener experiences a compelling, unified, transcending meaning that is inexpressible, or at least, inadequately expressible in words (2002, pp. 28, 39–40, 58). Moreover, this and other types of musical listening experiences can be important elements in the fashioning of personal identity, for like morality or science, music cuts deeply into the human bedrock that in many ways defines our existence (Kivy, 2002, p. 8).

II. Music and the fashioning of personal identity

For most music listeners it is the perceived powerful emotive qualities of music that capture their hearts and minds— "music sounds the way emotions feel" (ibid., p. 28). As Jourdain noted, research has suggested that "[I]t is the joy of so pure an expression of emotion ['emotions welling up through the mind's floorboards'] that draws musicians to the profession" (1997, p. 205). Marcel had a similar point of view when he wrote, "For the musician the work itself has been a certain way of living through an emotion, or more exactly super-eminently experiencing [*sur-vivre*] it, of finding for it a universal expression" (2005, p. 100). Musicians often speak of envisioning music, of "seeing music" with their internal senses, such as shapes of flow and structure (O'Donohue, 2004, p. 64), auditory images (Lipson, 2006) like the harmonies and tonal colour. Moreover, in terms of the personality of the typical musician, more than the self-discipline that is needed to practise long hours, and tenacity, independence, and confidence, Jourdain held that it was the quality of "tender-mindedness", defined as easily affected emotionally by other people's distress or by criticism, and more generally, "a sensitivity to emotional expression", that set musicians (and all artists) apart (1997, p. 231). Why one tender-minded artist turns to music versus painting, acting, dance, or litera-ture is not known, though a psychoanalytic study of the idi-osyncratic trajectory of the artist's personal life will surely provide some thought-provoking formulations. Speaking of psychoanalysis, especially in terms of understanding how identity is fashioned through and around music, Freud was famously indifferent to the evoked feeling associated with music listening, rather surprisingly because typically music is most impactful on people who are characterised by "a deep emotional existence" (ibid., p. 322). Even stranger, Freud's psychoanalysis was mainly based on "impressions received by hearing", that is, listening to his patients with empathic tenderness (Reik, 1953, p. 3). In fact, Freud suggested why he found music troubling and gravitated to other artistic forms:

> Works of art do exercise a powerful effect on me, especially those of literature and sculpture, less often painting. This has occasioned me, when I have been contemplating such things, to spend a long time before them, trying to apprehend them in my own way, i.e., to explain to myself what their effect is due to. Wherever I cannot do this, as for instance with music, I am *almost* incapable of obtaining any pleasure. Some rationalistic, or perhaps analytic, turn of mind in me rebels against being moved by a thing without knowing why I am thus affected, and what it is that affects me. (1914b, p. 211; my italics)[5]

As Reik perceptively pointed out, the most important word in Freud's statement is "almost". "The very wording of the statement about his restricted capability for enjoying music proves", said Reik, "that there was an emotional reluctance against this art operating in Freud." Freud resisted the emotional impact of music, he battled against his own sensitivity because he could not bear not knowing why he was so affected, this stated reluctance being an admission that he *was* in fact strongly affected by music, but he felt the need to wilfully resist music's emotional impact on him. Thus, Freud's reference to his rationalistic and analytic cast of mind is a rationalisation for his anxiety when strong feeling was generated in him while listening to music. As Reik concluded,

> It is likely that this turning away, this diversion was the result of an act of will in the interest of self-defense and that it was the more energetic and violent, the more the emotional effects of music appeared undesirable to him. He became more and more convinced that he had to keep his reason unclouded and emotions in abeyance. He developed an increasing reluctance to surrendering to the dark power of music. (1953, p. 4)

What Freud's self-observation puts into sharp focus is that there are probably many people who avoid music because they cannot tolerate, due to feeling threatened by, the strong feeling that it generates. In other words, the capacity to enjoy music, any kind of music, requires the willingness and ability to let it dramatically change one's experience of time. As O'Donohue perceptively noted,

> To enter a piece of music, or to have music enfold you, is to depart for a while from regulated time. Music creates a rhythm that beats out its own time-shape. Whilst theatre invites the suspension of disbelief as we enter and participate in the drama the characters create, in music there is a suspension of the world. We are deftly seduced into another place of pure feeling. (2004, p. 61)

Thus, one can plausibly say, following Marcel, that music, specifically classical instrumental music, does not merely "express" strong feeling; rather, it "is" strong feeling. That is, it is feeling that is so radically liberated from its psychosomatic matrix in which it is usually imprisoned that "[I]t clarifies itself to the point of becoming structure—structure in time and above time" (Marcel, 2005, p. 49). There is probably no artistic medium that condenses and purifies feeling in the manner that music does, this being one of the sources of its emotional command over us.[6] What is so remarkable about music is that despite its incredible intellectual complexity it can flourish in the most lyrical way. "[M]usic is depth in seamless form," and it is therefore no surprise that all poetry aims towards the condition of great music, namely, that it should communicate prior to being comprehended (Zatorre & Salimpoor, 2013, p. 12). As Kivy noted, music does not move us by stimulating an emotion that it is expressive of such as the garden-variety representational "content" associated with feelings of, for example, happiness or sadness; rather, music profoundly moves and enlivens us by its "pure formal structure", its sonic and aesthetic sensual structure, and by "its serene, tranquil beauty" (2002, pp. 129, 158, 255, 262).[7]

One of the important aspects of music's communication, that is, the way it plays with our sense of time, is its capacity to induce a retrospective consciousness in the listener. Oscar Wilde, for example, noted,

> After playing Chopin, I feel as if I had been weeping over sins that I had never committed, and mourning over tragedies that were not my own. Music always seems to me to produce that effect. It creates for one a past of which one has been ignorant, and fills one with a sense of sorrows that have been hidden from one's tears. (Redman, 1959, p. 88)

Thus, music evokes a wide range of memories, both happy ones—they are "playing our song", as paramours say—and sad ones, like those associated with painful losses and other wounding moments, including those that may have a bittersweet resonance.[8] In this sense, as Susanne Langer noted, music aptly depicts the double structure to existence, the ambivalence that humans manifest towards their wishes, anxieties, and fears:

> The real power of music lies in the fact that it can be "true" to the life feeling in a way that language cannot, for its significant forms have that ambivalence of content which words cannot have ... The possibility of expressing opposites simultaneously gives the most intricate reaches of expressiveness to music. (1957, p. 243)

What Langer was saying is that what makes music so enormously appealing, especially when it is wordless music, is that it provides us with an acoustical experience of the conflicting nature of our internal lives, one that offers the possibility of some kind of resolution, or partial resolution, albeit a fleeting one. As Pinchas Noy noted, music does not simply induce strong emotion, but it reproduces the "'sum total' of all the disparate emotions" (unpublished, p. 1; quoted in Nagel, 2013, p. 34). Moreover, Noy claimed, great music is a medium for an integrated gratification of primary and secondary processes, "to be sublimely integrated without contradicting each other" (2013, p. 34). By emanating from the palace of simultaneity, as Langer called it, music transports us to a dimension where time is experienced like "a circle". O'Donohue further elaborated,

> Here one thing does not follow another in a regular line of sequence. Somehow at that depth, all times are present together; the joys and losses of your past, the wonder of the present and the unknown possibilities of the future;

music plays out of this profound simultaneity. (2004, p. 63)

Thus, when one is gripped by great classical or jazz music, or for that matter, any music by which one is enthralled, one feels as if one is cradled by one's loving mother, "cradled in a sublime Now" (ibid.) of a "Thou" moment. That is, the listener enters a place where there is no "before" or "after", "otherwise" or "elsewhere". Rather, both memory and possibility merge in what feels like an invisible embrace. Music facilitates such a sublime experience by coaxing us into this transfigured time by clarifying and purifying feeling in the most immediate, unique, and hard-to-pin-down way—"Music", and I would add, the music listener, magically "dwells in a world of its own" (ibid.), a "fairy space", as Marcel evocatively called it (2005, p. 128). This is the moment when we experience the transcendent, transforming spiritual power that great music tends to evoke in the skilful and empathic listener. Such a "surrendering" involves letting oneself enter into that enchanting "fairy space", a realm, said Marcel, "in which the near and the far pass into each other, in which through the irresistible efficacy of analogical correspondences [i.e., analogies], every note, every chord evokes an infinity of others". To allow oneself to experience music this way, to feel it as a "pure erotic", as "feeling itself", is most analogous to falling in love, and wholeheartedly residing in this love experience, "the limitless fecundity of the spirit", as Marcel (ibid., pp. 118, 128) beautifully put it. It is precisely the power and grace of music that has the capacity to generate this mood context, a depth experience "where presence awakens to its eternal depth", in which we feel a perspective-altering, life-affirming threshold that is joyfully transgressed, "where the soul dovetails with the eternal" (O'Donohue, 2004, p. 62). As the incomparable cellist Pablo Casals said, "Music is the divine way to tell beautiful, poetic things to the heart" (imdb.com/name/nm0142829/bio).[9]

III. Psychoanalytic musings on music listening

While Freud was put off by music listening, there have been some psychoanalysts who have investigated the psychological function and significance of music, and some of these interesting ideas have bearing on my focus: what are the psychological conditions of the possibility for the average person to experience the great pleasures of music listening, and even better, to experience music as a medium for glimpsing immortality?

In her thoughtful book, *Melodies of the Mind*, Julie Jaffe Nagel has aptly summarised the main function of music from a psychoanalytic point of view, a formulation that is in sync with many of the ideas I have presented above using more phenomenological language. Wrote Nagel,

> Music [especially its tonality[10]] "works" because it has the capacity to put us in touch with the vulnerabilities, strengths, and complexities of our own psyches, allowing for regression to primal instincts while also permitting ego mastery. Music resonates uniquely with each listener's inner life. (2013, p. 87)

In other words, it is the formal structure of music, its heard properties, that gives the listener the vehicle to better manage his internal conflict, his complicated ambiguities and ambivalences. Whatever the composer and the performer (who mediates the written music) are trying to communicate, we the listener have an opportunity to work through their message, that is, to psychologically metabolise its personal meaning. Said Nagel, "The music speaks for itself and for each of us" (ibid., p. 106).

Within the psychoanalytic context, what this boils down to is that the analysand's use of music in his life, such as his preferences and musical experiences, and as Theodor Reik (1953) pointed out, the melodies that spontaneously come into his mind,[11] allow him and the analyst to more deeply understand how the analysand's conscious mind, and more important, his unconscious mind, are structured—think, feel, and fantasise—and most important, animate his behaviour in the "real world". Psychoanalytically speaking, we can thus say that man is metaphorically like a musical instrument, one that can be either out of tune or finely tuned (Wigram, Pederson, & Bonde, 2002, p. 24).

The great self-psychologist, Heinz Kohut, has interestingly formulated how musical listening and other musical experiences impact the psyche from the "structural" point of view (i.e., the id, ego, superego, and "internal objects", the phantasised internal images that are experienced as real). Echoing Aristotle's views on the appeal of watching theatre, Kohut (1957) mentioned that from the point of view of the id, music has mainly a cathartic purpose. Whether as a "transference phenomenon, a compromise formation, or a sublimation", the idea here is that the tensions associated with repressed wishes are permitted vicarious gratification in the evoked musical emotion instead of being bottled up and menacing to the stability and integrity of the ego. For example, rhythm, a regular, repeated pattern of sounds calls to mind the pleasurable rocking and lullabies associated with childhood, while adult sexuality, its sexual thrusting, has primitive rhythmic patterns of tension and release rooted in one's childhood that are stirred up and gratified through music. Likewise, aggressive wishes, such as in military music, said Kohut, are another example of this childhood-animated "sexual-kinesthetic discharge" via music listening (ibid., p. 391).

With regard to the ego, music listening is a pleasurable type of mastery in that it is a way of enjoyably surmounting the threat of panic, similar to Freud's view of the purpose of a child's play. That is, wrote Kohut, "The archaic mental apparatus, whether in the infant, in primitive man, or, under special circumstances, in the adult, has the tendency to perceive sound as a direct threat and to react reflexly to it with anxiety" (ibid., p. 392). However, unlike the child, the adult ego has the capacity to comprehend the orderliness of form and content of musical sounds and it can better manage the heard sounds by noticing that the music has a beginning, an end, and that the sonic structure of the music includes an organised scheme of tones and discernible rhythms. As Kohut further pointed out, the repetition of sections of music that have already been heard, the familiarity of the form and style of the piece of music, and the use of well-known instruments, all contribute to ego mastery of the heard sound. Thus, a slight escalation of the tension in a passage of music is generated by its movement into dissonance, which is then followed by pleasurable tension-reduction as the music resumes its consonance. In short, it is the playful ego mastery of the threat of being traumatically overwhelmed by sound that adds to the overall enjoyment of the listening experience (ibid., p. 392).

Finally, music activates the superego, what can be called the "musical superego", when a listener's involvement in it tends towards the mindfulness of rules and obeying them. "The emotional place of the code of morals", said Kohut, "is taken in art by the aesthetic code, in music by the rule of form and harmony." In other words, musical activity, including listening to it, morphs into a type of work, and the adherence to a set of aesthetic rules gives to the performer and listener a sense of gratification and safety, which is analogous to the pleasurable feeling of having acted properly, of having done the "right thing", a common desire in childhood.

Thus, as Kohut summarised, from the point of view of structural theory, we can say that music fosters catharsis of primitive and infantile id impulses, and in this sense music listening can be described as an emotional experience. Musical activity is also fundamentally an application of substitutable ego mastery, that is, it is a mode of play. Finally, music is an expression of rules to which one adheres and thus becomes a task to be fulfilled, analogous to work, and it therefore can be said to be an aesthetic experience. With these points in mind, Kohut concluded,

> With the aid of the structural point of view we comprehend how the pressure of unacceptable strivings, the despair at being incapable of inner or outer mastery, and the demands of an outmoded or tyrannical sense of duty leads us in our musical activities to substitute forms of discharge, mastery, and compliance in a nonverbal medium that lies, usually, outside the field of most structural conflicts. (ibid., p. 394)

In terms of the quest for glimpsing immortality through music, for the psychoanalyst, this experience is perhaps best conceptualised in terms of the longing for what Nobel Prize-winning French dramatist, Romain Rolland, called an "oceanic feeling" in his December 5, 1927 letter to Freud. Drawing from Eastern spiritual tradition, Rolland defined "oceanic feeling" as that sense of cosmic limitlessness that he believed was the ultimate source of religious feeling and religious systems.[12] Freud reflected on this mystical emotion in *The Future of an Illusion* and *Civilization and Its Discontents*, and not surprisingly, considering what he said about music as leaving him cold, he was not able to feel this "oceanic" feeling in his own personal life. For Freud, the "oceanic feeling" was inaccessible to him and to others because it was a regression "to an early phase of ego-feeling" (1930a, p. 72), one that called to mind the infantile experience at the mother's breast during breastfeeding, and most important, at a time prior to the infant understanding that he and his mother were separate and different people. Thus, for Freud, the "oceanic feeling" is a residue, a leftover of infantile consciousness when the infant considers the mother's breast to be an extension of himself. The development of the ego, the sense of being a separate self, is a result of breastfeeding ending. Freud noted that while he was not able to access this "oceanic feeling", there were adults who could have the capacity to experience this residual feeling of primary oneness-with-the-mother while also functioning at a high level of ego capacity.

It is precisely this regressive experience of narcissistic equilibrium, or more accurately, "narcissistic elation", as Béla Grunberger called "the narcissistic situation of the primal self in narcissistic union with the mother", that music is capable of evoking. This sense of well-being, completion, and omnipotence is similar to the experience of love, especially passionate love, of victory and success, such as in war or athletic and business competitions, and via self-comprehension and insight, as in psychoanalysis and meditation (1970, pp. 6, 43, 93, 123). When music and religious ritual are combined in mystical ecstasy, such as through polyrhythmic music, monotonous drumming, Western pop, and Arab musical schemata, these too can evoke narcissistic elation (Aldridge & Fachner, 2001). In psychoanalytic language we can say there is a joining in music, if not a fusion of the ego (i.e., the self one believes/feels one is) and the ego-ideal (the self one would like to be), without any superego blunting (negative judgment and inhibition). As Henry David Thoreau noted, "When I hear music, I fear no danger, I am invulnerable. I see no foe. I am related to the earliest times and to the latest" (ibid., p. 177).

What Thoreau was pointing to has been described as a form of "ecstasy". Ecstasy, said Jourdain, is more than extreme pleasure associated with, say, observing a beautiful sunset or painting; in addition, it "melts the boundaries of our being, reveals our bonds to the external world, engulfs us in feelings that are 'oceanic'". Ecstasy has a felt immediacy and beauty to it, one that is experienced as occurring to ourselves, "a transformation of the knower, and not merely a transformation of the knower's experience" (though in many instances extraordinary experience is needed to induce ecstasy) (Jourdain, 1997, pp. 327–328). Jourdain elaborated the nature of ecstasy with reference to Mozart:

Mozart somehow ratcheted himself up to the point that he could create an artificial world of perfect proportions and exceedingly deep relations, found a way to embody those relations in sound, and jotted them down for future generations. The sounds began as intentions at the core of his nervous system, and after much ado they are replicated however imperfectly, in other nervous systems centuries later. We switch on a CD player and the man's ghost steps right into our bodies. It is surely as close as any human being can come to immortality. (ibid., pp. 328–329)[13]

Thus, as Nagel pointed out, from a psychoanalytic point of view music can serve many psychologically enhancing functions to the typical person: it can be like a good friend or companion during times of happiness, sadness, and loneliness, and other significant moments in the life cycle like weddings, funerals,[14] and parties; it can serve as a "transitional object" as Donald Winnicott described it. A "transitional object" is literally an object which the child treats as being midway between himself and another person, typically his mother, such as a beloved doll, teddy bear, or blanket, and which a child uses as a comforting object, though one that does not have to be treated with the care suitable to a person/mother. As a "transitional object," music can help the adult to make the transition from a narcissistic way of being to one of object-love (so-called "mature" love relations), and from a more dependent way of being to one that reflects greater independence and self-sufficiency. A transitional melody in a child, often at sleep time, can help him feel shielded against the loneliness related to separation from his parents as well as provide a degree of control over his anxiety related to the separation (Lipson, 2006, p. 868). "Music", said poet Maya Angelou, "was my refuge. I could crawl into the space between the notes and curl my back to loneliness" (Sweeney, 2002, p. 30). Finally, as Reik, Noy, and other analysts have pointed out, as with a composer whose internal psychological world is entwined and embedded in his musical works (recall the above example of Mozart), for a musician and listener music has dormant meanings that are similar to the structure of a dream, daydream, and joke, meanings that can be psychoanalytically explored, and thus provide a vehicle for deeper self-understanding (Nagel, 2013, pp. 1, 19).[15] As Lombardi pointed out, an analysand's or ordinary person's free association to a musical experience can serve a transitional purpose; it can "bridge the gap between the concrete and the abstract, body and mind, the nonsymbolic and the symbolic, as well as between internal and the external" (2008, p. 1199).

Before moving to the next section of this chapter, I think it will be useful to the reader if I gave a real-life vignette that suggests how some of these highfalutin psychoanalytic and other formulations can illuminate how musical experiences can unconsciously influence early psychological development and be used for positive psychological purposes in adult life. Thus, taking my lead from Freud who used his personal life as a source of analysis and insight, I will summarise some of the ways music has animated my life from the point of view of self-fashioning (after all, self-fashioning is a form of improvised "composing") (Wigram, Pederson, & Bonde, 2002, p. 98); meaning, I will offer some tentative observations into what role music and musical experiences have played in my early development and current efforts at artfully living the "good life" and, here and there, glimpsing immortality. As this is only an illustrative vignette meant to give some "flesh" and "nuts and bolts" meaning to the abstract theoretical formulations provided above, my vignette is necessarily schematic and incomplete.

Case vignette

I have no memories of my mother (or father) ever singing any lullabies to me, or my mother in any way interacting with me using music as a vehicle for play or parent/child interaction (like with a toy instrument); nor do my two siblings. In elementary and middle school I was forced to take music education, but it was incredibly boring and most of the time I was daydreaming. Not only that, my immediate peer group looked down on other kids who were into classical music, as being in the school band was not a "cool" thing to do. My parents never encouraged me to learn an instrument, and I did not show any interest in doing so, being a depressed child, mainly due to a number of early medical traumas.

My late mother, a narcissistic though engaging woman, an English major in college, was highly self-educated in the fine arts, and even lectured on music, literature, and art in adult education centres and at a local college. As a child growing up in an affluent suburb I knew from early on that she loved classical music because she always had the classical radio station, WQXR, playing during the day and early evening when she and my father, an emotionally remote, money-oriented dentist, would sit in the living room reading their newspapers.

My first emotionally significant contact with music was around the kitchen table with my (at times) "drama queen" mother, probably when I was about nine or ten years old, as I was captivated by her dazzling stories about opera, opera singers, and great classical composers, which she told me while I was gobbling down my cornflakes before I went to school. I often came to breakfast earlier than necessary to hear her stories. Indeed, my mother was an amazing storyteller, and for a variety of psychodynamic reasons, I became her audience for which she performed every morning, allowing me to face the oppressiveness of school (I was a terrible student through high school) with a cluster of emotionally evocative stories and tunes swirling around my head. I also felt incredibly special to my enlivened and enlivening mother (and for a depressed child this was crucial), as the one she chose to share all of this with, and this sense of being special compared to my two siblings and father became the basis for a whole range of oedipally tinged fantasies, if not enactments later in my life. My siblings had no interest in my mother's music shtick, nor did my father, who, like most men of the "Greatest Generation", as Tom Brokaw called the Depression and World War Two participants, regarded the quest for financial stability as his raison d'etre, this being equated with a feeling of safety in what he construed as a fundamentally menacing world. My father was intellectually very smart; he had gone to a top dental school, but he had the emotional range of a teaspoon and most of my childhood and young adulthood I was afraid of him, especially his negative judgment of me.

Not surprisingly, I found myself a few years later, and throughout my adolescence, getting intensely into opera, both listening and going to performances at the Metropolitan Opera. While I could not afford to pay for bona fide tickets, I got standing room tickets and eventually figured out a way to sneak into the opera house after the first act, and once there, the ushers who knew and liked me let me sit in an empty seat in the orchestra. My main interest in opera, following my mother's lead, was the works of the great Italians, like Verdi and Puccini. However, while the melodic music and passionate story lines of the operas deeply resonated to my, at times, melodramatic personality, there was one opera that stood out as the most important one in terms of my psychological development, namely, Ruggero Leoncavallo's *Pagliacci* ("Clown"). As this opera became something of an obsession with me, it deserves to be summarised (www. metoperafamily.org/metopera/historystories/synopsis. aspx?...10) and reflected upon.

Prior to the beginning of the opera, Tonio, the hunchback clown, steps in front of the curtain to tell the audience that the author has written this story about actors and actresses who know the same joys and sorrows of ordinary people. The story takes place in southern Italy in the late nineteenth century.

Canio, the leader of the newly arrived company, describes to the villagers what is playing that night, and when a villager jokingly insinuates that Tonio, another member of the troupe, is secretly sexually attracted to, if not in love with, Canio's young, pretty wife, Nedda, Canio sternly warns that he will not accept any flirting. Troubled by her husband's jealousy, Nedda envies the freedom of the soaring birds overhead. Tonio returns from the tavern and attempts to make love to Nedda, but she scornfully rebuffs him. Furious, he grabs her, and Nedda lashes out at him with a whip, getting rid of him but provoking an oath of vengeance. Ironically, Nedda does have a lover, a villager named Silvio, who now arrives and convinces her to abscond with him at midnight. However, Tonio, who has viewed them, scurries off to tell Canio. Shortly the jealous Canio bursts in on the guilty pair; Silvio escapes in the nick of time, and Nedda refuses to say who she was with, even when threatened with a knife. Beppe, another member of the troupe, has to restrain Canio, and Tonio counsels him to wait until the evening performance to catch Nedda's lover. Alone, Canio cries that he must play the clown even though he is brokenhearted, sobbing as he sings the famous aria, *"Vesti la giubba"* ("Put on the costume" or "On with the motley").

The villagers, including Silvio, gather to see the play *Pagliaccio e Colombina*. In the absence of her husband, Pagliaccio (played by Canio), Colombina (Nedda) is serenaded by her lover, Arlecchino (Beppe), who dismisses her servant, Taddeo (Tonio). The lovebirds eat dinner together and plot to poison Pagliaccio, who soon arrives. Arlecchino slips out of the window. With sharp hatred, Taddeo assures Pagliaccio of his wife's innocence, intensifying Canio's real-life jealousy. Ignoring the script of the play, Canio insists that Nedda reveal her lover's identity. She tries to carry on with the play as if everything is normal, the audience greatly impressed and applauding the realism of the "acting". Enraged, Canio stabs Nedda and then Silvio, who has hurried forward from the audience to help her as she calls out his name. Canio cries out, "*La commedia e finita*"—the comedy is over.

I must have seen this opera about fifteen times during my adolescence and listened to a wide range of recordings another hundred times, almost with the compulsion of an addict. In hindsight, the reason this opera had such a strong interpretive grip on me is obvious: I was reliving and trying to master the range of passionate feelings related to my own unresolved oedipal struggle, often playing the parts of the different characters from this opera in my lively phantasy life. For example, I felt like Silvio (Nedda's lover) in relation to my seductive, dramatically present mother (Nedda), vis-á-vis my judgmental father (Canio). That I thought my mother was a mesmerising woman who I fantasised had made me her special audience usually played out at the breakfast table during her presentations of great operas; and in my further imaginings, I was not only her favourite child, but the much more sensitive and therefore more appealing "man" to her than my boorish, money-chasing father. On the other hand, I empathised with the enraged and brokenhearted Canio/father who found his wife being unfaithful, a common fantasy of a child who feels that his father has edged him out of his wished-for and special erotically charged relationship with his mother. That I discovered at an early age that my mother was actually having an affair with a neighbour only further fired up my oedipal fantasy life in terms of identifying with my father, both of us being rejected by my mother for another man. Thus, for many of my formative years my relationship with my mother was intensely ambivalent. With all of this un-metabolised emotion going on inside me it is no wonder that *Pagliacci* captured my mind and heart, especially being a *verismo* masterpiece. *Verismo* was a musical style typical of the post-Romantic operatic tradition associated with Italian composers, marked by melodramatic, often violent plots with characters drawn from everyday life. I could easily relate to these simple rural characters and common, everyday themes.

Indeed, *Pagliacci* made me think deeply about myself as I left the opera house, and for days I was whistling the melodic tunes and reliving the desiring and painful emotions that the music inspired in me.

In late adolescence, there was a notable musically mediated experience between my father and me when my mother left town to visit my brother at university and the two of us had to make do. We went to the ballet together to watch Rudolph Nureyev dance in *Swan Lake*. Not only was Nureyev magnificent and Tchaikovsky's music gorgeous to listen to, but it was a particularly electrifying experience because I was sitting next to Paul Newman and his wife! What made this experience so memorable was that it was one of the few times my father and I did something together that we both thoroughly enjoyed. Moreover, it was one of the few times I viewed him as something besides an oedipally tinged, fantasised adversary who was out to kill me. After all, I unconsciously felt some relief knowing that my father could "fall in love" with the same male Apollonian dancer as I did, so how dangerous a man could he really be? For a moment my fear of my father subsided.

When I was aged about sixteen I went with a few friends to the Woodstock Festival that took place for three rainy days in the Catskill area of upstate New York in 1985. I do not remember much in terms of the details of the festival, though as is well-known, many of the most important rock and roll groups played there. Not only did the Woodstock Festival decisively alter the history of rock and roll, it was a watershed of the counterculture movement with which I to some extent identified, at least in my fantasies. The one group that I recall hearing was Sly and the Family Stone; indeed their combination of body-pulsing rock, funk, soul, Latin, and psychedelic sounds, combined with their flamboyant costuming and messages of love and peace, was electrifying to my adolescent self. Even today, when I hear such songs as "Dance to the Music",

155

"Stand", "Everyday People", and "I Want to Take You Higher", I can't help but get a rush of extremely pleasant memories as well as feel the throbbing excitement that I associate with this thrilling music. For a developing teenager, the music of Sly and the Family Stone was a perfect psychological fit.

At around the same time I became heavily interested in Motown music. The Four Tops, Temptations, Stevie Wonder, and The Supremes were some of my favourites, but I became extremely familiar with many other singers and groups and read up on the history of the genre. Motown music, with its combined rhythm and blues and pop, or gospel rhythms and modern ballad harmony, affected me deeply, especially as a late adolescent and young adult when being and feeling "cool" was so important in terms of peer relations and relations with girls. Moreover, the typical themes of Motown, of love found and lost, resonated deeply with me, especially because the accessible music was typically produced using the "KISS principle", as the Motown producers of the music conceived it—"keep it simple, stupid". In addition, this music had another important personal connection to me, namely, that my father was one of the first white dentists to work in Harlem, then an almost totally black enclave, and this music and the blues were part of the fabric of his experience, and indirectly, mine, since these were the people with whom I hung out when I visited him at his office. The affection that his staff had for my father, whom he had trained and given a career to, and the black culture that they personified, included the then popular musical context of Motown and blues, and this music became a way of being positively connected to my father who, while at work, was an impressive figure who I looked up to.

In my mid-twenties and beyond, I became very interested in the work of Beethoven, Bach, and Brahms, though of the three composers, Beethoven most touched me. I had decided to study his music in depth and I listened to just about everything I could get my hands on as well as read many books about him. During this period of my life I was mainly focused on getting my Ph.D. at the University of London and negotiating an ill-conceived, ill-fated marriage, and the Third "Eroica" symphony, Beethoven's favourite symphony, as he told the poet Christian Kuffner, was the one symphony that I loved more than all the others. When I ask myself now, why the Third symphony?, I surmise that I identified with Beethoven's psychological calamity of 1802 when he understood that he was losing his hearing (in my unconscious mind, a castration equivalent). As a result of this suffering and struggle with his gradually developing disability, Beethoven seemed to find inside himself a new strength and upsurge of creativity, and this "new path" as a composer, said musicologist Robert Greenberg, "paralleled his own life in its heroic battle with and ultimate triumph over adversity" (1998, pp. 68, 75, 132). As Beethoven said in one of his letters, and I thoroughly identified with his words, "I will seize fate by the throat; it shall certainly never wholly overcome me" (Kalischer, 1909, p. 36).

Similarly, the other Beethoven symphony that I loved was the Fifth, in part because the musical and expressive content, in particular Beethoven's use of rhythm (separated from melody), "as a narrative element in its own right", was crafted by him as a medium for a dramatic struggle "in which light and hope were victorious over forces of darkness and despair". All of this, to a doctoral student who was struggling to complete his very challenging thesis, amid a failed marriage and lots of heartache in a foreign country, helped me to metabolise my painful feelings and offered me a sense of hope that all would work itself out. Beethoven's use of music as self-expression, part of his mature compositional style (Greenberg, 1998, p. 135), was exactly where I was at in terms of my own existential odyssey, trying to find a balance, if not integration, between the many conflicting parts of myself that often left me feeling as if my unyielding passions had got me smack in the middle of a "pooh storm". As Beethoven noted, "Music is the mediator between the spiritual [i.e., the psychological] and the sensual life" (Wood, 1923, p. 287).

Somewhere in my late twenties to early thirties I continued to listen to various types of classical music, dabbling in particular composers that I was drawn to depending on what was going on in my often roller coaster emotional life. For example, there was a Mozart phase, especially the concertos of his mature style, where "balance, lyricism, elegance and good taste" (Greenberg, 2006, p. 39) characterise his compositional work. For someone who was trying to maintain an inner centre of gravity, Mozart's concertos were a good place to go. During my various romances, with their emotional swings and roundabouts, I often found myself listening to some of the great romantic composers like Max Bruch, Edvard Grieg, and most of all, Chopin, including his two piano concertos. Chopin's rhythms rooted in Polish dance, his skilful use of Slavic-sounding melodies, his remarkably flexible use of rhythm, his authentic "bel canto lyric sensitivity, and pianism" (ibid., p. 71) made his music irresistible to me. Likewise, during self-explorations of my Jewish identity, I found myself listening to the gorgeous *klezmer* music, especially that of Giora Feidman, the Argentine-born Israeli clarinetist and member of the Israeli Philharmonic Orchestra, whom Steven Spielberg chose to play the clarinet solos in the soundtrack for the Oscar Award-winning *Schindler's List*. One of the moments when I experienced a glimpse of immortality was when I saw Feidman in a concert. The lights in the auditorium went out, and from the back of the hall he slowly walked to the stage playing one of the most beautiful and haunting *nigunim* (Hebrew for "tunes", more generally religious or folk melodies) I have ever heard as the lighting gradually shone on him until he graced the stage. Indeed, the social setting (e.g., a concert hall versus a rock stadium) and function of a musical experience can amplify the music listener's pleasure. When I am nervous,

I often call to mind the transcendent realm that Feidman took me to, a "fairy space" of pure loveliness.

Worth mentioning is the music to which I exposed my two children. While my daughter never had the interest and discipline to continue with her piano instruction, and my son was into painting, both of my children loved, as did I, the music of "Raffi", the award-winning, Egyptian-born Canadian children's singer and songwriter. Raffi's music was characterised by its simple folk instrumentations and displayed his sweet, lively voice and playful guitar playing. His songs, like "Baby Beluga", "Down by the Bay", and "Bananaplane" are marvellous children's music that show great empathy for the inner world of the child. Moreover, many of his songs have the message of honouring the world of the child by making our communities and ecosystems better places for them to grow up in. For me as for most engaged parents with young children, some of the most enlivening moments occurred during long drives singing along with Raffi, memories that are preciously heartwarming.

Finally, we come to the present. I continue to be open to all of the music described above, depending on the context I am in, that is, what I want to feel. As with other people, my music serves many personal functions; it can be a stimulant, a tranquilliser, a quest for intensity or beauty, a distraction, a wish to immerse myself in symbolism or abstraction (Jourdain, 1997, p. xvi). This includes pushing myself outside my comfort zone and familiar tonal system, and developing receptivity to music from around the world that often sounds like noise to me, at least at first hearing.

However, at the age of sixty I am feeling as if I am in the "fourth quarter" of my life and the music that seems to most include me is the blues. The blues has a near universal appeal in its ability to express the outrageousness of ordinary life, something that in my more maudlin moments speaks to me. Blues is musically characterised by usually strong 4/4 rhythm, flatted thirds and sevenths, a twelve-bar structure, and lyrics in a three-line stanza in which the second line repeats the first. Through its spirituals, work songs, field hollers, shouts, and chants, and rhymed simple narrative, "... the passion, the humor, the sorrow, the joy all seem to communicate on a subliminal, non-intellectual level" (Iglauer, 2012, p. x)—important truths about the art of living the "good life". As Ralph Ellison noted, "The blues is an art of ambiguity, an assertion of the irrepressibly human over all circumstances, whether created by others, or by one's own human failing" (ibid.). One song that particularly comes to mind is Ray Charles's version of "That Lucky Old Sun". Charles's soulful fusion of rhythm and blues and gospel, and the powerful lyrics that juxtapose the singer's hard, sweat-filled work and the adversity of his life with the indifference of the natural world, make this brutally honest though redemptive music utterly appealing to this old man. As the great Lutheran German pastor/theologian and anti-Nazi, Dietrich Bonhoeffer, said, "Music ... will help dissolve your perplexities and purify your character and sensibilities, and in time of care and sorrow, will keep a fountain of joy alive in you" (www.christianmusings-brian.blogspot.com/2013/01/the-power-of-music.html).

IV. Music as a gateway to immortality

For Marcel, the Catholic existentialist, the magisterial music of, say, Bach, Mozart, and Beethoven is "a pledge of eternity, like the active inmost depths of our life and thought" (2005, p. 114). It has this transcendent spiritual function because music, and all musical genres at their deepest and best, is like prayer. This should not be too surprising since "The harmony of virtually all the music we hear, whether Chopin or Elvis, is rooted in chants sung by medieval Christian monks" (Jourdain, 1997, p. 93). "Prayer", said Marcel, "is the purest form of invocation," a calling upon God or a spirit as a witness, or for inspiration, and while prayer is "embodied imperfectly in the uttered word", it "is a certain kind of inner transfiguration, a mysterious influx, an ineffable peace" (1964, p. 32). Most important, the spirit of prayer is its "receptive disposition" (Marcel, 2001, p. 195):[16]

> ... whether or not expressed by words, because it aims at a response or the granting of a request that is not a sensory order, if it is not itself silent, is at the very least indissolubly wed to silence. It is no doubt for that reason that it is music and also that of any music in its profoundest depths is prayer. (Jourdain, 1997, p. 139)

The difficult to grasp but vitally important link between silence and prayer involves understanding silence not merely as the absence or lack of noise, but rather, as a mode of engagement to people and things that is radically open and creative, including to the deeper patterns of the heard sound, as with skilful music listening.[17] Such a mode of listening, of creative receptivity, has been described by one Marcellian scholar as "expectant listening for the most basic" (Wood, 2005, p. 33). This way of listening means being excitedly aware that something is about to happen, though paradoxically, "the deepest pleasure" in listening to music "comes with deviation from the expected", such as "dissonances, syncopations, kinks in melodic contour, sudden booms and silences" (Jourdain, 1997, p. 319).[18] For Marcel, when music is approached with creative receptivity and responsiveness we enter into that psychological state of enhanced self-cohesion, of deeper inwardness and self-affirmation, and plenitude, that sense of "fullness" and completion that underlies the superficial and empty that constitutes living merely "on the surface of life" (Wood, 2005, p. 33). This is the difference between listening to music that is characterised by "moment-to-moment variations on a simple theme" versus music that has relational depth and complex musical structures (Jourdain, 1997, p. 266). Thus, similar to prayer, "immersion in music" becomes "a kind of response to a call, an openness to being seized and simultaneously coming into possession of oneself" (Wood, 2005, p. 16). We can call this moment of "interior foraging" (digging beneath the surface of everyday experience) (Marcel, 2005, p. 41), communion, "being-with", the sharing or exchanging of intimate thoughts and feelings that occurs in emotional or spiritual closeness.

When music is approached with creative receptivity, from the dimension of the spirit that is radically open and responsive, one is most likely to experience the transcendent significance of music. What are some of the key general characteristics of creativity that Marcel suggests make the transcendent in music accessible?

Creativity is associated with "novelty, freshness, revelation" (Gallagher, 1962, pp. 84–85). Creativity is novel in the sense that it points to that which is new, original, and different, always in a thrilling, self-renewing way. It is fresh in the sense that it calls to mind that which is eternal, that is, the creative experience is unaffected by the passage of time, like creating or encountering a great piece of music or art. Finally, creation gives one the feeling that one is in a "beholding", hearing, or looking at something that is amazing and exciting, the sense that one has been given an irresistible, quasi-magical "gift" that makes one feel "anew and beyond beginnings" (ibid., p. 85). In creation, whether one is the creator or the person who witnesses creation and its product, like listening to music, the experience is that one has engaged "the source, the beginning, which is also the end". As Gallagher further noted, "one who stands in the source transcends time"; however, paradoxically "[W]e need time to stand in the source" (ibid.). Put somewhat differently, in creativity, the creator surrenders himself to something other. He puts himself at the service of something, a source that transcends him, while at the same time it depends on him (Cain, 1995, p. 104). Marcel noted, for example, that for the composer and musician there is an encounter with "the original mystery, the 'dawning of reality' at its unfathomable source". Moreover, he said, "[T]he artist seems to be nourished by the very thing he seeks to incarnate; hence the identification of receiving and giving is ultimately realized in him" (Marcel, 2005, p. 92).[19]

In the act of creating, including listening to music, ironically, one does not feel as though one is giving up anything vital of the self, even as there is hard work and output required to create something (such as listening to complex music with deep relational patterns). Rather, creation feels as though one has become more bountiful, has a more plentiful supply of something that is judged by the creator as good and feels significantly healing. The psychoanalyst Melanie Klein and her followers have provided an intriguing psychoanalytic formulation that may further illuminate this point. In their view, creativity is a way of dealing with infantile depressiveness associated with normal development. It signifies an effort to make reparations for destructive unconscious phantasies that feel real and are imagined to have caused harm which have been directed at an ambivalently related-to object (originally the mother or primary caregiver whom one both intensely loves and hates). The experience of creativity is thus a curative act of uplifting restoration.[20]

The upshot of all of this is that, as most great composers will tell you, creation relies on and draws upon "a superior order" (ibid., p. 25),[21] a hard to describe transcendent realm; perhaps, as Bach and Michelangelo thought and felt, God, or the unconscious or collective unconscious, as Freud and Jung might have called it. Indeed, music history is full of stories of creative inspiration that call to mind this "superior order": when someone enquired of Mozart what the source of his musical ideas was, he replied, "Whence and how they come, I know not; nor can I force them" (maybe this is why occasionally Mozart would choose "melody notes by rolling dice"). Likewise, Beethoven's explanation for his creativity was similar: "They come unbidden." Handel, who by a servant was found sobbing while he was composing the whole *Messiah* in what appears to have been a manic state, said, "I thought I saw all of heaven before me, and the Great God himself." More recently, Puccini commented, "The music of this opera was dictated to me by God, I was merely instrumental in putting it on paper and communicating it to the public." Finally, Brahms said, "I felt that I was in tune with the Infinite, and there is no thrill like it" (Jourdain, 1997, pp. 60, 170).[22]

Thus, the "royal road" to glimpsing immortality through attentive music listening requires that one fashion a receptive spiritual setting. That is, the psychological conditions of possibility for making oneself a more fertile breeding ground for the experience of the transcendent requires "spiritual availability", a readiness, openness, and receptivity to the other with the fullness of one's whole being, whether it be to music or in love. When this occurs, we experience the music as a spontaneously undetermined, timeless/spaceless happening/event, one that feels like there is a mutual, life-affirming presence among the composer/musician/music and the listener. Such a confirming inter-human between-ness is a moment of genuine dialogue that calls to mind a transcendent, absolute presence (Kramer, with Gawlick, 2003, pp. 18, 142), one that makes one feel utterly grateful to be alive amid music's invisible embrace. As Nietzsche said, "Without music, life would be a mistake" (Gabrielsson, 2011, p. 446).

Notes

1. For example, in Celtic thought the wind personifies "the spirit-sound of the ancient earth" that gives the earth a sense of intimacy (O'Donohue, 2004, p. 60). With regard to ordinary speaking, Pinchas Noy, a psychoanalyst, has suggested the relationships among tone, nuance, and inflection constitute the "music of speech" (Nagel, 2013, p. 57).

2. Some music therapists have conceptualised sound in terms of "vibrations", that is, "inherent universal energy forms" that are believed to be in music and which are healing to body, mind, and spirit (Wigram, Pederson, & Bonde, 2002, p. 148).

3. For example, during the Holocaust, artistically talented Jews and non-Jews from diverse backgrounds functioned to help preserve the inmate's autonomy, integration, and humanity. By creating original music, sometimes writing passages on toilet paper, these inmates maintained their pre-incarceration artistic selves. Interestingly, these works were not only sad pieces or works that conveyed their awful ordeal, but in addition, their pieces included humour, whimsy, and sarcasm. What this documentation indicates, among other things, is that great beauty can be created within the context of great evil, and by so doing, an individual can save his soul (see Shapiro, 2013, pp. 12–17).

4. How words and music are merged and produce expressive beauty is an important question, though one that is outside the scope of this chapter.

5. It is worth mentioning that compared to sculpture and painting, music is probably more reflective of the "reign of the spirit", as it does not suppose a pre-existing object that the artist gives to himself (Marcel, 2005, p. 106).

6. Brain imaging has indicated that emotionally evocative music activates the reward system in the brain, stimulating subcortical nuclei that are related to reward, motivation, and emotion. Indeed, listening to "peak emotional moments in music", that is, music that evokes a "chill" of pleasure, increases dopamine levels, a vital signalling molecule in the brain (Zatorre & Salimpoor, 2013, p. 12).

7. A skilful listener can "hear simultaneous melodies, simultaneous rhythms" and "simultaneous harmonies", "the relations among relations" (Jourdain, 1997, pp. 5, 63).

8. To Marcel, music also reflects the "tragic tension implicit in the struggle against time, the contrast between musical matter that, through the actualized sound, exists only in the present, and its form that can constitute its unity only beyond durations,

within the immobile and silent judgment". In this sense, said Marcel, music is an "*ersatz* of eternity" (2005, p. 118).

9. In a sense we can say that music tells a story, a musical story with "musical plots", sound patterns, though without content, in contrast to fictional works (Kivy, 2002, p. 79). Music that involves improvisation is a more obvious form of storytelling and is a more immediate type of self-expression. Psychoanalytically speaking, improvisation, such as is used in music therapy, but also in jazz, can be usefully conceptualised as the expression of modes of relating and experiencing that replicate mother and child interactions (including free and directed play). These improvised pieces give insight into different aspects of self-experience and "different ways of experiencing how-to-be-with-another" (Wigram, Pederson, & Bonde, 2002, pp. 85, 257).

10. Tonality is "the dominance of tonal centers in harmony", a tonal centre is "the first note of the scale that underlies prevailing harmony" (Jourdain, 1997, p. 342).

11. Research has shown that most often adult musical preferences are based on one's earlier musical experiences. Moreover, most people choose music that is conformist, "taking on music that is an emblem of social solidarity with their peers", and each generation embraces its own distinct style (Jourdain, 1997, p. 263).

12. There is an infinity to primitive unconscious affects in that they ignore the distinguishing and dividing limits of secondary process thought, that is, they are not representable, thinkable, or containable (Lombardi, 2008).

13. Interestingly, Marcel believed that music could be "a victory over death". That is, "It is a transmutation by which life simply lived becomes thinking or, more exactly, illuminating in such a way that the other recognizes himself in it beyond all the changes, all the destructions of what we call history" (2005, p. 49).

14. In one of his plays, Marcel has a character ask, "Isn't music like the immortality of everything we think is dead but in fact lives on?" (2005, p. 55).

15. Maurice Ravel noted that "Music is a dream crystallized into sound" (O'Donohue, 2004, p. 64).

16. For Marcel, "I can pray to be more, not to have more," it is "basically the act by which I affirm myself dependent" on God, and "it is essential to religion" as autonomy is to ethics (Cain, 1995, p. 5).

17. The relationship between silence and music (and silence and speech in psychoanalysis) is an important one in terms of the structure of music and the listening experience, a subject that is beyond the scope of this chapter. It is worth mentioning that the most appealing music often has "spatial complexity, but with a clear sound source", or put differently, "carefully ordered experience" with "immaculate deep relations". Jourdain thus describes the experience of great "beauty" as "unsullied order persisting simultaneously at every perceptual level" (1997, pp. 51, 330).

18. Kivy has an interesting critique of this view that the pleasure of music is based on aroused, tension-filled expectations that are satisfied (2002, pp. 96–97).

19. The "giving" side of the artist can be formulated as resembling maternal function, said Marcel elsewhere (2005, p. 109).

20. Marcel described music as "a restitution", that is, "a releasing of what one has breathed in" (2005, p. 124).

21. My bet is that most composers, like authors, have an unconscious longing for immortality through their creations.

22. In some sense, music creation feels more like a "finding" and "revealing" than a "creating", though both processes are obviously in play.

CHAPTER SIX

"Once upon a time there was …"
On storytelling

Creating Heaven on Earth

"And so, from hour to hour, we ripe and ripe,
And then from hour to hour, we rot and rot;
And thereby hangs a tale."

—William Shakespeare (*As You Like It*, Act II, scene ii)

W e all listened spellbound", said Anna Freud, "to the revelations made by the patients, their dreams, delusions, fantastic systems, which the analytically knowledgeable among us fitted into a scheme" (Geissmann & Geissmann, 1998, p. 85). It is Anna Freud's use of the word "spellbound", defined as holding the complete attention of someone as though by magic, that caught my "inner eye", for it dovetails with the main question of this chapter: what is it about certain types of conversation, which I am calling storytelling, that has the effect of making us feel as if we have been put into a lovely spell, one that magically transports us far away from our routine lives, and once we return, we feel as if our existence has been wonderfully expanded and deepened? As J. K. Rowling, the author of *Harry Potter* noted, "There's always room for a story that can transport people to another place" (www.biographyonline.net/writers/j_k_ rowling.html), an imaginative realm that transforms us in a life-affirming manner, even if the conversation is painful to experience. While Rowling's stories transport us to another place, to Harry's wizarding world, all of us have had so-called "ordinary" conversations that morph into the extraordinary, conversations that give us a sense that we have crossed a powerfully meaningful existential threshold. Such "crossing worlds", from humdrum conversation into deeply significant conversation, has been conceptualised from diverse perspectives: those lodged in the professional oral storytelling tradition have described the power of telling a good story; it "grounds us", that is, "It gives us a sense of purpose, identity, and continuity between the past and present" (Harvey, 2012, p. 4). Performers of theatre improvisation ("improv") have described their storytelling as "storymaking", the result of spontaneous individual and group processes—as the "high priestess" of improv, Viola Spolin, noted, "A story is an epitaph; the ashes of the fire" (Marcus & Marcus, 2011, pp. 93–94). Psychoanalysts, like Roy Schaefer, have described psychoanalysis as a transforming narrative process, one in which the analysand is a "reteller" of his life story, and through his conversation with the analyst he develops new psychoanalytically glossed "storylines" (analogous to plots in literature), and modes of experience, that increase agency and expand and deepen subjectivity, including helping the analysand to love and work better. Donald Spence has discussed the difference between narrative and historical truth in psychoanalysis: "[N]arrative truth", the kind of truth that psychoanalysis deals with, "is what we have in mind when we say that such and such is a good story, that a given explanation carries conviction, that one solution to a mystery must be true" (1982, p. 31). Gabriel Marcel has described such threshold-crossing conversation in terms of being creatively receptive and responsive to the unique transforming presence of a "charming" person, especially a person who often makes us smile and laugh (Marcus, 2013b, p. 80). And finally, Martin Buber has described such face-to-face experiences as "genuine dialogue", as "I–Thou" moments characterised by "directness and wholeness, will and grace, and the presence of mutuality" (Kramer, with Gawlick, 2003, p. 20).[1] While all these "storying" experiences have their unique context-dependent, setting-specific rhythms of perception and emotion, what they have in common is the power to galvanise, to stimulate great internal activity that feels not only uplifting but also transformative. In short, as Lipman, a professional storyteller, has pointed out, both participants in the storytelling experience—whether the performer and the audience, the analysand and analyst, the charmer and the charmed, or two lovers—are positively changed internally and in terms of their relationship. While this change is hard to account for let alone put into intelligible words, one feels an enlarged and deepened consciousness, an "expanded awareness" that can be conceptualised depending on the context and the "language game" one is steeped in, "… as a leap in understanding, as a miracle, as an experience of 'flow,' as a sense of being 'right with the world,' or merely as an unnoticed window through which they have viewed some large or small piece of life." Sometimes this transformation is not only temporarily meaningful, but is also deeply significant as it ripples through one's outlook, such as a pronounced change in a person's sensibilities, being "reminded of some aspect of who they really are" or would like to become, or "form[ing] a connection with a [perspective-altering] body of traditional lore," like the storytelling literature. And as in all moments of glimpsing immortality, these felt changes amid the "storying" experience bring about an upsurge of "joy, gratitude and humility" (Lipman, 1999, pp. 207–208) among other positive emotions.

I will structure this chapter mainly in terms of the problem of creative self-fashioning, how a person can inventively constitute himself with an eye to glimpsing immortality through telling and listening to stories in various settings. What are the psychological conditions of possibility for attaining the sense of transcendence, well-being, and appreciation of life that emanates from authentic conversation? Specifically I will focus on the four relational settings mentioned above, storytelling settings where such positively transformational dialogue frequently occurs: (1) professional storytelling and theatre improv; (2) child psychoanalysis; (3) at a party or gathering where one encounters a disarmingly appealing, "charming" person; (4) in a deep friendship or love relationship.

"Once upon a time there was …"

I. The art of professional storytelling and theatre improv

Professional storytelling

The great religious studies scholar Huston Smith noted that "[E]xclusively oral cultures are unencumbered by dead knowledge, dead facts. Libraries, on the other hand, are full of them." The reason for this is that speech is "not only alive, it *is* life", that is, it cannot be detached from the living individual in one mode of his own being (Paine, 2012, p. 43). Indeed, different from literature, it is through oral storytelling that people in every culture "remember and record the peak" experiences of their personal lives, both inside and outside their families and communities. Storytelling, in other words, "is the commonality of all human beings, in all places, in all times. It is used to educate, to inspire, to record historical events, to entertain, to transmit cultural mores" (Collins & Cooper, 2005, p. 1). As Harvey has aptly summarised, unlike stories that exist in print, oral stories "live in conversation in our memories" and are enlivened through the storyteller's voice and body in the process of telling the story (2012, p. 4). Compared to acting, where one has memorised lines to precisely say while remaining concentrated on the role and place in the story, in storytelling the performer has greater freedom and power, for in narration he has "to make the light, sound, the action and all the characters" come alive (ibid., p. 61).[2] Stories can also define and demarcate relationships and generate parameters; they give a sense of self-coherence, self-continuity, and self-esteem, for they provide an account of who we are, where we came from and where we want to go, including conveying our most cherished values. In this sense, said Harvey, stories are the repository for our most profound "longings, hopes, and fears"; stories also interrogate life by encouraging critical self-reflection and "put[ting] up a mirror to yourself and to culture". Finally, more than so-called "facts", stories reveal "usable truths" as philosopher Richard Rorty called them, truths that convey meaning to our experiences and direction to our lives (1989, pp. 4–6).

The aspect of professional storytelling that I want to focus on is based on the claim that what makes storytelling so compelling is that there are three interdependent and interacting elements that are synergistically unfolding: the teller, the audience, and the story. Somewhere amid this storytelling triangle, the teller and the audience join forces to imaginatively co-produce what is like a collective dream, one that is magical in the delight it evokes. That is, when a well-chosen, well-crafted story is skilfully told by a passionate narrator to an engrossed audience, the effect is a dreamlike sense of enchantment (Collins & Cooper, 2005, p. 31). Joseph Conrad has called this dreamy storytelling quality "being captured by the incredible which is the very essence of dreams" (Goonetilleke, 2007, p. 105).

Like any performance art, to be a good professional storyteller requires training, devotion to practice, and the integration of constructive criticism by colleagues and audience reactions. Moreover, the "nuts and bolts" of the art form, such as creating evocative visualisations, manipulating time and focus, and developing complex and interesting characters, plot, and story structures, are necessary to maintain the audience's attention and provide a satisfying, transformative listening experience. However, the most important aspect of storytelling is the way the storyteller uses emotion to captivate the listener, that is, the way he psychologically connects to the story and the audience. For a good storyteller is not simply telling the plot, the main events of the story devised and presented by the teller as an interrelated sequence, often using an Aristotelian trajectory of beginning, middle, and end, or the Gustav Freytag Pyramid of plot development: exposition, rising action, climax, falling action, and *denouement*. More important, the storyteller is deliberately trying to evoke strong, well-placed emotion, for this is what makes an audience member feel he is "included" in the story. Understanding how the storyteller skilfully does this and its favourable impact on the receptive audience, that is, this magical dynamic between the storyteller and listener, can teach us something important about what is required when one wholeheartedly engages the other in a manner that positively transforms both participants and thus points to immortality.

"All great literature", said Leo Tolstoy, and I would add, all great storytelling, "is one of two stories; a man goes on a journey or a stranger comes to town" (www.badenstorytellers. wordpress.com/2013/10/15/469/). This being said, what makes a good storytelling experience for both the listener and teller is not the content alone, but the way it is animated by feeling and textured with emotional significance. While Tolstoy is certainly right, that for the most part, there is nothing new under the storytelling sun, the fact is that there is an infinite variety of ways to tell a story, and therein lies one of the unique qualities that make it potentially transformative. For example, take the *Cinderella* fairytale; depending on his perspective, the teller can narrate the story in terms of Cinderella's sadness, making us feel very sorry for poor Cinderella who is at the mercy of abusive adults. Another storyteller might emphasise Cinderella's self-assurance and boldness, getting us to root for her and applaud her victory. Still another teller might narrate the story with a good dose of irony or sarcasm, even mock-ing the fairytale convention itself, causing amusement at our own unrealistic wishes that everyone lives happily afterwards (Lipman, 1995, p. 31). Storytellers need to find the right rep-ertoire that is most in sync with their outlook on life and that uses emotions that the teller can comfortably work with. That is, the teller must be able to create, sustain, and bring to culmi-nation the "emotional arc"—the listener's belief and emotional connection to the events being told (Harvey, 2012, p. 317)—in a manner that is convincing and does not feel too manipulated. Indeed, while professional storytelling, similar to acting and stand-up comedy, manipulates the audience's emotions, at its best there is a sublime point in the storytelling experience when both the teller and the listener have given up their narcissistic stake in the story—the teller's exhibitionistic need for recognition and approval and the listener's wish to be stimulated and gratified without having to make much effort—and they suddenly reside in the interhuman realm of immediate presence and togetherness, of "address and response", as Martin Buber called it (Kramer, with Gawlick, 2003, pp. 58, 78).

Thus, what constitutes a good story is the teller effectively differentiating between the factual happenings in the plot and what is most emotionally important to the teller (and thus the audience) in the story. In other words, the teller needs to make a strong "emotional investment" (Harvey, 2012, p. 312) in the story he chooses, one that deeply resonates within him so that he can tell it in a compelling and truthful manner. "The truth of art", including storytelling, said the magisterial actor/director Constantin Stanislavski, "is the truth of your [given] circumstances" (Marcus & Marcus, 2011, p. 50). The "given circumstances" are the situations in which the actor (or storyteller) finds himself during a play or "storying" situation. This includes everything that the actor comes upon while he creates his character (e.g., "the plot, the epoch, the time and place of the actions, the conditions of life, the director's and the actor's interpretations, the setting, the properties of lighting and effects", etc.). Only once the actor is thoroughly immersed in the circumstances of the play or story, only after he has made it part of himself, will he be able to choose the apt actions that convey the believable and truthful manner of the psychological experiences of the character. Stella Adler and Sanford Meisner, both students of Stanislavski, further elaborated Stanislavski's performance axiom: "To defictionalize the fiction" was the actor's goal, said Adler, while Meisner noted that "living truthfully in the imaginary circumstances" means living the imaginary circumstances on stage as if they were real. To do this precisely and effectively, and be able to repeat it at will, requires considerable training and rehearsal, Stanislavski emphasised (ibid., p. 70).

In the context of acting, and I would include storytelling, Stanislavski said that the apt emotions must "grow out of your living them", of choosing the fitting action or behaviour (in storytelling, this includes the way one uses the body and the words chosen) that will convincingly express the feeling of the character. "The more delicate the feeling, the more it requires precision, clarity and plastic quality in its physical expression." While the authentic feeling will occur "spontaneously"—"… an emotion, if it is sincere is involuntary," said Mark Twain—the best the actor can do is "prepare the ground" via well-chosen and elaborated physical actions for the upsurge of truthful feeling to take place. Such a psychological scenario, Stanislavski said, is an important condition of possibility for the experience of "inspiration". Inspiration, what every actor and storyteller dreams of, is "when an actor is completely absorbed by some profoundly moving objective, so that he throws his whole being passionately into its execution" (Stanislavski, 1936, pp. 41, 107, 189, 280, 310).

Thus, said Stanislavski, "… *one cannot play or represent feelings, and one cannot call forth feelings point blank*" (italics in original). Rather they emerge when the actor wilfully does the right physical action which "prods" his conscious and unconscious "creative fantasy", which then "stirs up" emotion memory, which has the "echo" of appropriate feelings to the circumstances of the scene (1958, p. 87). When this happens, the actor or storyteller and the audience are amid a profound moment of presence and togetherness. Whether actor or storyteller, such an inspiring moment can be described as "spirit coming into form", that is, the artist encounters "something", and via his creativity fashions into form what he has encountered while unable to materially represent precisely what was encountered (Kramer, with Gawlick, 2003, pp. 60–61). While there is always a sensed limitation of language when directed to ultimate

177

concerns (Paine, 2012, p. 128), the audience feels that they are witnessing something transcendent.

It is not clear how this moment of presence and together-ness happens, but it does seem to require in both the story-teller and listener what has been called a "reverential mind". "[A] reverential mind can let things be and celebrate a per-son's presences or a thing's beauty without wanting some-thing from them." Most important, "It respects the otherness and the beauty of the world and endeavors to transfigure the desire to define oneself through possessions, achievements and power" (O'Donohue, 1998, pp. 111–112). In the context of the storytelling experience, what this means is that there is an unconscious internal "clearance", a stepping back that occurs, a psychological bracketing of everyday and banal concerns and a willingness and ability to fully engage the experience on its own terms, that is, its point and essential meaning. A reverential mind means respecting an experi-ence, having a depth of presence to the mystery of what is happening (O'Donohue, 2004, p. 31). At these moments of "sublime objectivity", we view things precisely as they are, without the distortions and disfigurations of our personal preferences, narcissistic desires, and neurotic needs (Paine, 2012, p. 51).[3] As Blake famously said, "If the doors of percep-tion were cleansed every thing would appear to man as it is, Infinite. For man has closed himself up, till he sees all things thro' narrow chinks of his cavern" (Swinburne, 1868, p. 215). When the storyteller and listener co-produce this clarifying and purifying moment of otherness and intimacy, of awaken-ing and belonging, the "real presence" of the story is in the foreground of the experience, and this feels extraordinary, as if "eternity" has become radiantly revealed via the "gran-deur" of co-creation (O'Donohue, 1998). Such a feeling can be psychologically described in terms of being bathed in an all-embracing sense of life continuity and a vital and endur-ing self. Most important, what all of this implies for the art of living the "good life" is that it is necessary to engage what we see and what we do with "a creative and kind eye" and with "passion and urgency", and by doing so, we are more likely to experience the beauty of the world, this being one of the points of entry to glimpse immortality (O'Donohue, 1997, p. 158; 2004, p. 13).

Theatre improv

Perhaps the essence of improv is the ability to create new realities, to actualise what is unthinkable and unimaginable, what is "not yet". In a certain sense, all of us produce and co-produce new realities as we go through our everyday lives, for most of what we say and do with others is not rehearsed, but is a function of responding in the moment to what is happening. And yet, when we see great improv, we feel there is something rather remarkable going on, as if what is a normative aspect of social interaction has morphed into something appealingly otherwise, something new. In short, great improv is fundamentally great "storymaking" (Wiener, 1994, p. 89).

It is mainly through stories that we live our lives, what in psychological parlance is called a narrative of self-identity. In other words, it is through "metaphoric redescriptions", as philosopher Mary Hesse noted (Rorty, 1989, p. 16) or what Roy Schafer (1983, p. 255) called "retellings", that new experiences and new insights can emerge, which is exactly for what improv aims. Richard Rorty has pointed out that a "… new vocabulary makes it possible, for the first time, a formulation of its own purpose. It is a tool for doing something which could not have been envisaged prior to the development of a particular set of descriptions, those which it helps to provide" (1989, p. 13). It is via these "retellings", as in improv, that we are able to see the material in question from a different slant, in a "new" way that gives "reality" to, or puts into sharp focus what was previously not seen. This is precisely what Spolin meant when she wrote that the main goal of theatre games and improv is transformation, that is creation, the emergence of a new reality.

To tell a great story in the improv context requires a number of creative skills such as cultivating adult playfulness, deepening interpersonal trust, increasing spontaneity, expanding creativity, and developing greater sensory, physical, and emotional expressiveness (Marcus & Marcus, 2011, pp. 77–97).[4] A good improvised story, one that helps make an aspect of life more intelligible, meaningful, and pleasurable, requires the ability to generate a "greater coherence in its structure, a greater universality in its message, and greater artistry in its performance" (Wiener, 1994, pp. xii–xv). To accomplish all of this, Spolin (1999) noted, requires the capacity to deal spontaneously with what is unforeseen and new; in fact, this is one of the main reasons improv is so compelling to watch—we are curious to see if the player will succeed or fail in his boldness and fearlessness as he engages his fellow players and the emerging, often challenging, situation. The parallel to ordinary life is obvious—we are all thrown into situations and circumstances that require us to spontaneously manage, hopefully inventively, while at the same time to generate a symbolic structure, that is, a story that makes better sense of what we are experiencing. As the Baal Shem Tov said, "Telling proper stories is as if you were approaching the throne of Heaven in a fiery chariot" (www.aaronshep.com/storytelling/quotes.html).

Perhaps the most important aspect of telling a good story in the improv context was captured by the British pioneer of improv theatre and the "Impro System", Keith Johnstone, when he wrote, "If you improvise spontaneously in front of an audience you have to accept that your innermost self will be revealed." Moreover, in order to enter domains that "would normally be 'forbidden', [such] spontaneity means abandoning some of your defences" (Johnstone, 1992, p. 111), not an easy thing to do by any means. Indeed, continued Johnstone, when a player says that he or she "can't think up a story", it is not because of a lack of talent but rather a decision not to put oneself out there (ibid., p. 116). Johnstone described the many types of defences that players use to avoid spontaneous self-creation and self-revelation, especially in the group context, defences that have their counterparts in real life. For example, there is "blocking", that which inhibits or stops action from progressing or that eradicates your partner's premise or offering; "sidetracking", offering a side-plot instead of going with the main theme of the story; "being original", which acts as a diversion or interruption from the main mood or energy of the story; "gagging", which uses gags or jokes to shift "the context away from the adventure within the story toward amusement at it".[5]

The upshot of all of this is an obvious, simple, but underappreciated truth: to be able to tell a great story in the improv context requires a feeling of emotional and spiritual closeness to one's fellow players, to the audience, and towards oneself (e.g., openness to one's otherness). Indeed, Spolin made this point when she wrote that "[I]mprovisation is not exchange of information between players; it is communion" (Spolin, 1999, p. 45). That is, "[I]ndividual freedom (expressing self) while respecting community responsibility (group agreement) is our goal" (ibid., p. 44). The implications of these insights derived from the world of improv have their obvious correlations for ordinary life, namely, in order to produce and co-produce new realities, realities that are spontaneously creative and enhancing, requires that one obtain a high degree of "openness to contact with the environment and each other and willingness to play" (ibid., p. 25). To achieve this kind of openness to the otherness of one's players, the audience, the material, and oneself, requires a diminution of one's narcissism, one's need for self-aggrandisement and the like. As Spolin noted, to fill a pail full of apples requires an empty pail, a kind of "unselving or transelving", a jettison of the selfish ego. It is only then, when one has generated a less self-centric subjectivity, that one is properly receptive to the other. Moreover, this inner state is a kind of waiting, an openness and accessibility that is different than ordinary waiting: "[T]he improviser is in waiting, not waiting for," said Spolin. As with the queen of England who has "ladies in waiting", whose function is to attend to the queen's needs as they arise, so the improviser must attend to the other, in service.

II. Child psychoanalysis

"She loved repeating stories the children told her," said Greta Bibring of Anna Freud. "She saw how 'wise' children can be, and she looked for that side of her patients" (Coles, 1992, p. 89). Children can sometimes teach adults how to better cope with the harshness of life, and even surmount terrible hardship, through informal storytelling in the form of creative actions that communicate more than words do. At times, the best storytelling is told by silence rather than by speech, a kind of "wordless saying". Anna Freud told such a story to Robert Coles and his wife who interviewed her:

> There is the observation made by one of our colleagues during a day-light air raid in a surface shelter [during the Blitz] into which a mother had shepherded her little son of school age. For a while they both listened to the dropping of the bombs; then the boy lost interest and became engrossed in a story book which he had brought with him. The mother tried to interrupt his reading several times with anxious exclamations. He always returned to his book after a second, until she at last said in an angry and scolding tone: "Drop your book and attend to the air raid." (ibid., p. 86)

Compared to his mother's ordinarily highly valued "clever awareness" and her reality-oriented approach to the terrifying

Blitz, this boy's practical wisdom helped him to find his own way of managing the situation that was far more adaptive. As Coles noted, there was a "transcendence of the child reading a book [his way of telling his story of how best to cope] while loony adults bomb adults, and anxious adults pay exacting attention to such a reality". Specifically, it was the boy's life-sustaining use of denial while facing his unchangeable, terrifying ordeal that was a much superior way of coping compared to his mother's hyper-attentive, hyper-anxious, reality-based approach (ibid., p. 87).

Salman Rushdie's thoughtful observation about the importance of storytelling in adult life has applicability to the above story and to those professionals engaged in child psychoanalysis and child psychotherapy: "Those who do not have power over the story that dominates their lives, the power to retell it, rethink it, deconstruct it, joke about it, and change it as times change, truly are powerless, because they cannot think new thoughts" (Hassumani, 2002, p. 104). Stories and storytelling have been used in child psychoanalysis and child psychotherapy for many decades as they are, like dreams of adults, ways of accessing a child's internal world. That is, for a young child a story is a vehicle for verbalising fantasy that reveals his sexual and aggressive wishes, his conflicts, and his anxiety and guilt, among other imaginings of his mind. Stories have thus been used both as evaluative and diagnostic tools and as an augmentation to treatment. As Nathan I. Kritzberg has pointed out, listening to and telling formal and informal stories in child psychoanalysis is especially useful with children because it is connected with earlier development, "with emotionally charged bodily activities such as feeding, eliminative actions, and hypnagogic [drowsiness before sleep] activities". Moreover, a number of activities in school, like "show and tell", "where I went on vacation", and "what I got for my birthday" are also connected with listening to or telling creative stories (Brandell, 1984, pp. 54–62).

In this section, I want to focus on how a child telling and listening to a story can help him to better cope with his psychic pain and/or blocked development. For it is often through a formal or informal story (the latter is much more the case in child analysis), that a child is better able to put his "worries and troubles" into words, and by doing so, and with the help of a skilful and kind analyst, he can both begin to reduce his subjective distress and unblock that which impedes his development. The totality of circumstances that constitutes this co-produced storytelling/listening/retelling between the child and the analyst is a form of experience-near communication that, at its best, allows a child to transcend his predicament. How this communication that moves between primary and secondary process thinking occurs has something to teach us about adult immortality-strivings, for it requires the capacity to flexibly and creatively reside in the transitional space between the unconscious and the conscious, between being and becoming. As Carl Jung noted, "The difference between most people and myself is that for me the 'dividing walls' are transparent" (Paine, 2012, p. 183).

In child analysis and therapy, toys, dolls, role play, verbal devices, and of course, stories are used in diverse ways to prepare the ground for "interpretation", roughly making the unconscious conscious, or to bring it about, this being the main mechanism of change (Sandler, Kennedy, & Tyson, 1980, p. 164). Interpretation has both an historical-developmental and narrative aspect to it (Brandell, 2000, p. 69). As Sandler and colleagues noted, what makes these techniques so useful is that they allow for a modicum of displacement and externalisation of the child's self and other representations and of the interplay between them. In other words, it is safer for the child if his inner experience, especially of his sexual and aggressive wishes, is discussed via displacement and externalisation, that is, using puppets, dolls, or characters in a story (or through events pertaining to another child). As Anna Freud pointed out, offering interpretations about a person or figure onto whom the child has externalised aspects of his own self is a most useful way of helping the child approach "threatening mental content gradually", for it is mindful of the child's ego readiness to hear and metabolise unconscious content. Moreover, such an approach permits the child to maintain his narcissistic equilibrium, self-esteem, and self-respect while appropriating the interpretation (Sandler, Kennedy, & Tyson, 1980, pp. 76, 164–165). When these interpretations, that is, the analyst's "storying" of the child's experience, hit their mark, when they deeply resonate in the person of the child, not only do they provide a degree of psychic relief but they can facilitate insight, that is, liberating change in those "deeper" layers of the child's mind that are contributing to his "worries and troubles", his behavioural problems, and developmental arrests.

In storytelling with children there are at least five "moving pieces" that the analyst must empathically engage in order to skilfully enter into, and understand, the inner world of the troubled child (Brandell, 2000, pp. 20–24).[6] First, the analyst must discern the central psychodynamic issue, theme, or conflict that animates the child's metaphoric story and that is likely to be the lynchpin of his psychological difficulties. Such central conflicts might be formulated in the analyst's mind in terms of various dualities, such as aggression-hostility versus guilt-anxiety, the desire to be assertive versus the fear of criticism, closeness and distance (e.g., intimacy versus fear of engulfment), or the wish to be autonomous versus a fear of rejection or abandonment. Second, children's stories almost always convey "a unique object relational experience" (i.e., a way of structuring and patterning relationships), one that is connected to earlier, emotionally supercharged events with family members and others. This includes transference attitudes, wishes, and fantasies directed at the analyst.[7] Often these stories give the analyst a view of how the child is likely to structure other non-familial relationships, especially in terms of problematic relationships with friends and teachers. Thus, it is important for the analyst to get a sense from the story which characters likely represent himself and other family members. Third, the analyst must be mindful of the emotional tenor of the child's story, what the main and subsidiary affects are that animate the story and particular characters. Fourth, a child's story frequently includes a number of sublingual vocal sounds, characteristic facial expressions, and illuminating body movements. Those sounds, facial expressions, and body movements that are out of sync with the story content and theme are usually the most instructive to the analyst in terms of getting a sense of what is bothering the child. Finally, the analyst must be attuned to the child's defensive regime, his self-protective behaviours and strategies, as well as his "conflict-free solutions" that develop as the treatment successfully proceeds. Stories like adult dreams contain "compromise solutions" to inner conflicts, that is maladaptive, pseudo-solutions to conflict between the three agencies of the mind—id, ego, and superego. Conversely, when the child strengthens his capacity for introspection and insight he develops "conflict-free solutions" to his internal conflict; that is, he crafts more adaptive strategies to better cope with life's challenges.

A vignette of this storytelling interchange between a troubled child and an analyst may be helpful to illuminate some of the unique features of this form of conversation.[8]

> Johnny, a four-year-old boy, was brought to treatment because he appeared to be always unhappy and sullen, which was evidenced in his chronic bad moodiness which frequently flared up into major temper tantrums that were very hard for his parents, babysitter, and teacher to effectively manage.
>
> Johnny had been told, as all children are, that the treatment room was a place where children talk about all their "worries and troubles". It is this process of the child

"telling", and the analyst's psychoanalytically glossed "retelling", always within in the context of a strong child/analyst attachment, that is the main mechanism of change. Johnny liked coming to treatment, at least most of the time, for he liked the child-centred ambience of the place and the engaged participation of the analyst in his psychic stream. Johnny unconsciously apprehended that the treatment room was a place where there was no "speechifying", talking past one another (Buber, 1999d, p. 79), or phoniness, even artificial tenderness. Rather, the analyst was an authentically gentle, compassionate, and smart woman who would carefully attend to his every word and gesture, and offered a special kind of intriguingly surprising, personally meaningful "truth telling" that was meant to help him feel better. One could say that Johnny unconsciously intuited that the "coming-to-be" of language, of putting his ambiguous and ambivalent feelings and thoughts into personally meaningful words, and that of the "coming-to-be" of himself, his self development, were inextricably connected (ibid., p. 154).

The stories can be as simple as the description of the wish to build a tower of blocks that never falls down, which might indicate to the analyst an anxiety in the child about people or things "being broken", damaged, or dying. In Johnny this story evolved into his wish for the tower to fall down at his command, which allowed the analyst to connect that it must feel much better to be big and strong and have the power to make things and people do what he wants when he demands it rather than have to worry about the tower killing him suddenly.

After a visit to the doctor, Johnny made a hospital out of paper for people with bone disease that then turned into a garbage dump. I [Irene Wineman-Marcus] said, "Sometimes people go to the doctor and they feel their body is damaged and they think it is like garbage." He

187

then made some cars out of Legos and began crashing them and putting them back together. I pointed out how nice it was to be able to crash things and put them back together when they broke. As Johnny was crashing the cars, a bit of Play-Doh that was on the table fell onto the rug and he became panicky that I would be annoyed. He commented that I had said that this place was for talking about his feelings but he wasn't doing that. I said that he sounded worried that I would be angry at him but he seemed to be showing me a lot about his feelings; he was showing me that he was worried that if he gets angry or excited, or crashes things, he might damage something and then get into big trouble. Johnny responded by telling me about a teacher who gets angry at the children when they misbehave and chases them.

Part of the challenge for Johnny, as it is for many children (and adults too), is to distinguish between fantasised wishes and reality, between internal imaginings and a mindfulness of how the outside world hangs together and works. Johnny made a "magic potent" out of water and washing-up liquid. He told me it was to be used to kill a girl in school. He then changed the story and said that he was going to "kill a doll with poison to make the doll dead". I said, "I know other children who thought they had a magic spell that could kill people and then they got really scared that they might be able to actually do it." Johnny then got on the play table, stood up with his chest bulging and told me he was "king of the castle" and I was "the dirty rascal", and I had to repeat this back to him many times at his order. He then found a dead fly that happened to be in the room which gave him a fright; he wanted to "bury it and hammer it"; he then pretended to be a statue that couldn't move.

I commented that this was the trouble with thinking that he had magic powers: because then, when he saw a dead fly he imagined that he had killed it, and then he had to turn himself into a dead statue who couldn't move in order to make sure that he couldn't do anything bad, or anything scary or dangerous.

More elaborate stories expressing more complex conflicts give greater understanding to both the analyst and child about what the child has to deal with internally, especially his inner demons.

Johnny drew a spider on the chalkboard. The spider had long legs and there was also a little spider that Johnny said "looked smart". Johnny then drew long legs on the little spider and added, "The little spider looked silly with such long legs," and he proceeded to erase the legs from the little spider. I asked Johnny if the little spider had wanted the long legs from the daddy spider, but then got frightened that the "daddy long legs would cut off the little spider's legs". Johnny asked if "the little spider got dead". I said to him, "In your story the little spider only wishes to have the daddy long legs's legs, but the daddy spider understands that the little spider was only wishing and nobody gets punished just for wishing."

"Human stories", said J. R. R. Tolkien, "are practically always about one thing, really, aren't they? Death. The inevitability of death" (Grotta, 1992, p. 105). In this vignette Johnny is full of omnipotent aggressive wishes, mainly intense anger, if not death wishes, directed at his father, though he also wants to steal or acquire his father's powerful masculinity, as symbolised by the "long legs". However, Johnny is terribly afraid of the implications in the real world of his aggressive wishes, of the imagined paternal retribution, thus he can be said to be in a highly ambivalent state of mind. As a result of his ambivalence and his anxiety about the devastating effect of his aggressive wishes in the real world, Johnny then attempts to inhibit his aggressive wishes mainly due to his fear of punishment by the "daddy long legs". Johnny is thus forced to turn his aggressive wishes against his father and others inwards, and is prone to moodiness and temper tantrums (psychoanalytically speaking, adult depression, or bad moodiness in a child, is aggression turned on the self; the aggression does a "u-turn"). It was through the analyst's labelling, clarifying, interpreting, and understanding Johnny's unconscious aggressive wishes, mainly directed at his father, that Johnny was able to begin to more adequately distinguish fantasy and reality and, therefore, reduce his subjective distress and better control his moodiness and temper tantrums.

There are a few aspects of this clinical vignette that suggest what is necessary to bring about a genuine dialogue between two people, either between an adult and a child or between adults. First, the analyst approached Johnny with a sense of immediacy and presence, without any preconceived notions or agendas (Kramer, with Gawlick, 2003, p. 22) about what should or should not occur in the session. The child led the "dance", while the analyst, with her whole being, tried to empathically follow Johnny's continually running present dialogue with the past (real and imagined events that have occurred in his life) and the future (his worries and longings in the future), and back again. Such dialogic wholeness on the part of the analyst involved "surrender" (ibid., p. 22) to the flow of the child's expression, his free flowing story and play, while being a listening, responsive, and responsible participant. In this sense the analyst must have a modicum of humility as he receives the child's verbal creations, including what in the theatre world is called a "willing suspension of disbelief" (Brandell, 2000, pp. 16, 71). In other words, the analyst and the child generated an interactive immediacy (Kramer, with Gawlick, 2003, p. 22) between them, each contributing their share to the dialogue of saying and meaning that gradually was expanded and deepened, and ultimately became illuminating and transformational for the child. It is through the analyst's creative responses using psychoanalytic techniques and understanding, a powerful form of storying in the context of the child's timeless, metaphoric, and primary-process-like (Brandell, 2000, p. 187) conscious and unconscious revelations, which gave Johnny the ability to transcend his pained condition. Moreover, in a secondary sense, the analyst himself was also positively changed by the interaction through his sense of togetherness with Johnny, a mutuality of contact, of trust, and of sharing of the child's pained existence (Kramer, with Gawlick, 2003, p. 197),[9] whose healing the analyst was privileged to help bring about and witness. As Erich Fromm noted, "My patients heal me" (Friedman, 1996, p. 362).

III. The experience of charm

"Laughter is the closest thing to the grace of God," said Swiss Reformed Church theologian Karl Barth (Fitzhenry, 1993, p. 223). Indeed, a person's storytelling ability to make us laugh allows us to feel, at least at that moment, that we have entered a domain of immediate, direct participation, a domain in which we feel the special presence of the humorist. Such a "felt presence refreshes me and reveals me to myself and makes me more fully myself" (Cain, 1995, p. 145). In addition, being in the presence of someone who can make us laugh feels like a privileged moment, as if we have received an undeserved and unexpected gift from that person, one that Marcel said feels like a moment of grace. While one can try to explain to oneself how and why someone makes us laugh, and the psychology of humour literature attests to this (Marcus, 2013a), the fact is that when we are in the domain of immediate, direct participation in which we laugh, the most natural response is not to try to "understand" what is going on, but rather to welcome this special presence—the wave of delightful laughter—with open arms (Cain, 1995, p. 145). Such encounters reflect "openness to the Open", as Marcel has called them (ibid., p. 121).

Marcel briefly discussed such moments of welcoming within the context of trying to understand the "storying" experience of charm, of being in the transforming presence of a charming person, including a person who often makes us smile and/or laugh. Charm, said Marcel, is "a quality immediately felt when it imposes itself on me. I note that we *have no charm for ourselves*, and that there is a tendency for charm to vanish when I, who am subjected to it, find out that the person who is employing his charm is aware that he is doing so" (1952, p. 300, italics in original).

What Marcel is getting at is that the experience of being in the company of a charming person takes place within the context of a spontaneously beckoning, inspiring relation. The experience of charm is not one that involves the other person trying to be charming, attempting to choreograph a certain kind of impression or image for the listener. Such narcissistic manipulation and display never feels charming; quite the opposite, it feels utterly forced and phony. "Nothing is less susceptible of being acquired than charm," said Marcel (ibid.). While "a slick politics of presentation and deliberateness" tends mainly to control the way in which many people present themselves in our digital mass society, the fact is that when we feel the direct, immediate "fluency of presence" of a charming person, we are struck by his or her summoning embrace. A truly charming person is spontaneously other-directed and other-regarding, and we strongly sense it when in his presence. There is a "dignity, grandeur and grace" to how such a person comes across, to how he moves us, and for the person who is receptive and responsive to welcoming the charming other, it is mysteriously magical (O'Donohue, 2004, pp. 15, 228–229). As Marcel put it, "There is a 'halo' round their acts and words … charm is as it were the presence of the person round what he does and what he says" (1952, pp. 300–301).

Marcel noted, "Charm only appears where we are directly aware of the margin that separates a person from what he does.

It is a 'beyond'; and hence it has no ethical equivalent." Thus, according to Marcel, an infant cannot be charming, though as is well known, a toddler can be adorably charming. "A person only has charm if he is 'beyond' his virtues if they appear to emanate from a distant and unknown source" (ibid., p. 301). It is not an experience that can be made objective without losing its compelling meaning, nor is it merely a projected quality of a person that can be definitively conceptualised. In other words, "Charm cannot be dissociated from the act of charming," it is an action that has a unique presence and, most important, "the reality" of charm *is* its "appearance" (ibid.). It is a "luminous moment" in which we feel "illuminated by a different light", one that makes us feel awakened to something remarkably outside our everyday experience, a glowing presence that we willingly surrender to in trust, sureness, and completion (O'Donohue, 2004, pp. 2, 6, 9, 11), at least for the duration of the encounter. As Marcel noted, for the person who is graced with encountering a charming person, it feels similar to a revelation, the revealing of something previously hidden or secret, that evokes "feeling another to be present, an infinite value in contact as such" (ibid.). For Marcel, the religiously animated believer, a charming person who touches one's existence is described as reflecting a moment of eternal resonance, of divine love; for the secularist, such a charming person might be called a "breath of spring" or "like fairy dust", as one of my patients described one of his delightful co-workers. In other words, when in the company of a charming person we feel, however brief the encounter, that we have spontaneously crossed a threshold, one that points to a different, transforming, order of being. Most important, to the extent that we learn to discern and participate in the luminous depths and ethico-lyrical presences that permeate our world, like when we happen upon a charming person, whether they be conceptualised as "divine love" or simply a "gift" by the believer and secularist respectively, one is more likely to experience a profound gratitude for being alive and for having been created. Marcel put this point beautifully when he further noted that we need to "open ourselves to the infiltrations of the invisible ... the radiance of that eternal Light" (2001, pp. 187–188).

IV. Love stories

I have never met a happy couple who did not thoroughly enjoy telling anyone who would listen the story of how they first met. Whether described in terms of chance, coincidence, or karma, the exuberant feeling is that the couple was somehow destined to meet. Dostoyevsky put the matter just right in *Crime and Punishment*: "There are chance meetings with strangers that interest us from the first moment, before a word is spoken" (1866, p. 10). Indeed, there is a mysterious quality to chance encounters, especially to those that morph into love relationships or good friendships. However, there is also a mysterious quality to any "genuine dialogue", to "being-directed-to-each-other", as Martin Buber called it (1999d, p. 88; 1999g, p. 153). In this section I want to describe some of the important aspects of conversations between lovers or good friends, a type of co-produced storytelling that is radically transformational and joyful. Buber has memorialised such powerful encounters in his discussion of "I–Thou" relationships and his philosophy of dialogue, though what is often underappreciated is that for Buber, and for that matter for Marcel and Emmanuel Levinas (though somewhat differently), the I–Thou relationship always includes the "Eternal Thou", Buber's term for God or the transcendent Presence, what I have called glimpsing immortality. In this section, I want to describe the conditions of possibility for an I–Thou relation, a living mutual relationship, to unfold where the sense of time and space vanish and one is fully engaged in the here and now of genuine dialogue with another person. What does it take, psychologically speaking, for two people to co-produce an authentic experiential meeting that significantly changes both participants for the better? Quite suddenly and miraculously, the world is no longer experienced as a wall but a gate.

I–Thou, I–It, and the Eternal Thou

"All real living is meeting," Buber famously wrote in his masterpiece, *I and Thou* (1958, p. 11).

What Buber was getting at was that the "royal road" to becoming a fully individuated and human person is through engaging another person (or animal or thing) as a Thou, as a highly valued, unique relationship rather than as a thing. The deep and affectionate bonding that Buber calls an I–Thou does not reside in one or the other of the two people, nor can it be reduced to the sum of the two; rather, it only spontaneously emerges and becomes fully present "between" them (Kramer, with Gawlick, 2003, p. 78). The "between" or "betweeness" is the interhuman realm of mutual presence and shared relationship, the "living mutual relation" (Buber, 1958, p. 45). It takes place on the "narrow ridge" between subject and object, "where I and Thou meet" (Buber, 1965a, p. 204).[10] As Buber evocatively said, "the between" can be described as "the mode of existence between persons communicating with one another, which cannot co-ordinate with either the psychic or the physical realms". It is "manifold togetherness and living with one another, as a light is kindled from leaping fire". It is the metaphor of "leaping fire" that best captures "the dynamic between persons in We" (Buber, 1999f, p. 108).

It is by relating with the fullness of one's whole being to the other as a uniquely whole person, not simply as an identity or thing to be used for instrumental purposes, that an individual becomes most human and most himself. Genuine meeting, conversation that is immediate, personal, and reciprocal, occurs when two people "enter into dynamic solidarity with each other", and through this spontaneous happening they become wholly, uniquely, and personally themselves (Kramer, with Gawlick, 2003, pp. 15, 43). As Buber wrote, "I become through my relation to the Thou; as I become I, I say Thou" (1958, p. 11). Moreover, phenomenologically speaking, I–Thou feels as if it is outside space and time (rather space and time are felt to be infusing the relationship), and it includes the past, present, and future possibilities, that is, it takes place in the sheltering intimacy of an impossible to adequately delineate numinous region that has an eternal resonance. I–Thou thus represents a basic life orientation or "way of speaking" in which one relates to others and things in a more immediate, mutual, and dialogical fashion.

In contrast to the "dialogical immediacy between men" (1974, p. 228) as Buber describes the I–Thou attitude, there is the I–It. The I–It depicts a way of speaking that is objectifying; it is monological and geared to using conversation as a means to an interpersonal end. I–It relations are characterised by a way of speaking that does not occur with the fullness of one's whole being; it is oriented to using, knowing, and experiencing the other, it is lodged in space and time, is one-sided and singular, tends to be controlling, and rather than reside in the "interhuman betweeness", it resides in the "subject-object duality" (Kramer, with Gawlick, 2003, p. 18). Where I-Thou moments are characterised by engaged listening, creative receptivity, and spontaneity, I–It relationships are geared to listening with a self-serving goal and objective in mind. As Kramer and Gawlick aptly summarise the I–It orientation, "The I–It relationship refers to a necessarily one-sided experience of 'knowing', 'using' and putting things in 'categories.' In this objectifying experience of the world, one does not venture outside self-reinforcing plans, schemes and purposes" (ibid., p. 26). Buber makes the important point that to function in the world one must live in the "It" realm, though every "It" can become a "Thou" if one approaches the person or thing as a Thou. Similarly, every Thou by necessity eventually becomes an It. However, what is crucial is whether one's life orientation is mainly a Thou or an It one, and whether one can fashion an internal world that makes one more likely to be able to engage the world in terms of an I–Thou way of speaking, of storytelling.

While genuine dialogue cannot be choreographed or coerced, there is a mode of being that tends to bring about an I–Thou moment and more generally contributes to the art of living the "good life". Such "spokenness to the Thou" (1999g, p. 154), "an elemental" or grounding "togetherness" (1999d, p. 87), as Buber called it, that animates a person's dealings with another requires a number of qualities of mind, body, and spirit, and it is this mode of attunement to the other that, following Buber, I believe is the prolegomenon to glimpsing immortality.

The act of "turning" to the other, that is, approaching an other with the fullness of one's whole being, has been described by Buber as follows:

> In genuine dialogue the turning to the partner takes place in all truth, that is, it is a turning of being. But where the dialogue is fulfilled in its being, between partners who have turned to one another in truth, who express themselves without reserve and are free of the desire for semblance [an outward appearance of imitation of something], there is brought into being, a memorable common fruitfulness which is to be found nowhere else. (1965b, pp. 85–86)

The gist of "turning" is that it is an internal transformation of making oneself open and porous, willing and able to enter wholly into the presence of the other without reservation or a preconceived agenda. Such a way of relating, of making the other "present", requires accurate empathy that intuits what the other is feeling, thinking, and experiencing without losing oneself in the process. Buber described this process in terms of a twofold moment, the "primal setting at a distance" and "entering into relation" (1999c, p. 4). By "setting at a distance" Buber means recognising the other person as a separate and unique other. This is the precondition for entering into genuine relation with another person; that is, one does not relate to a "part" of him that has a self-serving value to me, but with him as the unique person in all of his otherness. Entering into relation essentially involves being "present in my whole person, in relation", and "inclusion", that is, making the other present as a whole and a unity (ibid., p. 7; Graf-Taylor, 1999, p. 331). Presence thus has a duality of structure—it involves "being fully 'there'" without holding back, and "being fully 'open'" to engage others in ever-renewed genuine dialogue (Kramer, with Gawlick, 2003, p. 204).

Thus, such a mode of engagement requires a certain kind of daring to be vulnerable to rejection and other forms of "mis-meetings", as Buber calls them. Most of all, a "turning" requires an other-directed, other-regarding, and other-serving orientation. Where an It relation is centripetal, acting, moving, or pulling towards oneself, a mode of being that is highly narcissistic, the Thou relation is centrifugal, pulling away from oneself and is mainly "for the Other". Worthwhile as it is, conversation that is driven by self-expression and self-assertion, the quest for autonomy, integration, and maturity, or even inner serenity, as in psychotherapy, is not genuine dialogue as Buber conceives of it. "Turning" is a noble and ennobling act of the mind, body, and spirit, perhaps the "highest" expression of relational living, as it involves a significant self-donation while not losing oneself in the process.

When an individual has "turned" to the other in genuine dialogue, when he says Thou, "even when he stands in opposition to the other, [he] heeds, affirms, and confirms his opponent as an existing other" (Buber, 1974, p. 238). Such a capacity requires a "leap of faith", an existential trust in the humanising effect of authentic dialogue. The essential elements of "turning" include the capacity to be a fully present, whole person in the here and now, and making the other similarly fully present requires empathic listening (that is, listening that involves self-exposure, allowing oneself to be moved by the other), including affirming and confirming the other in all of his uniqueness and otherness, without relinquishing one's own self in the process. It demands that one does not hold back anything. It is a trusting but also trustworthy opening up. Finally, it requires a willingness and ability to be changed (Kramer, with Gawlick, 2003, p. 161), including in surprising ways. When this I–Thou encounter occurs, it is as if the veils that obfuscate and distort our clear vision of the other are removed and we feel the mystery of compassionate awakening to the otherness of the other, a mutuality of presences that calls to mind a transcendent realm that Buber designated as the "Eternal Thou" or God. It is this beautiful luminosity that radiates from genuine dialogue, from the mystery of mutual awakening and belonging that is a mainline point of entry into glimpsing immortality.

"Every particular Thou is a glimpse through to the eternal Thou," said Buber (1958, p. 75). God is the "source and presence reflected by" genuine dialogue. In short, God "is the immediate presence of the 'wholly Other,' who happens in every genuine relationship", whether with a person or thing, "and who creates, reveals, and redeems through each unique relational act" (Kramer, with Gawlick, 2003, p. 133). God is not merely a feeling, an intellectual notion or thought, or even a mystical experience of thrilling enmeshment, and he cannot be spoken about in the third person; rather, he is a living presence between I and Thou, a sacramental space that can never turn into an It.

What Buber's poetic language suggests in terms of our central concern, namely, the psychological conditions of possibility for glimpsing immortality through storytelling, is that it is through genuine dialogue with another person, animal, or thing that one is most likely to apprehend a transcendent presence. Most important, for Buber, and for that matter Marcel and Levinas, this centrally involves engaging in a creative partnership with God by becoming like him in terms of fashioning an ethical subjectivity that is mainly, and firstly, for the other before oneself, or at least, regards the other as important as oneself. As Buber said, "If you hallow this life you meet the living God" (1958, p. 79), and elsewhere he noted, "'God' ... enters into a direct relation with us men in creative, revealing, and redeeming acts, and thus makes it possible to enter into a direct relation with him" (ibid., p. 135). When a person makes God a living presence, one that centrally embraces and instantiates in real-life relations the heartfelt value of responsibility for the other, he is most likely to be blessed by grace. Grace for Buber refers to that "spontaneously undetermined presence of mutuality" which cannot be merely willed into existence (though it requires intention). Grace, in other words, is that transforming luminous spirit of "the between" that emanates from, creates, and sustains genuine interhuman encounters (Kramer, with Gawlick, 2003, pp. 22, 162). As Buber noted, "Love meets us through grace ... it is not found by seeking," that is, it is not an object but a sensed presence (1958, pp. 41, 44). Likewise, while affectionate feelings accompany love, they do not, in fact, "constitute it": "Feelings one 'has,' love occurs. Feelings dwell in man, but man dwells in love." While such love requires each party embracing "responsibility of an I for a Thou", ultimately it is a grace-moment (ibid., pp. 14, 66). It is precisely such grace that animates storytelling at its best. Most important, the affect-integrating, meaning-giving, and action-guiding nature of transformational storytelling is essentially about two people freely giving and receiving love, always as separate, independent beings. That is, love "storying" as I have called it, is not about being dependent on each other as a need-satisfying object, nor is it about forms of relational symbiosis and enmeshment, but rather, authentic love is interdependent. It relies on mutual assistance, support, cooperation, and interaction between two people through and through, or what can be called "reciprocal storytelling" (Brandell, 2000, p. 187). As Buber said, "man's loving speech" is the most direct route to the "presence of the Word" (Boni, 1996, pp. 242, 245), to glimpsing immortality.

V. Conclusion

A famous *hadith*, a saying of the Prophet Mohammed, beautifully makes the point about what the psychological conditions of possibility are for apprehending a sense of transcendence, well-being, and appreciation that constitute glimpsing immortality through storytelling.

> He who approaches Me [Allah] one span, I will approach to him one cubit; and he who approaches near to Me one cubit, I will approach near to him one fathom, and whoever approaches Me walking I will come to him running, and he who meets Me with sins equivalent to the whole world I will greet him with forgiveness to it. (Marcus, 2003, p. 166)

For the Muslim, God is not only the All-seeing, punitive though just Judge; He also is merciful, compassionate, long-suffering, gracious, and eager to forgive. Salvation—success in paradise, as the Muslim would describe it, and the peace of mind that goes with it—is possible if one tries with utter sincerity and honesty to live according to God's will, despite episodic failures in one's conduct.

Recasting this ancient religious wisdom in a modern psychological idiom as it pertains to storytelling, we can say that along with all the emotionally intelligent interpersonal skills mentioned throughout this chapter, what is most needed to glimpse immortality is the willingness and ability to enter into the ethical realms of the intersubjective, this being the opposite of self-centredness and selfishness. As in love, fidelity, faith, hope, and, I would add, storytelling, this involves the capacity for openness to others, "to welcome them without being effaced by them", as Marcel aptly puts it (Marcus, 2013b, p. 29). In other words, while the intersubjective is the prerequisite of human awareness, communion, that mode of engagement that facilitates a sense of deep emotional and spiritual closeness, it is also profoundly creative as it transforms and enhances both people. It is the form that an authentic life takes and points to the transcendent. As Allah suggests in the above *hadith*, it is intersubjectivity, receptiveness, responsiveness, and responsibility to and for the other that is most needed to know Him and experience His blessings. Huston Smith elaborated this insight when he boldly stated that all humans want one thing more than anything else: to "consciously or unconsciously seek to overcome the separation between us and God who is the true object of our desire, whether we envision that God as within or without", or don't even call him God. Storytelling, at its best, moves against the tragedy of separation. It lets us be co-creator, to bear witness to a creation that satisfies "the ultimate object of our desire", namely, "to be joined to the Reality for which we have been created" (Paine, 2012, p. 154).

Notes

1. While not always appreciated, it was Gabriel Marcel who used the term I–Thou relationship to describe the love experience prior to Martin Buber, though after Kierkegaard (Thomas C. Anderson, personal communication, April 2010).
2. Quoted from storyteller Donna Washington.
3. In a certain sense, it is not possible to achieve "sublime objectivity", for there is always a conscious or unconscious narcissistic investment in our actions, as even the wish to achieve

"sublime objectivity" and the pleasure associated with doing so has a narcissistic pay-off. Moreover, experience is always mediated by a person's subjective world, that is, it is socially constructed. In actuality, the point is to eliminate the inordinate personal preferences, narcissistic desires, and neurotic needs that keep a person on the "surface" of experience and reactive in a structure-bound and stereotyped manner. The goal is to be open and responsive to the unique otherness and presence of people and things.

4. I am summarising Wiener's formulations.

5. I have drawn from Wiener's summary of Johnstone's twelve ways that improvisers inhibit, if not prevent, narratives from evolving (1994, pp. 92–93).

6. I have drawn from Brandell's summary of the most useful components of a child's self-composed story.

7. For Anna Freud, transference as it relates to children compared to adults has its unique aspects. She said it is best conceptualised in terms of transference of habitual modes of relating, transference of current relationships, transference of past experiences, and transference neurosis (Sandler, Kennedy, & Tyson, 1980, pp. 78–104).

8. This vignette is based on a child that my wife, Irene Wineman-Marcus, a child analyst trained by Anna Freud, treated.

9. In any kind of psychotherapy, though especially with children, there is not a "complete mutuality", for the participants do not come to each other as equals, that is, the analysand (or patient or client) is in need of professional help and the focus of the meeting is on his personal life, not the analyst's. In the context of psychotherapy, Buber called this the "normative limits of mutuality" (1999a, p. 145).

10. Cited in Kramer, with Gawlick, 2003, p. 78.

CHAPTER SEVEN

Conclusion
Reflections on creating earthly immortality

Creating Heaven on Earth

> "Abide, moment—but if you cannot abide, at least return
> eternally!"
>
> —*Frederick Nietzsche* (Edwards, 1967, p. 512)

I don't want to achieve immortality through my work," said
Woody Allen, "I want to achieve it through not dying"
(Swedene, 2009, p. 79). What makes Allen's quip so amusing is that obviously, not dying is not an option. It does point,
however, to the idea that I have elaborated throughout this
book that although the way of achieving immortality is usually construed as leaving behind good work or deeds that are
recognised and appreciated by one's descendants and others,
I am suggesting that it is through engaging life with the fullness of one's whole being, with a gracious receptivity in the
immediacy of the here and now, that one can sense the force,
freshness, and depth (Buber, 1999e, p. 102) of an Infinite Presence, of glimpsing immortality.

Thus, my take on immortality in everyday life is not geared
to exploring the many religious and non-religious "immortality narratives" that have been generated by those who desire
to live forever. Throughout history, many have judged their
self-regard by the calculus of how they will remain symbolically alive after they die, whether it is the search for fame and
glory, or through their offspring. Some more secularly minded
people want to leave behind a personalised legacy in one form
or another, while the religious-minded want to leave the world
behind and enjoy a heavenly bliss (Swedene, 2009) or some
form of earthly resurrection.

I have taken a different path in my treatment of immortality
than most secular philosophers and theologians, as I have recast
the problem in mainly psychological terms, which in question
form is as follows: how does one best fashion an internal world,
a personal identity, that creates the conditions of psychological possibility to apprehend the intangible, ineffable, almost

magical Infinite—conceived as something-outside-everything, God, or the Other—amid everyday living? That is, following the wisdom of the poets, how does one engage and fully participate in the "infinite sea of being underlying the waves of our finite selves" (Smith, 1991, p. 33)? How does one cast off the ball and chain of deadening perceptions, and thereby become attuned to glimpsing immortality in the immediacy of our ordinary experience, and allow these eternal presences to bathe us in their sheltering and healing Infinite Light?

My angle of vision on immortality is rooted in a parable from the Talmud. To paraphrase: when you die and you are facing the Pearly Gates before God himself, hoping to be allowed into Heaven, the first thing He will ask you is, "Let me see your shoes." Why shoes? Because, say the ancient rabbis, God wants to see if you have danced at enough weddings. In other words, have you engaged the pleasures of life with your whole soul? To not do so is to mock Creation and desecrate God. The glory of God, an Episcopalian friend told me, is in being a fully alive person.

I have suggested within the context of easily accessible, everyday activities—gardening, baseball spectatorship, coffee drinking, music listening, and broadly conceived storytelling—how best to engage these activities in a way that can be aptly called a "spiritual" sensibility, one that points to Transcendence, to Presence, to the Absolute or Eternal Thou, or whatever word one uses to characterise the undefinable and unfathomable, "eternally nameless", "unknown something" (Buber, 1999b, pp. 36, 43, 48) for which humans long. Psychologically speaking, this spiritual sensibility includes such elements as the striving for integration, wholeness, and balance, the generation of a creative life that is saturated with meaning and significance, a capacity for unity, integration, and sense of interdependence in one's self-world relationship, especially as it relates to the many relationships, commitments, and responsibilities throughout one's life (Applebaum, 1985, p. 152). By way of concluding my study of immortality in everyday life, I want to summarise a few of the "take home" points as to what seems to be critically important in terms of self-fashioning, to make oneself most likely to encounter "a spiritual dynamism" that is driven by, and found in, "transcendence" (Marcel, 1964, p. 221), as reflected in everyday activities. These points in no way are a complete rendering of the psychological conditions of possibility for glimpsing immortality, but they do represent some of the most important interwoven aspects that constitute the fertile "internal" breeding ground for making these epiphanic moments more likely to happen.

As we have seen, when engaging in gardening, baseball spectatorship, coffee drinking, music listening, and storytelling, it is essential for a spiritual aspirant to be radically emotionally and intellectually open, to be ready, receptive, responsive, and responsible to what he encounters. This is easier said than done, for as Freud has noted, we are inherently ambivalent and ambiguous beings, marked by contradictions and paradoxes, who are chronically struggling between being "permeable" and "porous" versus impenetrable and closed-off. Being "spiritual" requires a deeply felt commitment of our whole self, our mind, body, and spirit to that which is before us, to that which calls out or summons us. In its polemical extreme, this is the difference between making a commitment with the fullness of one's whole being versus being indifferent or offering up a half-hearted form of engagement; it tends to strive for something beyond one's egotistical and self-centric concerns, it seeks "something more". In its polemical extreme this is the difference between being self-directed and for-oneself, while being only, and absolutely, wedded to the material world, versus being other-directed, other-regarding, and other-serving while also being mindful of there being more to existence than what one can see and manipulate; it requires a faith that the love of life, the creative urge, and the divine presences in the world are stronger than their opposites. This means siding with Eros, what Freud broadly meant by the life instincts, the sexual and self-preservation instincts, versus siding with Thanatos, the unconscious drive towards dissolution and death, the forms of aggression that are directed at oneself and others.

"All spiritual life is essentially a dialogue," said Marcel, Buber, and Levinas. That is, "The relationship that can be said to be spiritual is that of being with being ... What really matters is spiritual commerce between beings, and that involves not respect but love" (Marcel, 1952, pp. 137, 211). Respect of the other's "primally deep otherness" (Buber, 1999e, p. 96), of course, is part of an honourable, if not effective and satisfying person-to-person relation (to dishonour otherness is a form of barely sublimated aggression), but what is being emphasised here is that there must firstly be the will to do good to the other, whether a person or thing. Saint Augustine famously made this point in his *Confessions*: "My weight [motivational power] is my love" (1991, p. 228). To experience in oneself the love and joy of communing with the Infinite, that is, a sense of infinite being, knowledge, and bliss, requires a state of mind that nurtures the transcendent urge through compassion (Smith, 2012, p. 47).

An "intraworldly mysticism" is also a part of engaging the Infinite, of glimpsing immortality (Yearley, 1983, p. 131). This mystical outlook has an inward and outward aspect to it. It is inward-looking in that it moves consciousness away from the material world and strives towards a union with the transcendental central reality of the universe which is often referred to by the spiritual aspirant as the Infinite, Divine, or God, though it can be called by other, less religious names. In its outward aspect, the spiritual aspirant senses a unity with the universe with all there is; that is, the transcendent central reality is experienced everywhere, even in a $2 cup of coffee. This "superconsciousness" is known internally when the person becomes aware of his identity with the central reality of the universe and discerns the illusory character of the world of space and time. Moreover, he experiences this state more as a "gift" than an acquisition. Externally, the person's actions in the world reveal the Infinite, Divine, or God that can be said to reside in us. This is a form of concrete mysticism that makes the hallowing of everyday life its main goal (Friedman, 2002, p. 337). (In religious lingo, following Paul Tillich, this is equated with revelation, conceived as God's self-manifestation.) That is, the aspirant imitates God's most essential qualities by being compassionate, loving, gracious, and long-suffering, qualities that, in psychological terms, can be said to reflect the highest degree of character development, personality integration, and selfhood.

On a practical level, such a mystical way of being calls to mind Eastern religious wisdom. For such a spiritual sensibility means focusing intensely on the perceptions that are directly present before the aspirant, only moving on to another perception when a new perception enters consciousness or the old one wanes and disappears. This "hold and let go" approach, as it has been called, involves seeing life as a movie, a series of changing frames. Unlike other forms of mysticism in which union with the absolute reality or higher being is sought, intraworldly mysticisms mainly aim to see the world in a new way, to create "a way through the world". As Yearley further noted, "One neither obtains union with some higher being, nor unification with the single reality. Rather, he goes through a discipline and has experiences that allow one to view the world in a new way." In common parlance this form of mysticism aims to attain a oneness with the universe. In this view, whatever the activity, "… life … is a series of esthetically pleasing new beginnings, and all such beginnings should be grasped and then surrendered as change proceeds" (1983, pp. 130–131, 136).

Conclusion

The point here is the need to heighten our sensitivity in order to experience reality more directly and intensely. As is common in our technology-driven mass society, we psychoanalysts, like our analysands, are often full of false intellectualisations, heavy discursive reasoning, and defensive emotional reactivity, rather than being immediately present. As a result we are less likely to grasp reality in full conscious awareness, one of the important goals of any mode of psychoanalysis. Where psychoanalysis mainly uses abstraction and conceptualisation as its mode of engaging the world, the best way to go through the world is to experience life as it is lived, on its own terms, and without trying to hold on to experience. With this kind of moment-to-moment awareness which is a form of mindfulness, the mind is less likely to be ensnared by any experience and instead, can move effortlessly and continuously, seeing the world as a series of movie frames, some more pleasing than others but always changing. "To be interested in the changing seasons", said George Santayana, "is a happier state of mind than to be hopelessly in love with spring" (Wita, 1982, p. 41). Thus, to be open to the mystery of being, the mystery of identity, and the mystery of life itself, means developing a spiritual sensibility of knowing that provides authentic knowledge of reality (Jones, 2001, p. 805). Indeed, as the psychoanalyst Hans Loewald noted, this can mean being open to the gracious love of God:

> As the unconscious becomes transformed into ego-freedom ... the images and concepts of this relatedness [to the dynamic unconscious] also change into higher forms. The deepest inner knowledge of such relatedness is the experience of relation to a universal being ... The mature individual being able to reach back into his deep origins and roots of being, finds in himself the oneness from where he stems, and understands this in his freedom as his bond of love with God. (ibid., pp. 807–808)[1]

211

As I have already insinuated, to be most receptive to the Infinite, to glimpsing immortality, requires fashioning a different subjectivity than what is typical: it means giving up, or at least "toning down" our passion for the operative paradigm of an irreversibly self- and ego-centred subjectivity, a separate self, guided largely by self-interest. It is this narcissistic mode of subjectivity that is "for itself" firstly, and only, that prevents one from encountering the Infinite in its purest and most clarified form. Whether one calls them selfish cravings, inordinate needs, or infantile narcissism, developing a spiritual sensibility that points to the Infinite involves reconfiguring one's subjectivity, especially relating oneself to a transcendent realm with a strong ethical dimension that is fundamentally other-directed, other-regarding, and other-serving. Moreover, this new type of ethically animated subjectivity is based on the fact that more than anything else, humans are sentient beings before we become a thinking ego (Critchley, 1999, p. 239). That is, we are fundamentally geared to "response [which is a kind of 'response/ability' says Carol Gilligan], availability, openness, welcoming and abandonment to" (Guerriere, 1999, p. 718) what is before us, to the other, including the something-outside-everything, the eternally nameless that I have called the Infinite. Without such emotional attunement one is left with experiencing the world as a mere object of knowledge, and one will miss glimpsing the glorious subtle presences that we are privileged to apprehend, presences that are, to use Levinas's wonderful phrase, a "trace" of the Infinite.

One day one of the masters of tragicomedy, Samuel Beckett, and a friend were walking in a Paris park on a perfect spring morning. The warm sun was brilliantly shining, flowers were blooming with lovely colours and fragrances, parents and children were laughing while walking hand in hand, while young lovers were kissing on benches. Beckett's friend said, "Doesn't a day like this make you glad to be alive?" to which Beckett

Conclusion

responded, "I wouldn't go as far as that." While this response is, at first, funny, my hope is that this book about glimpsing immortality in everyday life has convinced the reader that the capacity for experiencing the world as a "Garden of Eden" entirely depends on how one looks at things.

Note

1. Jones is quoting from Loewald, 1953, pp. 1–15.

WEBSITE RESOURCES

Chicago Tribune (1989, 26 February). In bloom again. Gertrude Jekyll's cult status is in full flower. www.articles.chicagotribune.com/1989-02-26/news/890323038 .... Retrieved 20 August 2013.

Cultural Studies Reader, The. (n.d.). www.culturalstudies now.blogspot.com/2011/06/gaston-bachelar .... Retrieved 28 October 2013.

Inside "Gnomeo and Juliet" with Elton John, James McAvoy and Emily Blunt. (n.d.). http://movies.about.com/od/gnomeoanjuliet/a/elton-john-jame ... . Retrieved 10 July 2013.

Jones, J. M. (n.d.). Nearly half of Americans are baseball fans: Football is the top sport. www.gallup.com/poll/22240/nearly-half-americans-baseball-fans.aspx. Retrieved 28 October 2013.

Mahler, J. (2013). Is the game over? The *New York Times* Sunday Review, www.nytimes.com/2013/09/29/opinion/sunday/is-the-game-over.html Retrieved 1 October 2013.

Messi, L. (n.d.). www.lushquotes.com/author/lionel-messi/. Retrieved 28 January, 2014.

National Coffee Drinking Trends, 2013. (n.d.). www.ncausa.org/i4a/pages/index.cfm?pageID=731. Retrieved 29 October 2013.

Pelé. www.theguardian.com:Sport:Football. Retrieved 28 January, 2014.

People Magazine. (2008, 20 March). www.people.com/people/article/0,,20185337,00.html. Retrieved 12 June 2014.

www.360soccer.com/pele/peleplay.html. Retrieved 28 January 2014.

Redmon, E. (n.d.). Too much coffee: The United States of Starbucks. www.hobotrashcan.com/toomuchcoffee/archive/070215.php. Retrieved 25 October 2013.

Ronaldo, C. (n.d.). www.ronaldo7.net/extra/quotes/cristiano-ronaldo-quotes.html. Retrieved 28 January 2014.

Sartre, J. -P. www.sartre.org/quotes.htm. Retrieved 27 July 2014.

Shankly, B. www.shankly.com/article/2517. Retrieved 1 February 2014.

Solo, H. www.npr.org › Arts & Life› Books› Author Interviews. Retrieved 28 January 2014.

Sydney Morning Herald. (n.d.). Interview: Chad Harbach. www.smh.com.au/.../interview-chad-harb. Retrieved 26 January 2014.

TCM.com. (n.d.). They were expendable (1945). www.tcm.com/tcmdb/title/2070/They-Were-Expendable. Retrieved 30 September 2013.

Treanor, B. (n.d.). Gabriel Marcel. *Stanford Encyclopedia of Philosophy.* http://plato.stanford.edu/entries/marcel/#13. Retrieved 29 October 2013.

Warner, C. D. www.quotegarden.com/gardens.html. Retrieved 21 July 2014.

www.aaronshep.com/storytelling/quotes.html. Retrieved 19 January 2014.

www.backpagefootball.com/clean-sheet-grand-final-countdown/56929/. Retrieved 30 January 2014.

www.badenstorytellers.wordpress.com/2013/10/15/469/. Retrieved 21 July 2014.

www.betweenthelines.in/2014/01/book-review-s0ccer-sun-sha .... Retrieved 30 January 2014.

www.biographyonline.net/writers/j_k_rowling.html. Retrieved 17 December 2013.

www.christianmusings-brian.blogspot.com/2013/01/the-power-of-music.html. Retrieved 9 December 2013.

www.dailymail.co.uk/.../Pele-wants-Escape-Victory-again.ht. Retrieved 27 January 2014.

www.eng.aphorism.ru/author/horace/. Retrieved 15 June 2014.

www.fifa.com/.../players/player=63869/. Retrieved 17 June 2014.

www.fifa.com/world-match-centre/.../7/. Retrieved 27 January 2014.

www.geniusrevive.com/en/geniuses.html?pid=142&sid... Football. Retrieved 28 January 2014.

www.goodreads.com/.../537494-coffee-and-chocolate-the-inventor-of-m... Retrieved 11 November 2013.

www.hdfootballwallpaper.com/quotes.php. Retrieved 28 January 2014.

www.ifhof.com/hof/banks.asp. Retrieved 1 February 2014.

www.imdb.com/name/nm0142829/bio. Retrieved 3 December 2013.

www.isleofholland.com/read/sports/14-classic-johan-cruyff-quotes-explained. Retrieved 29 January 2014.

www.izquotes.com/quote/291919. Retrieved 15 September 2013.

www.izquotes.com/quote/293033. Retrieved 29 October 2013.

www.izquotes.com/quote/52360. Retrieved 30 January 2014.

www.manchester.com: Sport:United. Retrieved 27 January 2014.

www.metoperafamily.org/metopera/history/stories/synopsis.aspx?...10. Retrieved 5 December 2013.

www.pinterest.com/pin/259308891017930436/. Retrieved 29 January 2014.

www.pinterest.com/pin/508273507916040657/. Retrieved 30 January 2014.

www.quotegarden.com/gardens.html. Retrieved 21 July 2014.

www.sportsillustrated.cnn.com/.../siflashback_p .... Retrieved 28 January 2014.

www.thedivineponytail.com/.../roberto-baggio-and-the-moment-that-def .... Retrieved 29 January 2014.

www.theglobalgame.com/.../shostakovich-football-is-the-ballet-of-the-m .... Retrieved 27 January 2014.

www.thegoaldiggers.weebly.com/legends-of-the-game.html. Retrieved 28 January 2014

www.topendsports.com/sport/soccer/quotes.htm. Retrieved 27 January 2014.

www.vanguardngr.com/2013/01/messi-ive-changed-so-much/. Retrieved 28 January 2014.

REFERENCES

Adler, S. (2000). *The Art of Acting.* H. Kissel (Ed.). New York: Applause.

Aldridge, D., & Fachner, J. (Eds.) (2001). *Music and Altered States: Consciousness, Transcendence, Therapy and Addictions.* London: Jessica Kingsley.

Alford, F. (2002). *Levinas, The Frankfurt School and Psychoanalysis.* Ithaca, NY: Cornell University Press.

Andrews, A. (2012). *Baseball, Boys, and Bad Words.* Nashville, TN: Thomas Nelson.

Applebaum, S. W. (1985). The rediscovery of spirituality through psychotherapy. In: M. H. Spero (Ed.), *Psychotherapy of the Religious Patient* (pp. 140–152). Springfield, IL: Charles C. Thomas.

Augustine, St. (1991). *Confessions.* H. Chadwick (Trans.). Oxford: Oxford University Press.

Austin, M. W. (2011). The necessary ground of being. In: S. F. Parker & M. W. Austin (Eds.), *Coffee: Philosophy for Everyone: Grounds for Debate* (pp. 25–33). Chichester, UK: Wiley-Blackwell.

Bachelard, G. (1969). *The Poetics of Space.* M. Jolas (Trans.). Boston: Beacon.

Barwell, I., & Powell, J. (2010). Gardens, music, and time. In: D. O'Brien (Ed.), *Gardening: Philosophy for Everyone* (pp. 136–147). Malden, MA: John Wiley & Sons.

Benedetti, J. (1998). *Stanislavski and the Actor.* New York: Routledge.

219

References

Bennett, J. (2001). *The Enchantment of Modern Life: Attachments, Crossings, and Ethics*. Princeton, NJ: Princeton University Press.

Bernstein, L. (2004). *The Joy of Music*. Pompton Plains, NJ: Amadeus.

Betts, E. M. (Ed.) (1999). *Thomas Jefferson's Garden Book*. Charlottesville, VA: Thomas Jefferson Memorial Foundation.

Bisgrove, R. (1988). Preface. In: G. Jekyll, *The Illustrated Gertrude Jekyll: Colour Schemes for the Flower Garden*. Boston: Little, Brown and Company.

Bisgrove, R. (1992). *The Gardens of Gertrude Jekyll*. Berkeley, CA: University of California Press.

Bisgrove, R. (1995). Gertrude Jekyll: A gardener ahead of her time. In: M. Tooley & P. Arnander (Eds.), *Gertrude Jekyll: Essays on the Life of a Working Amateur*. Durham, UK: Michaelmas.

Boni, P. (1996). Martin Buber and King Lear. In: M. Friedman (Ed.), *Martin Buber and the Human Sciences* (pp. 237–248). Albany, NY: State University of New York Press.

Borghini, A., & Baldini, A. (2010). When a soccer club becomes a mirror. In: T. Richards (Ed.), *Soccer and Philosophy: Beautiful Thoughts on the Beautiful Game* (pp. 302–316). Chicago: Open Court.

Bouton, J. (1984). *Ball Four Plus Ball Five*. Aurora, ON: Canada.

Brandell, J. R. (1984). Stories and storytelling in child psychotherapy. *Psychotherapy, 21*(1): 54–62.

Brandell, J. R. (2000). *Of Mice and Metaphor: Therapeutic Storytelling with Children*. New York: Basic Books.

Bronson, E. (2004). Baseball and aesthetics. In: Bronson, E. (Ed.), *Baseball and Philosophy, Thinking Outside The Batter's Box*. Chicago: Open Court.

Brook, I. (2010). The virtues of gardening. In: D. O'Brien (Ed.), *Gardening: Philosophy for Everyone* (pp. 11–25). Malden, MA: John Wiley & Sons.

Brooke, S. L. (Ed.) (2006). *Creative Arts Therapies Manual: A Guide to the History, Theoretical Approaches, Assessment, and Work with Special Populations of Art, Play, Dance, Music, Drama, and Poetry Therapies*. Springfield, IL: Charles C. Thomas.

Bruscia, K. (2000). The nature of meaning in music therapy. *Nordic Journal of Music Therapy, 9*(2): 84–96.

Buber, M. (1958). *I and Thou*. R. G. Smith (Trans.). New York: Charles Scribner's Sons.

Buber, M. (1964). *The Way of Man: According to the Teaching of Hasidism*. New York: Hope, Rinehart & Winston.

Buber, M. (1965a). *Between Man and Man*. R. G. Smith (Trans.). New York: Macmillan.

Buber, M. (1965b). *The Knowledge of Man: A Philosophy of the Inter-human*. M. Friedman & R. G. Smith (Eds.). New York: Harper & Row.

Buber, M. (1974). *Pointing the Way: Collected Essays*. M. Friedman (Ed. & Trans.). New York: Schocken.

Buber, M. (1999a). Afterword to I and Thou. In: J. B. Agassi (Ed.), *Martin Buber on Psychology and Psychotherapy* (pp. 139–148). Syracuse, NY: Syracuse University Press.

Buber, M. (1999b). Buber and Jung. In: J. B. Agassi (Ed.), *Martin Buber on Psychology and Psychotherapy* (pp. 34–71). Syracuse, NY: Syracuse University Press.

Buber, M. (1999c). Distance and relation. In: J. B. Agassi (Ed.), *Martin Buber on Psychology and Psychotherapy* (pp. 3–16). Syracuse, NY: Syracuse University Press.

Buber, M. (1999d). Elements of the interhuman. In: J. B. Agassi (Ed.), *Martin Buber on Psychology and Psychotherapy* (pp. 72–88). Syracuse, NY: Syracuse University Press.

Buber, M. (1999e). Images of good and evil. In: J. B. Agassi (Ed.), *Martin Buber on Psychology and Psychotherapy* (pp. 21–33). Syracuse, NY: Syracuse University Press.

Buber, M. (1999f). What is common to all. In: J. B. Agassi (Ed.), *Martin Buber on Psychology and Psychotherapy* (pp. 89–109). Syracuse, NY: Syracuse University Press.

Buber, M. (1999g). The word that is spoken. In: J. B. Agassi (Ed.), *Martin Buber on Psychology and Psychotherapy* (pp. 149–160). Syracuse, NY: Syracuse University Press.

Burman, H. (2012). *Season of Ghosts: The '86 Mets and the Red Sox*. Jefferson, NC: Mcfarland.

Burroughs, W. S. (1994). *Esquire: The Magazine for Men, 122*: 98.

Cain, S. (1995). *Gabriel Marcel's Theory of Religious Experience*. New York: Peter Lang.

References

Camus, A. (1960). *Resistance, Rebellion, and Death: Essays.* J. O'Brien (Trans.). New York: Vintage International.

Cohen, M. (1974). *Baseball the Beautiful.* New York: Links.

Coles, R. (1992). *Anna Freud: The Dream of Psychoanalysis.* Reading, MA: Addison-Wesley.

Collins, R., & Cooper, P. J. (2005). *The Power of Story: Teaching through Storytelling (2nd ed.).* Long Grove, IL: Waveland.

Cooper, D. E. (2006). *A Philosophy of Gardens.* New York: Oxford University Press.

Critchley, S. (1999). The original traumatism: Levinas and psychoanalysis. In: M. Dooley & R. Kearney (Eds.), *Questioning Ethics: Contemporary Debates in Philosophy* (Ch. 8). New York: Routledge.

Crowe, J. (2010). The loneliness of the referee. In: T. Richards (Ed.), *Soccer and Philosophy: Beautiful Thoughts on the Beautiful Game* (pp. 347–356). Chicago: Open Court.

Cyclical Time. Flow Psychology, at www.flowpsychology.com/circular-time/. Retrieved 31 July 2013.

Davis, C. (1996). *Levinas: An Introduction.* Cambridge: Polity.

Dawson, K. J. (1990). Nature in the urban garden In: M. Francis & R. T. Hester (Eds.), *The Meaning of Gardens* (pp. 138–143). Cambridge, MA: MIT Press.

Day, J. (2010). Plants, prayers and power. In: D. O'Brien (Ed.), *Gardening: Philosophy for Everyone* (pp. 63–78). Malden, MA: John Wiley & Sons.

Dickson, P. (Ed.) (2008). *Baseball's Greatest Quotations.* New York: HarperCollins.

Dostoyevsky, F. (1866). *Crime and Punishment.* New York: Macmillan.

Dura-Vila, V. (2010). Why playing beautifully is morally better. In: T. Richards (Ed.), *Soccer and Philosophy: Beautiful Thoughts on the Beautiful Game* (Ch. 11). Chicago: Open Court.

Durvasula, R. (2013). *You Are WHY You Eat: Change Your Food Attitude, Change Your Life.* Guilford, CT: Globe Pequot.

Edwards, P. (Ed.) (1967). *Encyclopedia of Philosophy (Vols. 5 & 6).* New York: Prentice Hall.

Elcome, T. (2010). Is Ronaldo a modern Picasso? In: T. Richards (Ed.), *Soccer and Philosophy: Beautiful Thoughts on the Beautiful Game* (Ch. 13). Chicago: Open Court.

References

Esar, E. (1995). *20,000 Quips & Quotes*. New York: Barnes & Noble.

Festing, S. (1992). *Gertrude Jekyll*. New York: Viking.

Fitzhenry, R. I. (1993). *The Harper Book of Quotations*. New York: Collins Reference.

Foucault, M. (1989). The ethics of the concern for self as a practice of freedom. S. Lotringer (Ed.). *Foucault Live, Collected Interviews, 1961–1984*. New York: Semiotexte.

Francis, M. (1990). The everyday and the personal: Six garden stories. In: M. Francis & R. T. Hester (Eds.), *The Meaning of Gardens* (pp. 206–215). Cambridge, MA: MIT Press.

Francis, M., & Hester, R. T. Jr. (1990). *The Meaning of Gardens*. Cambridge, MA: MIT Press.

Frankl, V. (1963). *Man's Search for Meaning*. New York: Pocket.

Freud, S. (1914b). The Moses of Michelangelo. *S. E., 13*: 211. London: Hogarth.

Freud, S. (1916–1917). *Introductory Lectures on Psycho-Analysis. S. E., 15–16*. London: Hogarth.

Freud, S. (1919h). The "Uncanny". *S. E., 17*. London: Hogarth.

Freud, S. (1930a). *Civilization and its Discontents. S. E., 21*: 72. London: Hogarth.

Friedman, M. (1996). Reflections on the Buber-Rogers dialogue: Thirty-five years after. In: M. Friedman (Ed.), *Martin Buber and the Human Sciences* (pp. 357–370). Albany, NY: State University of New York Press.

Friedman, M. (2002). Martin Buber and Emmanuel Levinas: An ethical query. In: M. Friedman (Ed.), *Martin Buber: The Life of Dialogue (4th ed.)* (pp. 116–129). London: Routledge.

Gabrielsson, A. (2011). *Strong Experiences with Music: Music is Much More than Music*. R. Bradbury (Trans.). Oxford: Oxford University Press.

Galeano, E. (2009). *Soccer in Sun and Shadow*. M. Fried (Trans.). New York: Nation.

Gallagher, K. T. (1962). *The Philosophy of Gabriel Marcel*. New York: Fordham University Press.

Geissmann, C., & Geissmann, P. (1998). *A History of Child Psychoanalysis*. London: Routledge.

Geisz, S. (2011). Samsara in a coffee cup: Self, suffering, and the karma of waking up. In: S. F. Parker & M. W. Austin (Eds.),

Coffee: Philosophy for Everyone: Grounds for Debate (pp. 46–58). Chichester, UK: Wiley-Blackwell.

Gentile, D. A. (Ed.) (2003). *Media Violence and Children: A Complete Guide for Parents and Children*. Westport, CT: Praeger.

Giamatti, A. B. (1998a). *A Great and Glorious Game: Baseball Writings of A. Bartlett Giamatti*. K. S. Robson (Ed.). Chapel Hill, NC: Algonquin.

Giamatti, A. B. (1998b). *Take Time for Paradise: Americans and their Games*. New York: Summit Books.

Goonetilleke, D. C. R. A. (Ed.) (2007). *Joseph Conrad's Heart of Darkness: A Routledge Study Guide*. Oxford: Routledge.

Gould, S. J. (2003). *Triumph and Tragedy in Mudville: A Lifelong Passion for Baseball*. New York: W. W. Norton.

Graf-Taylor, R. (1999). Philosophy of dialogue and feminist psychology. In: M. Friedman, *Martin Buber and the Human Sciences* (pp. 327–334). Syracuse, NY: Syracuse University Press.

Greenberg, R. (1998). *The Symphonies of Beethoven (Parts 1–4, Course Guidebook)*. Chantilly, VA: The Teaching Company.

Greenberg, R. (2006). *The Concerto (Part 3, Course Guidebook)*. Chantilly, VA: The Teaching Company.

Grimes, W. (2013, October 10). Holding court in all their petaled glory. *New York Times*, Weekend Arts, p. C2.

Grotta, D. (1992). *J. R. R. Tolkien: Architect of Middle Earth*. Philadelphia, PA: Running Press.

Grunberger, B. (1970). *Narcissism: Psychoanalytic Essays*. Madison, CT: International Universities Press.

Guerriere, D. (1999). Continental theistic philosophers. In: R. Popkin (Ed.), *The Columbia History of Western Philosophy* (pp. 712–720). New York: Columbia University Press.

Hadot, P. (1997). *Philosophy as a Way of Life*. Oxford: Blackwell.

Hagman, G. (2005). *Aesthetic Experience: Beauty, Creativity, and the Search for the Ideal*. Amsterdam, The Netherlands: Rodopi.

Hall, M. (2009). *Plants as Persons: A Philosophical Botany*. Albany, NY: State University of New York Press.

Hall, M. (2010). Escaping Eden. In: D. O'Brien (Ed.), *Gardening: Philosophy for Everyone* (pp. 38–47). Malden, MA: John Wiley & Sons.

References

Hamilton, M. J. (2004). There's no lying in baseball (wink, wink). In: E. Bronson (Ed.), *Baseball and Philosophy* (pp. 126–138). Chicago: Open Court.

Hand, S. (Trans.) (1987). *The Levinas Reader*. Oxford: Basil Blackwell.

Harvey, H. B. (2012). *The Art of Storytelling: From Parents to Professionals* (Transcript Book). Chantilly, VA: The Great Courses.

Hassumani, S. (2002). *Salman Rushdie: A Postmodern Reading of His Major Works*. Cranbury, NJ: Rosemont.

Henneberg, S. (2010). *The Creative Crone: Aging and the Poetry of May Sarton and Adrienne Rich*. Columbus, MO: University of Missouri Press.

Hibberd, S. (1871). *The Amateur's Flower Garden: A Handy Guide to the Formation and Management of the Flower Garden*. London: Groombridge & Sons.

Hobhouse, P. (Ed.) (1993). *Gertrude Jekyll: On Gardening*. New York: Vintage.

Hobhouse, P. (2008). *The Art and Practice of Gardening: England, Ireland and America*. (Two DVD set.)

Hoyningen-Huene, P. (2010). Why is football so fascinating. In: T. Richards (Ed.), *Soccer and Philosophy: Beautiful Thoughts on the Beautiful Game* (pp. 7–22). Chicago: Open Court.

Hutchinson, A. C. (2000). *It's All in the Game: A Nonfoundationalist Account of Law and Adjudication: The Game*. Durham, NC: Duke University Press.

Iglauer, B. (2012). Foreword. In: J. R. Steinberg & A. Fairweather (Eds.), *Blues: Philosophy for Everyone: Thinking Deep about Feeling Low* (pp. x–xv). Malden, MA: John Wiley & Sons.

Ilundain-Argurruza, J. M., & Torres, C. R. (2010). Embellishing the ugly side of the beautiful game. In: T. Richards (Ed.), *Soccer and Philosophy: Beautiful Thoughts on the Beautiful Game* (Ch. 15). Chicago: Open Court.

Imre, R. (2010). Hungary's revolutionary golden team. In: T. Richards (Ed.), *Soccer and Philosophy: Beautiful Thoughts on the Beautiful Game* (Ch. 23). Chicago: Open Court.

James, H. (1881). *The Portrait of a Lady*. New York: Serenity Publishers, 2009.

References

Jekyll, G. (1899). *Wood and Garden*. G. S. Thomas (Ed.). Salem, NH: Ayer, 1983.

Jekyll, G. (1901). *Home and Garden. Notes and Thoughts, Practical and Critical of a Worker in Both*. London: Longmans Green.

Jekyll, G. (1908a). *Children and Gardens*. Woodbridge, UK: Antique Collector's Club, 1982.

Jekyll, G. (1908b). *Colour in the Flower Garden*. London: Country Life.

Jewett, S. (2005). *God's Troubadour, the Story of Saint Francis of Assisi*. Chapel Hill, NC: Yesterday's Classics.

Johnson, N. (1999). *Fresh Brewed Life*. Nashville, TN: Thomas Nelson.

Johnstone, K. (1992). *Impro: Improvisation and the Theatre*. New York: Routledge/Theater Books.

Jones, J. W. (2001). Hans Loewald: The psychoanalyst as mystic. *Psychoanalytic Review, 88*(6): 793–809.

Jourdain, R. (1997). *Music, the Brain, and Ecstasy: How Music Captures Our Imagination*. New York: Avon.

Kalischer, A. C. (Ed.) (1909). *The Letters of Ludwig van Beethoven (Vol. 1)*. New York: E. P. Dutton.

Kaplan, R., & Kaplan, S. (1989). *The Experience of Nature: A Psychological Perspective*. New York: Columbia University Press.

Kent, M. A. (2010). Aristotle's favorite sport. In: T. Richards (Ed.), *Soccer and Philosophy: Beautiful Thoughts on the Beautiful Game* (Ch. 17). Chicago: Open Court.

Kirkwood, K. W. (2011). Higher, faster, stronger, buzzed. Caffeine as a performance-enhancing drug. In: S. F. Parker & M. W. Austin (Eds.), *Coffee: Philosophy for Everyone: Grounds for Debate* (pp. 205–216). Chichester, UK: Wiley-Blackwell.

Kivy, P. (2002). *Introduction to a Philosophy of Music*. Oxford: Oxford University Press.

Kohut, H. (1957). Observations on the psychological functions of music. *Journal of the American Psychoanalytic Association, 5*: 389–407.

Kolpass, N. (2005). *Practically Useless Information: Food & Drink*. Nashville, TN: Thomas Nelson.

Kramer, K. P., with Gawlick, M. (2003). *Martin Buber's I and Thou: Practicing Living Dialogue*. New York: Paulist Press.

References

Kraus, J. (2004). There's no place like home! In: E. Bronson (Ed.), *Baseball and Philosophy* (pp. 7–19). Chicago: Open Court.

Kunitz, S., with Lentine, G. (2005). *The Wild Braid: A Poet Reflects On A Century In the Garden*. New York: W. W. Norton.

Lambert, A. (2010). The evolution of the football fan and the way of virtue. In: T. Richards (Ed.), *Soccer and Philosophy: Beautiful Thoughts on the Beautiful Game* (Ch. 17). Chicago: Open Court.

Langer, S. K. (1957). *Philosophy in a New Key: A Study in the Symbolism of Reason, Rite, and Art*. Cambridge, MA: Harvard University Press.

Lawrence, E. (Ed.) (1964). *The Gardener's Essential Gertrude Jekyll*. Boston: Nonpareil.

Laxness, H. (1996). *Independent People*. New York: Vintage.

Lever, J. (1983). *Soccer Madness: Brazil's Passion for the World's Most Popular Sport*. Long Grove, IL: Waveland.

Levinas, E. (1985). *Ethics and Infinity: Conversations with Philippe Nemo*. R. A. Cohen (Trans.). Pittsburg, PA: Duquesne University Press.

Levinas, E. (1987a). There is: Existence without existents. In: S. Hand (Trans.), *The Levinas Reader* (pp. 29–36). Oxford: Basil Blackwell.

Levinas, E. (1987b). *Time and the Other*. R. A. Cohen (Trans.). Pittsburg, PA: Duquesne University Press.

Levinas, E. (1989). *Difficult Freedom: Essays on Judaism*. S. Hand (Ed.). Baltimore, MD: Johns Hopkins University Press.

Levinas, E. (1994). *Nine Talmudic Readings*. A. Aronowicz (Trans.). Bloomington, IN: Indiana University Press.

Levinas, E. (2001). *Is it Righteous To Be? Interviews with Emmanuel Levinas*. J. Robbins (Ed.). Stanford, CA: Stanford University Press.

Lifton, R. J. (1976). *The Life of the Self: Toward a New Psychology*. New York: Basic Books.

Lipman, D. (1995). *The Storytelling Coach: How to Listen, Praise, and Bring Out People's Best*. Atlanta, GA: August House.

Lipman, D. (1999). *Improving Your Storytelling: Beyond the Basics for All Who Tell Stories in Work or Play*. Atlanta, GA: August House.

References

Lipson, C. T. (2006). The meaning and functions of tunes that come into one's head. *Psychoanalytic Quarterly, LXXV*(3): 859–878.

Loewald, H. W. (1953). Psychoanalysis and modern views on human existence and religious experience. *Journal of Pastoral Care, 7*: 1–15.

Lombardi, R. (2008). Time, music and reverie. *Journal of the American Psychoanalytic Association, 56*: 1191–1211.

Maberry, J., & Kramer, D. F. (2007). *The Cryptopedia: A Dictionary of the Weird, Strange, and Downright Bizarre*. New York: Citadel.

Macdonald, E. (2010). Hortus incantans. Gardening as an art of enchantment. In: D. O'Brien (Ed.), *Gardening: Philosophy for Everyone* (pp. 119–134). Malden, MA: John Wiley & Sons.

Mahler, M. S., Pine, F., & Bergman, A. (1975). *The Psychological Birth of the Infant. Symbiosis and Individuation*. London: Karnac, 1985.

Manhattan Murder Mystery. (1993). TriStar Pictures.

Marcel, G. (1952). *Metaphysical Journal*. B. Wall (Trans.). Chicago: Henry Regnery.

Marcel, G. (1964). *Creative Fidelity*. R. Rosthal (Trans.). New York: Farrar, Straus and Giroux.

Marcel, G. (2001). *The Mystery of Being, Volume II: Faith and Reality*. South Bend, IN: St. Augustine.

Marcel, G. (2005). *Music and Philosophy*. S. Maddux & R. E. Wood (Trans.). Milwaukee, WI: Marquette University Press.

Marcus, P. (2003). *Ancient Religious Wisdom, Spirituality and Psychoanalysis*. Westport, CT: Praeger.

Marcus, P. (2008). *Being for the Other: Emmanuel Levinas, Ethical Living and Psychoanalysis*. Milwaukee, WI: Marquette University Press.

Marcus, P. (2010). *In Search of the Good Life, Emmanuel Levinas, Psychoanalysis and the Art of Living*. London: Karnac.

Marcus, P. (2013a). *How to Laugh Your Way through Life: A Psychoanalyst's Advice*. London: Karnac.

Marcus, P. (2013b). *In Search of the Spiritual: Gabriel Marcel, Psychoanalysis and the Sacred*. London: Karnac.

Marcus, P., & Marcus, G. (2011). *Theater as Life: Practical Wisdom Drawn From Great Acting Teachers, Actors and Actresses*. Milwaukee, WI: Marquette University Press.

References

Massingham, B. (1973). *Miss Jekyll: A Portrait of a Great Gardener*. Newton Abbot, UK: David & Charles.

Miller, L. (2013, July 17). Pitching God. *New York Times*, p. 22.

Miller, M. (1993). *The Garden as an Art*. Albany, NY: State University of New York Press.

Miller, M. (2010). Time and temporality in the garden. In: D. O'Brien (Ed.), *Gardening: Philosophy for Everyone* (pp. 178–191). Malden, MA: John Wiley & Sons.

Moeller, C. (2001). *Chasing Lighting: The Pursuit of Successful Living in America*. Lincoln, NE: iUniverse.

Moore, B. E., & Fine, B. D. (Eds.) (1990). *Psychoanalytic Terms and Concepts*. New Haven, CT: Yale University Press.

Moore, P. (2000). Soccer and the politics of culture in Western Australia. In: N. Dyck (Ed.), *Games, Sports and Cultures* (pp. 84–95). Oxford: Berg.

Morgan, W. J. (2004). Baseball and the search for an American moral identity. In: E. Bronson (Ed.), *Baseball and Philosophy* (pp. 157–168). Chicago: Open Court.

Myers, M. (2013). *How to Grow Anything: Your Best Garden and Landscape in 6 Lessons*. Chantilly, VA: The Great Courses. (DVD.)

Nagel, J. J. (2013). *Melodies of the Mind: Connections between Psychoanalysis and Music*. Chichester, UK: Routledge.

Nguyen, A. M. (2010). Barça's treble or: How I learned to stop worrying and love the heat. In: T. Richards (Ed.), *Soccer and Philosophy: Beautiful Thoughts on the Beautiful Game* (Ch. 21). Chicago: Open Court.

Nichols, A. (2006). *Emerson, Thoreau, and the Transcendentalist Movement* (Course Guidebook). Chantilly, VA: The Teaching Company.

Noy, P. (2013). A theory of art and aesthetic experience. *Psychoanalytic Review, 100*(4): 559–582.

Noy, P. (n.d.). *Art and Emotion*. Unpublished manuscript.

O'Brien, D. (2010a). Cultivating our garden: David Hume and gardening as therapy. In: D. O'Brien (Ed.), *Gardening: Philosophy for Everyone* (pp. 192–203). Malden, MA: John Wiley & Sons.

O'Brien, D. (2010b). Planting the seed. In: D. O'Brien (Ed.), *Gardening: Philosophy for Everyone* (pp. 1–10). Malden, MA: John Wiley & Sons.

References

O'Donohue, J. (1997). *Anam Cara: A Book of Celtic Wisdom*. New York: Harper Perennial.

O'Donohue, J. (1998). *Eternal Echoes. Exploring Our Hunger to Belong*. London: Bantam.

O'Donohue, J. (2004). *Beauty: The Invisible Embrace: Rediscovering the True Sources of Compassion, Serenity, and Hope*. New York: HarperCollins.

Olaya, C., Lammoglia, N., & Zarama, R. (2010). A "Messi" way of life. In: T. Richards (Ed.), *Soccer and Philosophy: Beautiful Thoughts on the Beautiful Game* (Ch. 22). Chicago: Open Court.

O'Neil, B., with Wulf, S., & Conrads, D. (1996). *I was Right On Time*. New York: Simon and Schuster.

Ortiz, J. M. (1997). *The Tao of Music: Sound Psychology: Using Music to Change Your Life*. San Francisco: Weiser.

Paine, J. (Ed.). (2012). *The Huston Smith Reader*. Berkeley, CA: University of California Press.

Palmer, P., Gillette, G., & Shea, S. (2006). *The 2006 ESPN Baseball Encyclopedia (1st ed.)*. New York: Sterling.

Parker, S. F., & Austin, M. W. (2011). Editor's introduction. In: S. F. Parker & M. W. Austin (Eds.), *Coffee: Philosophy for Everyone: Grounds for Debate* (pp. 1–6). Chicherster, UK: Wiley-Blackwell.

Pendergrast, M. (2010). *Uncommon Grounds: The History of Coffee and How it Transformed Our World (Rev. ed.)*. New York: Basic Books.

Pendergrast, M. (2011). Black puddle water or panacea. In: S. F. Parker & M. W. Austin (Eds.), *Coffee: Philosophy for Everyone: Grounds for Debate* (pp. 9–24). Chichester, UK: Wiley-Blackwell.

Peperzack, A. (1997). *Beyond: The Philosophy of Levinas*. Evanston, IL: Northwestern University Press.

Pepple, J. (2010). *Soccer, the Left, & the Farce of Multiculturalism*. Bloomington, IN: AuthorHouse.

Person, E. S., Cooper, A. M., & Gabbard, G. O. (Eds.) (2005). *Textbook of Psychoanalysis*. Washington, DC: American Psychiatric Publishing.

Phillips, K. G. (2011). The unexamined cup is not worth drinking. In: S. F. Parker & M. W. Austin (Eds.), *Coffee: Philosophy for Everyone: Grounds for Debate* (pp. 34–45). Chichester, UK: Wiley-Blackwell.

References

Pratt, J. W. (2013). *Worship in the Garden: Services for Outdoor Worship*. Nashville, TN: Abingdon.

Price, J. L. (2006). *Rounding the Bases: Baseball and Religion in America*. Macon, GA: Mercer University Press.

Rattiner, S. L. (2004). *Food and Drink: A Book of Quotations*. Mineola, NY: Dover.

Ray, M. T. (2010). Cultivating the soul: The ethics of gardening in ancient Greece and Rome. In: D. O'Brien (Ed.), *Gardening: Philosophy for Everyone* (pp. 26–37). Malden, MA: John Wiley & Sons.

Redman, A. (Ed.) (1959). *The Wit and Humor of Oscar Wilde*. Garden City, NY: Dover.

Reik, T. (1953). *The Haunting Melody: Psychoanalytic Experiences in Life and Music*. New York: Farrar, Straus and Young.

Riley, R. B. (1990). Flowers, power, and sex. In: M. Francis & R. T. Hester (Eds.), *The Meaning of Gardens* (pp. 60–75). Cambridge, MA: MIT Press.

Roach, M. (2013). *The Backyard Parables: Lessons on Gardening, and Life*. New York: Grand Central.

Robbins, M. P. (1998). *A Gardener's Bouquet of Quotations*. New York: HarperCollins.

Robson, K. (1998). Introduction. In: K. S. Robson (Ed.), *A Great and Glorious Game: Baseball Writings of A. Bartlett Giamatti* (pp. 1–6). Chapel Hill, NC: Algonquin.

Romaya, B. (2011). The philosopher's brew. In: S. F. Parker & M. W. Austin (Eds.), *Coffee: Philosophy for Everyone: Grounds for Debate* (pp. 113–124). Chichester, UK: Wiley-Blackwell.

Rorty, R. (1989). *Contingency, Irony, and Solidarity*. New York: Cambridge University Press.

Rosen, M., with Bruton, J. (2012). *Best Seat in the House*. Minneapolis, MN: MVP.

Ruiz, J. A. V. (2010). *God is Round*. Ciudad de México, Mexico: Editorial Planeta Mexicana.

Rushing, F. (1997). *Gardening Southern Style*. Jackson, MS: University Press of Mississippi.

Rycroft, C. (1995). *A Critical Dictionary of Psychoanalysis*. London: Penguin.

Sadler, B. (2011). Café noir: Anxiety, existence, and the coffeehouse. In: S. F. Parker & M. W. Austin (Eds.), *Coffee: Philosophy for Everyone: Grounds for Debate* (pp. 100–112). Chichester, UK: Wiley-Blackwell.

Sandler, J., Kennedy, H., & Tyson, R. T. (1980). *The Technique of Child Psychoanalysis: Discussions with Anna Freud.* Cambridge, MA: Harvard University Press.

Schafer, R. (1983). *The Analytic Attitude.* New York: Basic Books.

Schaff, P. (Ed.) (2004). *Confessions and Letters of St. Augustine with a Sketch of His Life and Work: Nicene and Post-Nicene Fathers of the Church.* Whitefish, MT: Kessinger.

Schivelbusch, W. (1993). *Tastes of Paradise: A Social History of Spices, Stimulants, and Intoxicants.* D. Jacobson (Trans.). New York: Pantheon.

Schultz, H., with Gordon, J. (2011). *Onward: How Starbucks Fought for Its Life Without Losing Its Soul.* Chichester, UK: John Wiley & Sons.

Schwartz, B. (2004). *The Paradox of Choice: Why More Is Less: How the Culture of Abundance Robs Us.* New York: HarperCollins.

Seidel, M. (1991). *Ted Williams: A Baseball Life.* Lincoln, NE: University of Nebraska Press.

Senor, T. D. (2004). Should Cubs fans be committed? What bleacher bums have to teach us about the nature of faith. In: E. Bronson (Ed.), *Baseball and Philosophy* (pp. 37–55). Chicago: Open Court.

Sexton, J., with Oliphant, T., & Schwartz, P. J. (2013). *Baseball as a Road to God: Seeing Beyond the Game.* New York: Penguin.

Shakespeare, W. (1623). *As You Like It* (Act II, scene ii).

Shapiro, S. (2013). There was music amidst the misery: Holocaust art offers a reminder of life and loss. *B'nai Brith Magazine, Winter*: 12–17.

Shoemaker, C. A. (Ed.) (2001). *Encyclopedia of Gardens, History and Design (Vol. 2).* Chicago: Fitzroy Dearborn.

Simson, S., & Straus, M. C. (Eds.) (1998). *Horticulture as Therapy: Principles and Practice.* Binghamton, NY: Haworth.

Slung, M. B. (2005). *The Garden of Reading: An Anthology of Twentieth-Century Short Fiction about Gardens and Gardeners.* London: Overlook Duckworth.

References

Smith, H. (1991). *The World's Religions*. San Francisco: Harper.

Smith, H. (2012). *The Huston Smith Reader*. J. Paine (Ed.). Berkeley, CA: University of California Press.

Smith, R. (1951, 4 October). Miracle of Coogen's Bluff. *New York Herald Tribune*.

Spence, D. (1982). *Narrative Truth and Historical Truth: Meaning and Interpretation in Psychoanalysis*. New York: W. W. Norton.

Spolin, V. (1999). *Improvisation for the Theater (3rd ed.)*. Evanston, IL: Northwestern University Press.

Stanislavski, C. (1936). *An Actor Prepares*. New York: Routledge.

Stanislavski, C. (1949). *Building a Character*. New York: Routledge.

Stanislavski, C. (1958). *Stanislavski's Legacy. A Collection of Comments on a Variety of Aspects of an Actor's Art and Life*. E. R. Hapgood (Ed. & Trans.). New York: Theatre Arts Books, 1968.

Stanislavski, C. (1961). *Creating a Role*. New York: Routledge.

Stewart, M. (2012). *Team Spirit: The Houston Astros*. Chicago: Norwood House.

Stilgoe, J. R. (1969). Foreword. In: G. Bachelard (Ed.), *The Poetics of Space: The Classic Look at How We Experience Intimate Places* (pp vii–x). Boston, MA: Beacon.

Swedene, J. K. (2009). *Staying Alive: The Varieties of Immortality*. Lanham, MD: University Press of America.

Sweeney, J. (2002). *Quote-a-Day: Writing Prompts*. New York: Scholastic.

Swinburne, A. C. (1868). *William Blake: A Critical Essay*. London: John Camden Hotten.

Taylor, P. (Ed.) (2006). *The Oxford Companion to the Garden*. Oxford: Oxford University Press.

Thayer, R. L. Jr. (1990). Personal dreams and pagan rituals. In: M. Francis & R. T. Hester (Eds.), *The Meaning of Gardens* (pp. 194–197). Cambridge, MA: MIT Press.

The Week, 19 July 2013, p. 6.

The Week, 26 July 2013, p. 16.

The Week, 20 June 2014, p. 16.

Turnbull, J., Satterlee, T., & Raab, A. (Eds.) (2008). *The Global Game: Writers on Soccer*. Lincoln, NE: University of Nebraska Press.

References

Ukers, W. H. (1922). *All about Coffee*. New York: The New York Tea & Coffee Trade Journal Company.

Way, T. (2012). *Gertrude Jekyll*. Oxford: Shire.

Wear, A. (2011). The flavor of choice: Neoliberalism and the espresso aesthetic. In: S. F. Parker & M. W. Austin (Eds.), *Coffee: Philosophy for Everyone: Grounds for Debate* (pp. 152–165). Chichester, UK: Wiley-Blackwell.

Weissman, M. (2008). *God in a Cup: The Obsessive Quest for the Perfect Coffee*. Hoboken, NJ: John Wiley & Sons.

Wiener, D. J. (1994). *Rehearsals for Growth: Theater Improvisation for Psychotherapists*. New York: W. W. Norton.

Wigram, T., Pederson, I. N., & Bonde, L. O. (2002). *A Comprehensive Guide to Music Therapy: Theory, Clinical Practice, Research and Training*. London: Jessica Kingsley.

Wilbur, G. (2005). *Glory and Honor: The Musical and Artistic Legacy of Johann Sebastian Bach*. Nashville, TN: Cumberland House.

Wild, A. (2004). *Coffee: A Dark History*. New York: W. W. Norton.

Will, G. F. (1990). *Men at Work: The Craft of Baseball*. New York: Macmillan.

Will, G. F. (1998). *Bunts: Curt Flood, Camden Yards, Peter Rose and Other Reflections on Baseball*. New York: Charles Scribner's Sons.

Winnicott, D. W. (1971). *Playing and Reality*. London: Tavistock.

Winters, E. (2010). How to appreciate the fingertip save. In: T. Richards (Ed.), *Soccer and Philosophy: Beautiful Thoughts on the Beautiful Game* (Ch. 12). Chicago: Open Court.

Wita, B. S. (1982). *Dried Flowers for All Seasons*. New York: Van Nostrand Reinhold.

Wood, J. (Ed.) (1923). *Dictionary of Quotations from Ancient and Modern, English and Foreign Sources*. New York: Frederick Warne.

Wood, M. (Ed.) (2006). *The Unknown Gertrude Jekyll*. London: Francis Lincoln.

Wood, R. (2005). Introduction. In: S. Maddux & R. E. Wood (Trans.), *Music and Philosophy* (pp. 11–40). Milwaukee, WI: Marquette University Press.

References

Yearley, L. (1983). The perfected person in the radical Chuang-Tsu. In: V. H. Mair (Ed.), *Experimental Essays in Chuang Tzu* (pp. 125–139). Honolulu, HI: University of Hawaii Press.

Young, W. (2004). Taking one for the team: Baseball and sacrifice. In: E. Bronson (Ed.), *Baseball and Philosophy* (pp. 56–68). Chicago: Open Court.

Zatorre, R. J., & Salimpoor, V. N. (2013, June 9). Why music makes our brain sing. *New York Times*, Sunday Review, p. 12.

INDEX

Index

Index

Index

Index

Index

Index

ACKNOWLEDGEMENTS

A number of specialist scholars have graciously read chapters of my book and provided me with very useful feedback: David. E. Cooper (gardening), Peter J. Schwartz (sport/baseball), Scott F. Parker (coffee), Julia Jaffee Nagle (music), and Jerrold R. Brandell (storytelling). Two of my best friends have read every word of my book, the latter many times: sociologist professor William B. Helmreich, and my wife, child/adult psychoanalyst, Irene Wineman-Marcus. While I, of course, am solely responsible for what is contained in my book, I am most grateful to all these busy scholars in their willingness to take the time to read my material and provide me with constructive criticism and helpful suggestions to improve my manuscript.

ABOUT THE AUTHOR

Paul Marcus, Ph.D. is training and supervisory analyst at the National Psychological Association for Psychoanalysis in New York City and the author/editor of seventeen books including *In Search of the Spiritual: Gabriel Marcel, Psychoanalysis, and the Sacred* and *How to Laugh Your Way Through Life: A Psychoanalyst's Advice.*